Parliamentary Selection

Parliamentary Selection

Social and Political Choice in
Early Modern England

MARK A. KISHLANSKY

Department of History, University of Chicago

The right of the
University of Cambridge
to print and sell
all manner of books
was granted by
Henry VIII in 1534.
The University has printed
and published continuously
since 1584.

CAMBRIDGE UNIVERSITY PRESS

Cambridge
London   New York   New Rochelle
Melbourne   Sydney

Published by the Press Syndicate of the University of Cambridge
The Pitt Building, Trumpington Street, Cambridge CB2 1RP
32 East 57th Street, New York, NY 10022, USA
10 Stamford Road, Oakleigh, Melbourne 3166, Australia

First published 1986

Printed in the United States of America

Library of Congress Cataloging-in-Publication Data
Kishlansky, Mark A.
Parliamentary selection.
Bibliography: p.
Includes index.
1. England and Wales. Parliament – Elections – History – 17th century.   2. Elections – England – History – 17th century.   3. Great Britain – Politics and government – 1558– 1603.   4. Great Britain – Politics and government – 1603–1714.   I. Title.
JN945.K57   1986   324.942'06   86–11782

British Library Cataloguing in Publication Data
Kishlansky, Mark A.
Parliamentary selection : social and political choice in early modern England.
1. Great Britain – Parliament. *House of Commons* – History   2. Legislators – Great Britain – History – 17th century   3. Legislation – Great Britain – History – 18th century
I. Title
328.41'073   JN673

ISBN 0 521 32231 6 hard covers
ISBN 0 521 31116 0 paperback

For Jeanne M. Thiel

Then happy I that love and am beloved...
Sonnet XXV

Contents

Preface

THIS IS A STUDY in the social history of politics. It is a continuation of my interest in the nature of politics in early modern England – in the assumptions that underlay it, the practices that gave it form, and the structures through which it operated. Remarkably, given all the attention of preceding generations, we still have no very clear idea of the political process in the sixteenth and seventeenth centuries. The Marxist paradigm that politics is the history of class struggle has been too frequently disproved with regard to this historical period to command much attention. But in its place, residually, rests the assumption that politics is an instinctive activity that man brought to civilization from the state of nature. *Homo politicus* requires no special explanation and no critical treatment. His aspirations and his actions are historical constants readily explicable to anyone who has ever participated in a club, an educational institution, or a local council. And of all political instincts, none is more natural than the electoral one.

It is this assumption that I wish to challenge. I shall argue, instead, that politics is environmentally specific, that it is tied to its historical period and to its local context. Politics interacts with social organization and cultural categories, sometimes replicating them, sometimes throwing them into stark contrast. Political assumptions and political practices therefore change over time, and their changes can provide a window through which to view deeper social transformations.

In early modern England, political activity took place within the context of a hierarchical social structure and a theocentric universe. Governance, or magistracy, was guided by concern for maintaining the order of the social structure and the harmony of the universe. It was obsessed not with the structure of order but with orderliness itself. We tend to describe this form of social organization as profoundly conservative because a desire to maintain order is usually translated into the maintenance of the existing order. But this is not necessarily so, and the most

ix

important social development of this period is the increase in both numbers and power of the gentry, a group which took on many of the
attributes of the ancient aristocracy and became functionally indistinguishable from the peerage. Thus hierarchical notions about social organization need not make for a static society.

Nor do they necessarily make for static political participation. A top–
down process of social differentiation was mirrored by a top–down
process of political representation. But like the elite itself, this process
was in considerable flux. For one thing, political participation was an
ancient attribute of social distinction. If the number of people with claims
to such distinction increased, then so must competition for possession
of its marks. Gunpowder and gold were to devalue two of the most
reliable indicators of status – prowess and wealth – while demographic
attrition and geographic mobility eroded ancient standing. By the late
sixteenth century, service in the form of local and national office holding
had become a principal arena for social differentiation among the elite,
and over the succeeding century it became a principal battleground for
social competition.

In this book I am particularly concerned with the way in which individuals were chosen to become members of Parliament. Though this
is not the only test of service or the only avenue of approach to the
process of social differentiation, it is a particularly useful one. Unlike
the selection of magistrates or court office holders, selection of members
to Parliament was choice in a public sphere. Uncovering the process
exposes the aspirations of candidates and the values of the communities
that chose them. Unlike the choice of corporate officials, professional
dignitaries, or even church elders, the choice of members of Parliament
was irregular. Thus the social and intellectual shifts it reflected were
more jarring than those felt in permanent offices with patterns of con-
tinuous selection.

The subject is of interest for historiographical reasons as well as historical ones. For generations, Parliament and its members have been the
primary subject of political history. Its study is so well developed and
its empirical base so secure that analytic studies like my own can be
undertaken without years of preliminary exploration. In this regard I
must make special mention of the *History of Parliament Trust*, which
has served the early modern period so well. The volumes already published and those covering the periods 1603–28 and 1628–59 that are
under way will soon provide us biographies of members and histories
of constituencies as complete as we are ever likely to need. This book
would still be a pile of note cards without the trusty guidance of the
The House of Commons 1660–90 and would undoubtedly be better

had the early seventeenth-century projects been completed. In the same vein, the intense interest in parliamentary reform in the nineteenth century led local historians to scour archives and to publish documents relating to the selection of members to Parliament in preceding ages. This saved much material from the ravages of the two world wars and made much available for preliminary work in America.

Moreover, the work of others has allowed me to treat the subject in a way that would otherwise have been impossible. The ground-breaking work of earlier historians saved me from explaining the nuts and bolts of how representation came to exist, how parliament operated, or even what the representational system was like. More ambiguously, perhaps, earlier work on this subject has provided the skeptical impulse that led me to explore the primary material myself. Dissatisfaction with what is now called the Whig canon – particularly the work of J. E. Neale and D. M. Hirst – was the starting point for my investigation.

Yet no matter how vigorously one historian dissents from the work of another, he remains but a link in a historiographic chain, fastened to the questions and answers of his predecessors, forged from the metals of his own time and place, incapable of escaping either. To criticize the work of others, to offer alternative interpretations, even to expose errors, is a professional matter and not a personal one. It is also a matter of some delicacy. Where I am in consistent disagreement with my predecessors I have tried to refrain from persistent criticism. As so much of my argument is empirical rather than theoretical, many of my disputes are over matters of fact. I have tried to note these quietly in footnotes.

Stuart history has not been without its controversies or its controversialists. Though we might all wish to write the standard interpretation, we are all revisionists. In our own age of ideology it might be anticipated that our scholarship will be criticized in ideological terms. But to study a hierarchical elite and to portray its values in its own terms does not constitute a statement of modern political preferences, any more than a student of Ptolemy must believe that the sun revolves around the earth. A historian whose recent ancestors were Polish peasants is not predisposed to prefer hierarchies based on birth and breeding to those open to ability and achievement. The historian's primary obligation remains to understand the past on its own terms.

In hopes of achieving this I have decided to blend together two different modes of historical discourse: narrative and analysis. The book is organized into two parallel parts. In both I have attempted to use my evidence in three different forms. First, I have written in the traditional manner of analytic history, providing discrete pieces of evidence to illustrate concrete points. I have always tried to adhere to what might be called the best evidence rule; but the fact of the matter is that in thousands of selections across a period of more than a century, one can document almost anything by carefully culling examples. Though it is necessary to demonstrate that there are main lines to the structure of the process of parliamentary selection – and this can only be demonstrated by using isolated bits of information from across the country – this method by itself would be open to all the criticisms so frequently leveled at "impressionistic" history.

Therefore I have chosen, in the second instance, to illustrate the most important conceptual aspects of the process of parliamentary selection and its transformation by providing illustrative narratives. These detailed presentations speak directly to particular points in my argument but are presented within their historical context and are intended to illustrate other points as well. The principle of selection of these short narratives has been entirely based upon surviving evidence. Because I believe that what I am describing in this book is systematic, the more detail I can provide the stronger my case becomes. I have looked for situations in which there is sufficient material to reconstruct a reliable narrative. For the period before 1660 I have made very few choices, as there are few such instances from which to choose. In the period after the Restoration, where equally well-documented selections survive, I have tried to provide some examples that have not been previously narrated.

Finally, I have told two chapter-length stories – the elections at Somerset in 1614 and at Buckingham in 1685. Again the richness of detail is meant to illuminate the entire range of ideas and practices in the process of parliamentary selection, but unlike the briefer narratives it is meant to do so without the mediating authority of the historian. So far as I know, these are the two best-documented elections for their respective periods. Their great virtue as examples is that they contain papers written as events unfolded rather than retrospectively, and that they contain papers of more than one participant. Though the reconstruction of the Somerset election is largely from the Phelips manuscripts, the contribution of the few Poulett letters that survive is inestimable in balancing the point of view. The Buckingham archives are, to the best of my knowledge, unique in that papers of all three participants survive and survive in profusion. I do not regard either of these narratives as case studies: They are the historical reality from which analysis must be drawn and to which it must be held accountable.

The debts that I owe for all manner of aid can receive only the poor payment of acknowledgment. Librarians and archivists have been unfailingly kind in making materials available. To single out some is not to diminish the contributions made by others. The staff of the Joseph Regenstein Library at the University of Chicago, especially the interlibrary loan officers who processed my unending requests for town histories and county record society volumes, merits special mention. So too, in England, does the staff of the Institute for Historical Research. Mary Robertson at the Huntington Library endured my week-long blitz of that marvelous manuscript collection and promptly provided photocopies of the Temple–Stowe papers.

Among the many scholars who proffered advice and gave me the benefit of their criticisms I would like to thank Simon Adams, Julie Baskes, Ted Cook, Eveline Cruickshanks, Alan Davidson, Barbara Donagan, Charles Gray, Richard Hellie, Peter Lake, John Morrill, Virginia Moseley, Linda Peck, and Lawrence Stone. To John Ferris I must express more than the gratitude due for help and advice. He carefully read through the first draft of the manuscript and corrected more errors than I would like to admit could have been found. His unrivaled knowledge of this subject was generously placed at my disposal, and his assistance went beyond the call of scholarly aid.

Archival historians cannot work without the generous support of private and public philanthropy. Americans attempting to make a contribution to the history of England are still more dependent. The American Bar Foundation and the American Council of Learned Societies supported my initial trips to the English archives at a time when the project was differently conceived. The Chicago branch of the English Speaking Union and the College of the University of Chicago made possible summer sojourns to London for the collection of manuscript materials, and the American Philosophical Society provided travel funds for a visit to the Huntington Library. A senior research fellowship from the National Endowment for the Humanities and the generosity of the Division of the Social Sciences at the University of Chicago allowed for a year's leave during which research was concluded and the book substantially drafted. To all these agencies my debts are more than financial.

The dedication is my final, inadequate acknowledgment.

PART I

Selections and Social Choice

For though to be Knight of the Shire be a thing I much desire and even the highest mark of my ambition, yet I would be loath to purchase it with the loss of a friend.

From the Somerset election of 1614

1

Parliamentary Selection

I

THE MARTIAL FEATS of Caius Marcius earned him the appellation Coriolanus. When he returned to Rome after his greatest triumph his mother, Volumnia, exulted: "I have lived to see inherited my very wishes. ...Only there's one thing wanting, which I doubt not but our Rome will cast upon thee."[1] This crowning accolade was selection as consul, a veneration of honor and merit reserved for the noblest Romans. The process, in Shakespeare's Rome, was one of nomination by the senate and approbation by the citizenry. The body of senators would meet to select a candidate to be presented to the people. Marcius's heroism against the Volscians concluded a career of gallantry that even the aged Cominius felt himself unable to describe. He was nobly born and bred, and his valor – "the chiefest virtue" – could not "in the world be singly counterpoised."[2] He was adopted by the senate unanimously in the belief that "he cannot but with measure fit the honors which we devise him."[3]

It remained only for Coriolanus to present himself for the people's assent. This aspect of the selection process involved the symbolic humbling of the recipient of high honors. The nominee, in the "gown of humiliation," perambulated the public squares requesting the voices of the citizens. It was the act of petition that was paramount – "the price is to ask it kindly."[4] In turn, the people demanded some show of the nominee's merit. In the case of warriors, this meant the display of wounds suffered in the service of the state:

All dates are given in old style with the year reckoned to begin on January 1.
[1] William Shakespeare, *Coriolanus*, act II, scene i, lines 194ff. All references are to the Arden Shakespeare.
[2] Ibid., II, ii, 84ff.
[3] Ibid., II, ii, 123.
[4] Ibid., II, iii, 75.

Your voices: for your voices I have fought; watched for your voices; for your voices bear of wound two dozen odd; battles thrice six I have seen....for your voices have done many things; some less, some more: your voices: Indeed I would be consul."[5]

But Coriolanus did not ask it kindly. He implored the senators to dispense with the public rites and he discharged his obligation grudgingly. There was no false modesty in his abhorrence of the spectacle of his bravery; he eschewed it before the senate as well as before the citizens: "I had rather have my wounds to heal again than to hear say how I got them."[6] But his humility was not unadulterated. He despised the common people and deplored their role in affirming his elevation. He recoiled from begging their "needless vouches," and only stern persuasion could induce him "to crave the hire which first we do deserve."[7] As he moved from crossroad to marketplace performing the requisite obeisance, he mocked the plebians and derided their ceremony. Even the citizens' eager approval provoked his scorn.

Coriolanus's consulship was not to be. His haughtiness and his indifference to the welfare of the plebians – already demonstrated when he opposed the free distribution of grain to avert famine – had roused the tribunes, the representatives of the people, against him. His implacable foe, Brutus, precisely summarized Coriolanus's attitude toward selection: "He would miss it rather than carry it but by the suit of the gentry to him and the desire of the nobles."[8] He and Sicinius persuaded the citizens to withdraw their assent. As the senators convened to celebrate Coriolanus's elevation, the tribunes led a delegation to protest it. This unexpected reversal of fortune unleashed Coriolanus's deep-seated rancor: "Must these have voices that can yield them now, and straight disclaim their tongues."[9] Such dishonorable conduct was all that could be expected from unhonorable men. His tirade against the tribunes quickly passed the bounds of treason. The banishment, revenge, and tragic fall of Coriolanus all stemmed from his failure to be selected consul of Rome.

Shakespeare's account of the candidacy of Coriolanus is an apt starting place for a discussion of the process of parliamentary selection in early modern England. There is of course much in fiction that is not likely to be as sharply defined in life. The dramatist needs conflict to propel action. Few parliamentary selections make as good a story as does the tragedy

[5]   Ibid., II, iii, 125ff.
[6]   Ibid., II, ii, 69.
[7]   Ibid., II, iii, 113.
[8]   Ibid., II, i, 232.
[9]   Ibid., III, i, 32.

of Coriolanus. But in a play that rarely strays from the accounts of Plutarch and Livy, the episode of Coriolanus's consulship is entirely of Shakespeare's devising.[10] Moreover, these scenes so accurately portray the process by which officeholders were selected in the early seventeenth century that one must conclude that Shakespeare had first-hand experience, either of wardmote selections to the London Common Council or of parliamentary selections themselves. It is rare to have the testimony of so acute an observer. Thus it is worth reflecting on the central tenets of selection as Shakespeare recreated them.

First, selection was not resolved by choice. This is of paramount importance. If any choosing was done, it took place informally before Coriolanus's nomination:

1 Off.: How many stand for consulships?
2 Off.: Three they say: but tis thought of every one
Coriolanus will carry it.[11]

Nomination was made within the body of the nominators. It was their gift to bestow. The candidate neither presented himself, proclaimed his abilities, nor promised beneficial performance. It was only necessary that he have a sponsor among the senators to put forward his name. This was done in an encomium of those qualities that fitted the office to him – attributes already possessed, deeds already accomplished. There was no question of Coriolanus's seeking the consulship:

1 Cit.: Tell us what hath brought you to it.
Cor.: My own desert.
2 Cit.: Your own desert!
Cor.: Aye, not mine own desire.[12]

Secondly, selection took place without a contest. The senators made their nomination unanimously, endowing the candidate with the dignity of their office. When the tribunes sought to arrest Coriolanus after his treasonous speech, the senators pledged with one voice, "We'll surety him."[13] Indeed, the fact that the candidate did not seek his place meant that opposition was more an attack upon magistracy – "to unbuild the city and to lay all flat" – than upon the individual involved.[14] Not only was there every expectation that the candidate nominated by the senate would become consul, the entire process depended upon this result. The

[10] Plutarch's account, no less garbled as to procedure than Shakespeare's, is of an election among three candidates in which people made choice of the other two.
[11] Shakespeare, *Coriolanus*, II, ii, 2ff.
[12] Ibid., II, iii, 65ff.
[13] Ibid., III, i, 176.
[14] Ibid., III, i, 196.

senators never doubted the fulfillment of their wish. After his nomination Coriolanus was toasted: "To our noble consul we wish all joy and honor." The tribunes were apprised of the decision reached by the senate and directed to present it to the people: "We recommend to you, tribunes of the people, our purpose to them."[15]

It is the people's role, and Shakespeare's attitude toward it, that has so perplexed modern commentators. Certainly, there was nothing democratic about their participation; nor was there anything antidemocratic in Shakespeare's depiction of it. Like the senate, the plebians acted collectively, but they gave assent rather than consent. Coriolanus called their voices "needless vouches," and even the tribune Sicinius described the ceremony as "the custom of request."[16] They took no part in generating candidates, and they had no candidates from which to choose. The most they could do was to withhold their assent and bring the process to a halt. This colloquy among three citizens is the best possible description of how rights and responsibilities blended together in the selection process:

1 Cit.:   Once if he do require our voices, we ought not to deny him.
2 Cit.:   We may, Sir, if we will.
3 Cit.:   We have power in ourselves to do it, but it is a power that we have
          no power to do; for if . . . he tells us his noble deeds, we must also tell
          him our noble acceptance of them.[17]

It was participation that was essential to the plebians – "neither will they bate one jot of ceremony."[18] If selection affirmed honor, then those who participated in it, in whatever capacity, must be seen as honorable. This was precisely the objection that Coriolanus raised against participation by the multitude. Selection to office did not confer honor, it confirmed it. It recognized noble qualities and distinguished them. This was what Coriolanus meant by "the hire that first we do deserve." To seek for confirmation of honor among those least able to recognize it was to diminish both officeholder and office – "by Jove himself, it makes the consul base."[19] Though part of his own honor stemmed from merit, Coriolanus viewed birth and upbringing as more essential elements, and feared that these qualities were in danger of dilution by the masses:

> Thus we debase
> The nature of our seats, and make the rabble
> Call our cares fears; which will in time

[15] Ibid., II, ii, 151.
[16] Ibid., II, iii, 141.
[17] Ibid., II, iii, 1ff.
[18] Ibid., II, ii, 139.
[19] Ibid., III, i, 106.

> Break ope the locks of the senate, and bring in
> The crows to peck the eagles.[20]

Finally, in Shakespeare's recreation of the selection process failure equals catastrophe. Riot, near rebellion, death and destruction all flow from this one event. If selection affirms the honor of the individual and confirms the harmony between patricians and plebians – the underlying harmony of the state – then dissent forcefully expresses the opposite. The rage that overcame Coriolanus was in equal parts the fury of the individual and of the state. To allow the "mutable rank-scented many" a voice of assent was bad enough, but to allow them to reject a nominee was to create an equality as dangerous as it was unnatural. Coriolanus could predict only the most extreme consequences for the state and for his class:

> This double worship,
> Where one part does disdain with causes, the other
> Insult without all reason; where gentry, title, wisdom
> Cannot conclude but by the yea and no
> Of general ignorance; – it must omit
> Real necessities, and give way the while
> To unstable slightness.[21]

In this he was the prophet of his own doom.

Coriolanus is frequently described as Shakespeare's most political play, meaning that it raises issues most recognizably political to the modern mind. It can be read as a play about class struggle and as a play about liberty and oppression. A. C. Bradley, who rejected this view, nevertheless ascribed Coriolanus's fall to the tragic flaw of pride. He was a character out of step with his times, unlike Menenius, who could drink a cup of wine and flatter the commons even while lecturing to them on the virtues of nobility. If Coriolanus was not as ambitious as Macbeth, he was as unyielding as Othello. His rigid values were matched by those of Brutus and Sicinius. In their clash is found the central conflict of the play. By this reading, it is neither a great theme nor a great play.[22] But by elevating the episode of the consulship to the center of the action, we can see the tragedy in a different light – as that of a society whose structures and values are incapable of absorbing the tensions and conflicts within it.

The selection process depicted by Shakespeare depends upon an identity of interest within society. It is grounded upon participation rather

[20] Ibid., III, i, 134.
[21] Ibid., III, i, 141.
[22] A. C. Bradley, *Coriolanus* (1912).

than choice, and on unanimity rather than majority. The senate had no more right to dispense with the assent of the people than did the people to reject the nominee of the senate. It was their agreement that was mutually reinforcing and that defined honor and worth. Yet throughout the episode, Shakespeare presents an undercurrent of disharmony, an expression of views that would render traditional practice inadequate. While one citizen asserted that the people could not deny Coriolanus their voices, another believed that "we may, Sir, if we will." One asked the crowd, "Are you all resolved to give your voices?" He then answered the murmur of discontent: "But that's no matter, the greater part carries it."[23] There is even a hint that the individual voice is as important as the collective one: "He is to make his requests by particulars; wherein every one of us has a single honor in giving him our own voices with our own tongues."[24]

Similarly, Brutus and Sicinius are out of step with the common notion that selection is a celebration of honor. This is a view that both Coriolanus and the citizenry share, however different their notions of who should participate in it. Selection was a social distinction that affirmed virtue rather than a political act that necessitated performance:

2 Off.:   He hath deserved worthily of his country. . . . He hath so planted his honor in their eyes and his actions in their hearts that for their tongues to be silent, and not confess so much were a kind of ungrateful injury.[25]

But for the tribunes, the selection of Coriolanus was above all a political issue. "Our office may, during his power, go to sleep."[26] They could not be persuaded of his virtue by Menenius because it was not his virtue that they sought. They saw their own office in the same political sense that they projected his.

Honor and dishonor, virtue and power – these are at the core of the episode of the consulship and ultimately of the tragedy itself. More importantly, all are at the core of the process of parliamentary selection in early modern England. The clash of values at which Shakespeare dimly hinted would, over the course of the seventeenth century, emerge as one of the defining characteristics of the selection process. Assent would become choice, and the dire consequences of rejection would recede. For the first time election – that is, contests among candidates for majority decisions – would become an important element in the system by which men were chosen to Parliament. A process of social

---

[23]   Shakespeare, *Coriolanus*, II, iii, 37.
[24]   Ibid., II, iii, 44.
[25]   Ibid., II, ii, 24.
[26]   Ibid., II, i, 218.

distinction would give way to one of political calculation, and along the way England would be brought as close to collapse as was Coriolanus's Rome.

II

The selection of members to Parliament is a subject on which it is difficult not to be Whiggish. The electoral process is so fundamental to modern participation in politics that we have an intuitive understanding of its operation. Parliamentary elections are now elaborate events, carefully coordinated and even more carefully studied. The adversarial nature of the process, the competition among the candidates, the interest groups that form the electorate – these are the very stuff of politics itself. Psephologists with their computer graphics mesmerize us with predictions of marginals and swings, of issues and preferences, of winners and losers. It is only to be expected that efforts to study past elections take these categories as their starting point.

In studying the history 'of elections it is hard to view the past as anything less than an imperfect version of the present. The march of parliamentary reform is one of the cherished traditions of British democracy and one of the few that remains untarnished. The enfranchisement of class upon class of citizens opened the way for participatory democracy, for social equality, and for the liberation of women. It is a truism of modern politics that legitimacy is based on consent and that consent is given at elections. The principle of one person, one vote is no longer an issue of politics; it is an issue of justice.

Thus to enter into a discussion of a system in which none of these principles was yet recognized is necessarily to enter into an alien world. We cannot help but explore its features along the lines on which it ultimately developed. What were the requirements for participation at elections? Who held rights to elect, and who to be elected? Who nominated candidates and on what basis? What were the legal sanctions and safeguards of the system? Was it equitable even to those who participated in it? These are the questions that have dominated writing on the subject for generations, whether by local antiquarians, jurists, or professional historians. The classic work of the Porritts, *The Unreformed House of Commons*, crystallized generations of research and immortalized the anachronistic nature of the investigation.[27]

That work also froze into place the supercharged language in which the subject is discussed. Perhaps there is no more evocative phrase in

---

[27] E. and A. Porritt, *The Unreformed House of Commons*, 2 vols. (1903).

the history of political reform than "rotten borough." It calls to mind not only the inherent corruption in the old system of representation but also its inevitable decay. Against the disease of rotten boroughs there could only be purgatives, quarantines, or surgical cleansing. Indeed, the metaphor became more potent as the science of medicine advanced. Rotten boroughs, like lepers, were pariahs in a new age of political awareness. Once representation became the right of individuals rather than of communities and once participation became voting at elections, then rotten boroughs became as indefensible as the divine right of kings. Though they were not completely and immediately swept away, they were ultimately doomed.

The phrase rotten borough is but one example of how the language used to describe the old electoral system denies that system its own integrity. Because rotten borough is so obviously a metaphor, it is easy to call attention to the problems inherent in using it as a description of the early modern system. Since a borough existed by grant of rights from the Crown, and since one of those granted rights was to send representatives to parliament, a rotten borough is a contradiction in terms. What was later thought to be rotten about nineteenth-century boroughs was a conflation of two different things: that they had rights granted to them that were denied to others, and that they had rights they were no longer thought fit to exercise. In the early modern context, of course, the whole point about corporate rights, or chartered rights, or manorial rights, was just such exclusivity. They were granted in exchange for something of value – loyalty, service, fines, rents – and they were normally granted to communities in perpetuity. The point is perhaps made more forcefully when one realizes that in the Middle Ages the community of Torrington, Devonshire, was granted the right not to have to send members to Parliament.[28]

This problem of descriptive language pervades our subject. One obvious case is the use of the word *voting*. In early modern parlance, electors gave voices rather than votes and spoke of having voices to give. The distinction was never precise because the modern meaning of voting, let alone the process, remained inchoate. But giving voices had descriptive meaning, as voting does today, both rhetorically and actually. Rhetorically, giving voices meant giving assent, agreeing to something rather than choosing it. Actually, giving voices meant appearing at the place of election to shout or say aye to the proposal of the nominee's name. The shout was a ritual of affirmation and celebration. As a process, it

---

[28]   In 1661 Torrington petitioned, unsuccessfully, to have its members restored. *Calendar of State Papers Domestic Series 1661–62*, p. 579.

was both anonymous and unanimous. It was the very opposite of voting. The same difference can be observed between the early modern term *standing* for a seat and the modern term *running* for one. Running implies competition and competitors, standing implies individual worth and service. Men stood as the representatives of their communities, however defined, rather than running to represent constituencies within it. Neither the process nor the ideas are analogous, and even more neutral modern words like *candidacy* are fraught with implications of competition.

Yet it is not enough to point out that there are differences between our own language and that of our ancestors. Giving voices, or standing for a seat, are phrases sufficiently jarring to our ears that we can guard against their misconstrual. But there is other language, shared language, that is more complicated to deconstruct. It is not simply imprecision that is the problem. Unaware of how distinctions would evolve, and which ones would become important, contemporaries could mean both less and more by the phrases they chose. Take the phrase "free election." Both early modern and modern meanings impart a sense of equity, an absence of corruption or of overwhelming power. Free choice was un-pressured choice. Though the idea that selections should be uncon-strained was present, the definition of constraint had peculiar parameters. In the seventeenth century there was a clear notion – though not always a clear articulation – of what constituted laboring for voices and of what threatened a free election. That distinction was implicit, and we shall encounter it in its context. But there was another concept inherent in the early modern meaning of a free election, one entirely absent from our own. This was the notion that for an election to be free it was to be made without opposition. Listen to the Earl of Suffolk, in considerable fury, lecture the townsmen of Saffron Walden: "As I am Lord of the town and most of you my tenants (if there were no other respect) that you give your *free* consent and voices to my good friend, Sir Edward Denny, Knight, which if you shall not...I will make the proudest of you repent it."[29] Listen again to the Aldermen of Thetford who selected Sir Robert Cotton to be a member of Parliament in 1625:

Notwithstanding you are a stranger to us, yet upon the commendation of the right honorable, the Earl of Arundel, our most worthy Lord we have made choice of you to be a burgess for our borough of Thetford....Our election being so free and general that you had not one voice against you.[30]

[29] British Library, Egerton Mss., 2644, fol. 138. See Chapter 3 of this book for the context of this comment.
[30] Thomas Martin, *The History of Thetford* (1779), Appendix.

Most destructive of all the language that we bring to this subject is its identification as the history of elections. By labeling the process as electoral, we define it as competitive. Its two most important features become voters and voting. Although historians have chosen to devote most of their attention to them, electoral contests occurred only occasionally in early modern England.[31] What is less appreciated, however, is that these were truly exceptional events, events that violated anticipated patterns of behavior rather than fulfilled them, events that were aberrant rather than normative. Even as they became more common after the Restoration, they remained novel aspects of the process by which representatives were chosen.

That process is much better described as one of parliamentary selection. It was a process in which patrons and peers, civic dignitaries and officeholders, community leaders and community neighbors were designated members of Parliament without opponents, competition, or votes. Contemporaries did not make the linguistic distinction between selection and election, but it is a difference that they would readily have understood.[32] Elections involved divisive choices usually made at polls; selections involved harmonious choices usually made by acclamation. Thus a study of parliamentary selection will not be focused on contests or franchises, on freeholders or corporate freemen, but on the process itself. Only in that context will the importance of elections come to be apparent and their emergence in the late seventeenth century come to be appreciated.

III

In early modern England, political choice was subsumed within a wide system of social relations. Complex notions of honor, standing, and deference, shared but not always articulated, helped to regulate and absorb conflict between and within loosely defined status groups. The selection of members of Parliament, an intermittent event for county property holders and members of designated boroughs, was but one part of a continuing process of social distinction. Despite the uniqueness of Parliament in the political history of the nation, in the ongoing life of the communities that chose its members, parliamentary selection existed in a broader context. For peers of the realm, a summons to the House of Lords was a prescriptive right, another attribute of their nobility. For

---

[31]   It is of course impossible to prove a negative. Positive evidence of uncontested choice is unusual. Normal conduct is generally unremarkable and unremarked upon.

[32]   Indeed, in the seventeenth century the word *election* held religious rather than political significance.

members of the small group of dominant gentry families within the county communities, it was both a responsibility of service and a privilege conferred on them by kin and neighbors. For rich merchants of large boroughs, it followed as part of the *cursus honorum* of civic office; while for gentlemen and lawyers, who obtained the majority of borough seats parceled out to patrons, it was an occasion to follow their own businesses, advance their careers, or simply partake of the delights of the capital. The recurrent directives to sheriffs and returning officers for the selection of discreet and learned men to provide counsel to the monarch – "the Queen ... desires to be served with men of understanding and knowledge" – were inevitably met with the same mix of gentry, lawyers, and merchants whose education, wealth, and governmental experience rose at no greater rate than did that of the classes from which they were drawn.[33]

Although fitted within the common methods of choice and distinction that governed social relations, parliamentary selection had unique dimensions as well. It was hedged about by arcane legal rules that could be invoked or ignored according to whim and which took on increasing importance with the expansion of the common law. While it was the duty of the counties equally, it fell to boroughs in a haphazard fashion and with a dizzying complexity of customs to regulate participation. Patterns of representation had once been functional and had reflected the general distribution of human and material resources. But, like much else in the social system, this had been eroded by demographic and economic expansion. Over the centuries merchant guilds had grown into urban centers or had deteriorated beyond prospect of resuscitation; population shifts had stretched the flesh and muscle of the economic body away from an ossified distribution of seats. The forty shilling freehold which determined the county franchise had once identified men of substance, but it was now crippled both by price inflation and by changing concepts of tenurial relations.

In differing ways all these factors affected the methods by which communities selected members to Parliament. In the largest part, the process of selection conformed to patterns determined by local circumstance. Some corporations followed formulas for parliamentary selection that mirrored their more frequent processes of selecting civic officers. Broad or narrow participation by freemen, freeholders, or inhabitants had as much to do with their integration into corporate life – as jurymen, ratepayers, and minor officials – as with the prescription of ancient

[33] Historical Manuscripts Commission Reports, *Report on the Manuscripts of the Marquis of Salisbury*, VII, 410.

charters. The patronage of landed magnates depended upon some natural tie, either as high stewards, civic benefactors, or owners of town lands. But such influence equally turned upon the vagaries of mortality, minorities, or the competence of governmental officials, and these – combined with the irregular gaps between parliaments – prevented customary, informal arrangements from congealing into fixed patterns.

Similarly, county selections differed according to social structure, population, and wealth. In counties the keynotes of parliamentary selection were honor and deference. Men were chosen members of Parliament or given the right to nominate members on the basis of criteria largely social in nature. This was especially true of the senior knight of the shire, which by the early seventeenth century had become a mark of social distinction that outweighed all other factors. Counties whose internal social elites were dominated by one or two families – like Herefordshire or Surrey – honored these men and their heirs regularly. Counties like Kent or Somerset, which had more variegated elites, developed patterns of rotation. In many places the leading magistrates, perhaps at assizes or quarter sessions, met together in anticipation of the day of election and nominated the two candidates who would be chosen. In others, the candidates emerged in a less tidy manner, writing to each other and their friends, assessing the likeliest intentions of their equals and superiors, and adhering to a code of conduct that served to winnow the field to the two who were to be chosen at the county court.

Because boroughs comprised an exotic mixture of the great urban areas of the realm and the passing remnants of medieval prosperity, they made their selections more variously than did counties. In large and flourishing places – like York, Bristol, or Exeter – indigenous citizens could be honored in the same fashion as in counties. Distinguished alderman, past mayors and sheriffs completed their course of honor by selection to Parliament. A legal officer, especially a recorder, might be designated as one of the town's representatives, as was done at Reading, Bedford, and many other places. Communities might have specific individuals to whom honor was due for other reasons: a lord of the manor who had let the use of land and buildings at uneconomic rents; a neighboring gentleman who had established a local school; a privy councilor who had defended and procured a charter, as did Archbishop Laud for his birthplace of Reading. All of these categories of members or their nominees, though lumped together under the opprobrious label of "patronage," were part of the natural relationships – the symbiotic relationships – that protected the rights and privileges of communities on the one hand and extended the rank and standing of the individual on the other.

The Elizabethan innovation of creating the office of high steward at reincorporations is a case in point. High stewards were usually great men of the realm, socially superior to any within the borough and politically powerful in their own right. They performed service to the borough in a host of ways, including acting as arbitrators of local disputes. Their deeper interest might lie in the proximity of their estates to the borough or in an obligation, such as serving as county lord lieutenant, to ensure its good governance. From the borough they gained the privilege of recommending nominees for a variety of posts, of which parliamentary representatives were only the best known. They were not parliamentary patrons as we generally meet them – power brokers moving into weak and undefended territory to operate something akin to a protection racket. Nor, mutatis mutandis, were those government officials who were also given rights of nomination in specific and logical places like the Cinque Ports, the Isle of Wight, or the towns in the Duchy of Lancaster.

Like counties, boroughs organized their selections to provide the same number of candidates as there were places at their disposal, usually two. Indeed, the dyadic nature of parliamentary selections was a most effective safety valve. It allowed local interests, competing patrons, or distinguished individuals room to maneuver.[34] Until the new charter granted to Reading in 1637, the corporation always sent its recorder and a nominee of its high steward; Leicester generally accepted a nominee of the Earl of Huntington and one of the chancellor of the Duchy of Lancaster; Dover selected the lieutenant of its castle. Scores of other places worked out similar and changing patterns. There can be no question about the relationship between the putative franchise and the actual process of selection: There was none. The internal history of boroughs reveals the local context from which appropriate arrangements developed; among the more interesting were the lotteries organized in places like Cambridge, York, and Great Yarmouth.

None of these dimensions to the process of parliamentary selection can be usefully described as political. Of course, in one sense politics pervades all social relations. Categories such as sexual politics or the politics of the family remind us that no human relations are devoid of political meaning. But they also remind us that we cannot confuse generic and specific meanings of what is essentially an amorphous analytic category. The problem is complicated by the fact that in the early modern world there was no separation between the social and the political.

---

[34] In Wales the competitive pressures were much greater, as both shires and town were single-member constituencies. Welsh electoral contests were among the most brutal of the period. See especially J. E. Neale, *The Elizabethan House of Commons* (1949).

Authority was integrated. Personal attributes, prestige, standing, godliness – were all implicit in officeholding. Their presence qualified individuals for place, their absence disqualified them. Individuals represented communities by virtue of the possession of these qualities, not by reflecting the special interests or ideals of particular groups of constituents. In all but a handful of instances, most of which are extremely well documented, before 1640 ideology was absent from the process of parliamentary selection.[35]

There is almost no evidence upon which to base the assumption that there was a connection between the selection of members to Parliament and the activities of members of Parliament. It is certainly the case, especially in boroughs, that parliaments were occasionally seen as opportunities to present private bills or to complain about specific grievances. But this had little effect upon the patterns of selection. Patrons prefaced their commendatory letters with the promise that their nominees would actively follow the community's business. When Viscount Conway nominated Sir Fulke Greville to the town of Yarmouth in 1628, he recommended him as "well affected to the good of your town, will study and endeavor to advance it all in [his] power, and will give you a good account of anything you shall commit to [him]."[36] Given the choice between paying members of Parliament and paying lawyers to handle corporate business, most places chose the latter. Perhaps more than a few gained the advantages offered by Lord Cobham to New Romney in 1597: "And though I mean to make choice of such one, for that service, as shall specially regard the good of your town, yet (in the love I bear you all) I think fit to advise you to authorize some discreet burgess or other inhabitant of your town to attend here this Parliament to give instructions as occasion may fall out."[37] Even in cases in which members received "instructions" from grand juries or corporate magistrates there is rarely evidence that their selection, as distinct from that of others, hinged on their willingness to accept them.

The principle of parliamentary selection – and, judging from the available evidence, the reality as well – was unified choice. "By and with the whole advice, assent and consent," was how the town of Northampton

[35]   It must be stressed, here and elsewhere when this point is made, that the absence of ideological issues at parliamentary selections does not mean that they were absent from English society or from the communities that chose representatives. Nor does it mean that ideological issues simply burst forth, Athena-like, in 1640. There were no parliamentary selections between 1628 and 1640, but social and political developments were not frozen during that period. This point cannot be emphasized too strongly.

[36]   Public Record Office, State Papers, 16/92/6.

[37]   Kent Archive Office, New Romney Records, NR Aep/35.

put it when enrolling the selection of Christopher Sherland and Richard Spencer in 1626.[38] Communities avoided division over parliamentary selections for all the obvious reasons – cost, trouble, fear of riot, challenge to magisterial authority – and for one other: The refusal to assent to the choice of an M.P. was an explicit statement of dishonor. Freely given by the will of the shire or the borough, a place in Parliament was a worthy distinction. Wrested away from competitors in a divisive contest, it diminished the worth of both victor and vanquished.

This is why contests were so rare in early seventeenth-century selections. Most arose accidentally because of a failure of communication or the tardiness of one entrant or another. We can see many begin and then be composed, sometimes at the last moment, by the intervention of the magistracy, a leading peer, or even a concerned privy councilor. In 1588 the Privy Council directed Lord Rich to cease his activities at the Essex selection so that there would be neither opposition to Sir Thomas Heneage and Sir Henry Grey nor a large number of freeholders gathered at the county court.[39] Contests generally developed not only from their accidental first cause, but also from the subsequent suspicion, misinterpretation of personal slights, and hints of family discredit. Resolution of near-contests generally took the form of face-saving of one variety or another. The famous Essex selection of 1604 was composed on the night before the county day when one of the three aspirants agreed to stand down at the request of the sheriff and magistrates, and the other two threw dice for senior shire place.

The contests which did occur were bitter personal or local feuds that rent the social fabric of the community. They called upon primary allegiances and divided kin and neighbors. The cautious code of conduct that helped prevent contests continued in force until the day of the county court, but once contests became inevitable, all rules were abandoned. Contestants competed by fair means or foul with the single-minded purpose of inflicting as much pain as possible. This was why Star Chamber, far from being the ineffectual remedy that Neale believed it to be, was the perfect place to resolve contests.[40] What was at issue was not

---

[38] Northampton Record Office, 3/1 fol. 429. Northampton Assembly Hall Book.

[39] *Acts of the Privy Council 1588*, pp. 318–19.

[40] J. E. Neale, "Three Elizabethan Elections," *English Historical Review*, 46 (1931), pp. 209–38. Neale built much of his case for the inherent corruption of the electoral system upon its supposed absence of remedy. This was not a precise idea, although certainly it was difficult to obtain a seat on petition to the Lord Chancellor and impossible to gain a reversal on a writ from Star Chamber. Some reversals were being granted by the House itself in the very late Elizabethan period. Instead of reflecting upon why this should have been so, Neale simply concluded that it served the interests of the corruptors of elections. In fact, because contests were so rare and so divisive,

a seat in Parliament but an attack upon personal worth and magisterial authority. Cost, trouble, legal sanction, and loss of prestige were worthy punishments. Cases lasting years beyond the lives of the parliaments that generated them attest to the motives and aspirations of Star Chamber litigants. Contests resulted in riots, in ambushes, in lawsuits. They were the focal point of division that could last for decades, as did the bitterness of the 1614 election in Somerset. Contests were a catastrophe for the community and were seen as such both in the extraordinary efforts taken to avoid them and in their aftershocks. Because they are so rare and so extraordinary, contests are not a barometer either of normal social relations or of the level of social conflict within society.

The transformation of the process of parliamentary selection is first observable during the revolutionary era. "Between the Elizabethan era ... and the crisis of the Popish Plot something of decisive importance happened which changed the character of elections."[41] It is, of course, impossible to place precise dates upon shifts of practices and beliefs as deep-rooted as these. In the case of parliamentary selection the difficulty is complicated immensely by the fact that no parliaments occurred between 1629 and 1640. But beginning with the selections to the Short and Long Parliaments, and then expanding significantly during the Commonwealth, the underlying nature of the process of parliamentary selection began to change. These changes were caused, in the first place, by the introduction of an explicitly political dimension to choice that accompanied the belief that Parliament was a political institution in which the rights and liberties of the subject were protected. Again we can see the first stirrings of these beliefs in 1628, but their consequences do not appear and begin to spread until much later. More fundamentally, the transformation of parliamentary selection resulted from the infusion of political ideologies during the course of the Revolution. Under these pressures, not to mention a decade of civil war, the routines of the past could not survive unaltered.

This is not to say that parliamentary selections were transformed immediately, or that once political and ideological considerations invaded the process it was only a matter of time before all outposts were conquered. During the revolutionary period many saw an enhanced value in unified choice and in attaching themselves to the protection of local worthies. Nor should we discount the conscious efforts made at

---

it is not at all surprising that no immediate remedy existed to regulate them. To recognize that the House stumbled upon one in 1604 is not to say that one was actively being sought.

[41]   D. E. Underdown, "Party Management and the Recruiter Elections 1645–1648," *English Historical Review*, 83 (1968), p. 235.

the Restoration to undo the changes initiated, intentionally or not, by the Revolution. Still, the signs of change are unmistakable. They are best revealed in the new attitude toward candidacy. In the past men willingly abandoned their candidacies or never went forward at all if there was any danger that they would not be successful. They were more concerned to avoid the "foil" or the "repulse" than to secure the seat. But beginning in 1640, more and more candidates came to believe that it was more important to secure a seat than to avoid defeat. This was a purely political concern, especially in the 1650s when the lessons of the power of Parliament over men's lives and estates had been fully digested.

After the Restoration, the process of parliamentary selection became more systematic and more a subject of explicit attention than ever before. Throughout the nation, country gentlemen and men of affairs were absorbed by the subject of Parliament. In contrast to the earlier period, correspondence is filled with information collected from around the nation. In part this was because of the rhythm of parliamentary selections after 1661. The Long Parliament of Charles II removed selection from the general community and channeled it into by-elections. This created a pent-up demand for seats across the 1660s and 1670s and allowed for the kind of planning on the part of candidates and government officials that had never before been possible. Nevertheless, the politicization of the process had its own impact. The choices made in 1660 and 1661 were made with full cognizance of the political divisions that had dominated the revolutionary era. The reasons men had for standing and for participating were stated in political terms. The strategies they developed to gain their seats were no less political in tone.

The informal system of patronage that had existed in boroughs became solidified and fixed. No longer was there confusion over who might nominate and who might be nominated. Competition for the right to influence choices became intense, especially with the intrusion of Court officials into the quest. Individuals with natural holds on parliamentary seats, like lords of manors or dominant neighboring gentlemen, grasped them tightly. The increase in repetitive selections of individuals and of family members makes clear the enhanced value of a parliamentary seat. Never again would a Luttrell forget to send in a nomination at Minehead, as one did in 1601.[42] After the Restoration, Luttrells would make no nominations at all at Minehead: They would take the seats themselves. Moreover, patronage relations became more overtly reciprocal than they had been before the Revolution. Communities were only too happy to

---

[42] M. K. Mort, "The Personnel of the House of Commons in 1601," unpublished M.A. thesis, London University (1952).

put their seats up to bid, especially when aspiring patrons or candidates viewed a seat in Parliament as a valuable commodity. "This business is like to grow to a great height of expense and trouble," one of the candidates for a place at Dover was advised. "The Lord in Mercy send a time wherein Parliament men may be chosen with less."[43] The story of Buckingham's election in 1685, one of many with similar features, could not have been told of any parliamentary borough sixty years earlier.[44]

After the Restoration, candidates secured their seats by "building an interest," a process that combined natural ties, benefactions, and outright bribery. They did this in direct competition with others of their class and with a ruthlessness hitherto unknown. At Yorkshire in 1679 Sir John Kaye "met with great disappointments on the perfidiousness of persons who promised me their interests under their hands. What an age are we in when honor and honesty is laid aside by persons of good rank."[45] Building an interest involved obtaining a majority among the electorate rather than achieving unified choice.

This was one reason why elections became horrendously expensive after 1660. Costs increased ten- or twenty-fold, with no logical limit based on competition or constituency. Rising costs were simply the result of the presence of free-spending competitors trying to feed an insatiable electorate or, more commonly, competing electorates. Not until this transformation was well under way did the issue of franchises become potent. Once majorities were the requirement for selection then the question of who held rights of participation became paramount. One obvious consequence of building majority interests, of course, was that it undermined magisterial authority. By definition one candidate or another would be competing against the one supported by the governing officials, while in franchise disputes they would be competing against the rights of the governing body itself. Thus were the deep political and religious divisions of the post-Restoration era manifested in the rise of competitive parliamentary selections.

Though electoral contests – elections – never outnumbered selections in early modern constituencies, after the Restoration they were the expected outcome of every competition. Men made plans to stave off opponents or to defeat them. The death of a patron or of a father set off a flurry of inquiries among those likely to switch their support. The terms upon which contests were to take place were regularized and publicized. Polls, anathema before the Revolution, came to be established

---

[43] Kent A.O., Papillon Mss., U1015/020/14.
[44] See Chapter 8 of this book.
[45] Leeds Central Library, Mexborough Manuscripts, MX/R14/172c.

routines with elaborate rules governing oathtaking, counting, and venues. Candidates no longer opposed each other on personal grounds. Each recognized, perhaps even admired, the other's objective in gaining a seat and viewed the process of achieving victory more studiously and objectively. But achieving victory was the goal, and the late seventeenth century witnessed the beginnings of that violence and intimidation of electors that was to become so common in the succeeding half-century.

The depersonalization of the process of parliamentary selection is one of the most important elements of its transformation. It was made possible by the ideological and political divisions that allowed candidates to represent something more than themselves. As Lord Weymouth observed at the very end of our period: "The truth is if this election had been as others formerly, where affection to the persons standing, not interest to a party, had been the only competition, I believe my brother had carried it."[46] This was the shift from the social to the political, the compartmentalization of values that R. H. Tawney defined as the most important change of the seventeenth century.[47] Its consequences in the history of parliamentary selection were the multiplication of contests, the serious struggle to establish the electorate, and the emergence of professional politicians whose training ground was the House of Commons. It was the willingness of the elite to contend with each other that created the conditions for the expansion of political participation by other social classes and which, in the long run, made necessary both the party system of the eighteenth century and the franchise reforms of the nineteenth.

[46] Quoted in Henry Horwitz, "The General Election of 1690," *Journal of British Studies*, 11 (1971), p. 87.
[47] R. H. Tawney, *Religion and the Rise of Capitalism* (1922).

2

Counties and Boroughs

I

JUST AS THE SUMMONING of Parliament was occasional and intermittent, selections to the House of Commons were an unplanned part of a wider range of social and political choices made in local communities. Assembled together, members of Parliament acquired symbolic importance in uniting the King with his Lords and Commons. They also exercised legal and political functions and represented the community of the realm. They were part of an ongoing institution that was increasingly a part of royal government in the early modern era. Thus it is often assumed that members were individually suited to their collective responsibilities and that this was a result of the process by which they were selected. In fact, there is little that connects the selection process in the localities with the legislative process at Westminster. Parliamentary selections were part of a kind of social ecology in which elevations to titles and honors, appointments to the bench, the lieutenancy, or the assumption of corporate responsibility marked out the thriving species. They were subject to the inexorable laws of the life cycle and the land market – hostages alike to fortunes won and lost, ambitions grasped and dashed. Their determinants varied in place and time and conformed only to the ever-changing patterns of local leadership and social differentiation.

The normative process of parliamentary selection must be studied in this context of social standing and community service. Selection of members to Parliament could present the opportunity to honor natural leaders or could highlight ambiguities in the competition for local prestige. The moment of selection was the ever-present uncertainty. When a Parliament was summoned, traditional choices for representatives might be unavailable for selection because of elevation to the peerage, appointment to government service, or death. A borough may have recently received a charter, lost or gained a high steward, or had its chief manor

22

change hands – all circumstances that would alter its patronage. Re-shuffled government officials might forget to send in nominations or be unaware of the customs of boroughs within their purview, as was Sir Robert Cecil in 1597 when as Chancellor of the Duchy of Lancaster, he requested the right of nomination to nonexistent seats in the county of Durham.[1]

In county and borough alike, parliamentary selection was a process of affirmation rather than a struggle for power. "The country expects that Sir Edward Coke will be put by and that your worship shall have a place," Martin Man wrote to Sir Roger Townsend in 1616. "Which if it fall out you may take comfort in the love of the country and in so free an election, being more honorable than to obtain it by suit and labor." "Men should not stand to be knights," Sir Henry Poole argued in a Commons debate on parliamentary reform, "but they should be chosen whom the county chooses of itself, not they that desire it."[2] William Wiseman assured the electors at Maldon, "I mean to use neither art nor labor for a burgessship, for he that takes that course most commonly least deserves it." Rather he relied upon his known reputa-tion: "If you shall think my place among you or my service and love to the borough for many years to deserve your voices, I shall take it kindly."[3] Even in the very rare cases when malevolent spirits were hell-bent upon victory, language, actions, and behavior were molded into a decorum based upon mutual respect and deference.

These conventions of the selection process were not shadows behind which lurked ambition and the hunger for power. A seat in parliament, especially as knight of the shire, was an honor when freely given. Its

---

[1] Thus the Duke of Buckingham neglected to send nominations along with the writs for selection to the Cinque Ports in 1626. I cannot accept Gruenfelder's argument that Buckingham's nominations were rejected at this election. Sir John Hippisley warned Buckingham of the necessity of sending in his nominations. "I marvel that your letters have not come down ... for the writs to the parliament I have sent four days since and this is not to be delayed unless you intend to lose your right." He then explicitly analyzed the failure: "... all which was for want of your letters in time." Public Record Office, State Papers, 16/18/28; SP 16/18/58; J. K. Gruenfelder, "The Lord Wardens and Elections," *Journal of British Studies*, 16, 1 (1976), p. 20. In 1597 Sir Robert Cecil, newly appointed chancellor of the duchy of Lancaster, requested the bishop of Durham to grant Cecil a nomination in the county Palatine, to which Bishop Matthew responded: "I cannot learn that ever such [representatives from Durham] were allowed of in the Parliament House." Historical Manuscripts Commission Re-ports, *Manuscripts of the Marquis of Salisbury*, VII, 405.

[2] Wilfred Prest, "An Australian Holding of Norfolk Manuscripts," *Norfolk Archae-ology*, 37, 1 (1978), p. 122; W. Notestein, H. Simpson, F. Relf, *Commons Debates 1621*, II, 460.

[3] Essex Record Office, Maldon Corporation Mss., bundle D/B 3/3 no. 1; V. Hodges, "The Electoral Influence of the Aristocracy 1604–1640," unpublished Ph.D. disser-tation, Columbia University (1977), p. 217.

value rapidly diminished when sullied by competition: "For though to be knight of this shire be a thing I much desire and even the highest mark of my ambition, yet I would be loath to purchase it with the loss [of] . . . a friend."[4] After all, sessions were of uncertain duration; and the preparation and pains of travel could be repaid by sudden dissolution, as in 1584 or 1614, or by unanticipated costs, as in the marathon sessions of the 1604 Parliament. Men would decline service for an array of reasons, from responsibilities to family and estate to the financial burdens a seat imposed. For most it was an experience to add to the variety of others that marked a gentleman in this Renaissance age: "For some private occasions I should now gladly be a spectator, and give my son a little breeding there."[5] Each House had as many one-time members as it did men with parliamentary experience.[6] This was the more remarkable given the established interest of patrons, the formulas that elected particular borough officials, and the general disinclination to reject magistrates who performed their trust. The undeniable fact that the early modern period witnessed increased interest in and competition for parliamentary seats, especially by the gentry, should not lead to the conclusion that the desire for seats was universal and unrelenting.

In fact, the sounding-out process that preceded nominations in counties and boroughs frequently elicited responses of disinclination or irresolution. When Sir John Poulett heard that he was to be advanced as a candidate to the county seat in Somerset for the 1624 selection, he had his servant Robert Hackshaw "desire his friends and well-wishers by all means possible to excuse him and free him from that place at this time for that he hath already served twice . . . and there are many more gentlemen of worth in the country worthy of the place."[7] The calamitous contest in Somerset prior to the 1614 Parliament had its origins in Sir Robert Phelips's initial disinclination to stand; and the 1597 contest in

[4] Somerset Record Office, Phelips Mss., DD/PH 216/89.
[5] Historical Manuscripts Commission, *12th Report*, Appendix I (Coke Manuscripts), p. 253. Sir George Chudleigh to Sir John Coke, February 1, 1626.
[6] See compilations in N. M. Fuidge, "Personnel of the Parliament of 1563–67," unpublished M.A. thesis, London University (1950); Hazel Matthews, "Personnel of the Parliament of 1584–85," unpublished M. A. thesis, London University (1948); R. C. Gabriel, "Members of the House of Commons 1586–87," unpublished M. A. thesis, London University (1954); E. E. Trafford, "Personnel of the Parliament of 1593," unpublished M.A. thesis, London University (1948); M. K. Mort, "The Personnel of the House of Commons in 1601," unpublished M.A. thesis, London University (1952).
[7] Somerset R.O., DD/PH 219 fol. 63. Also see William Leonard's letter declining a nomination for Dover in 1621: "I am moved . . . to stand for a place which I do not greatly desire in regard I have formerly been a burgess of the parliament." PRO SP 14/117/74.

Yorkshire turned on Sir John Saville's similar disavowal.[8] Contemporaries were better equipped to read and hear the nuances in demurs and refusals than we are, but they had no difficulty in accepting the likelihood that given individuals at given moments were not interested in being selected.

Yet beyond actual disinclination there were many reasons for candidates to proceed cautiously while their ranks were being sifted. Especially in counties with a large and prosperous gentry class there were more suitable aspirants than places available, and even elaborate rotations could not alone resolve all legitimate claims. What prevented free-for-alls, then, was a set of conventions by which the relative merits of competitors could be evaluated; the shared assumption that an actual test of strength was to be avoided whenever possible; and a recognition of the stakes. "I am absolutely certain Sir John Saville will not stand when it comes to the upshot," Sir Henry Saville wrote to Sir Richard Beaumont in 1621. "When he shall well understand his friends' and neighbors' engagements, he will think it more wisdom and safety for his reputation to go to his grave with that honor the country hath already cast upon him, than to hazard the loss of all at a farewell."[9] Simply put, there was more to lose by losing than there was to win by winning.[10]

II

In the counties, initiative for selecting representatives of necessity fell upon the gentry. Selection to the county's seats was a mark of social distinction within the hierarchy of the elite. Although residency was not a requirement – it was one of the statutory regulations that the common lawyers had agreed to ignore – by the 1580s only a handful of knights of the shire were selected for counties in which they did not hold a landed estate. The country gentry were the class from which the representatives would be drawn, and they had the responsibility for setting the selection process in train. "We doubt not that the principal persons in the county will see to the choice of men meet to serve as knights of the shire," the Privy Council wrote to returning officers in its election

---

[8] See Edith Farnham, "The Somerset Election of 1614," *English Historical Review*, 46 (1931), pp. 579–99, and Chapter 4 of this book; J. E. Neale, *The Elizabethan House of Commons* (1949), p. 91, and Chapter 3 of this book.

[9] J. J. Cartwright, *Chapters in Yorkshire History*, (1872), p. 201. Though related, these two Savilles nested in remote branches of the family tree.

[10] Thus Bacon's dictum: "A man is an ill husband of his honor that enters into any action, the failing wherein may disgrace him more than the carrying of it through can honor him."

circular of 1597.[11] Methods differed not only according to local custom, but also according to the changing circumstances of the social hierarchy within the county. Patterns of geographical rotation, which become apparent when they are violated, appear to have existed in many counties: east and west in Sussex, Kent, and Northamptonshire; vale and forest in Berkshire and Gloucestershire.

Small counties, like Rutland and Herefordshire, usually found the selection process uncomplicated. In Rutland, Haringtons and Noels shared county honors and only the exceptional circumstances of Sir Andrew Noel's shrievalty in 1601 created difficulties.[12] In Herefordshire, a Croft had sat for one county seat in every parliament but one between 1563 and 1621, and a Scudamore in all but three. Sir Herbert Croft's conversion to Catholicism in 1617 and subsequent retirement from public affairs, and Sir James Scudamore's death in 1619, transformed a settled pattern into a fluid one. Disagreement over candidates in 1614, for which no details have come to light, was likely to erupt into county-wide divisions in 1621. The magistracy moved quickly to prevent them. Shortly after the writs were issued, the leading gentry of the county were called together to consider "what was fit to be done as well for the election of knights to serve at the next approaching parliament as for future time. Weighing and considering the great inconveniences which have heretofore happened by faction and opposition in the said election," the county leadership determined "that whensoever hereafter notice shall be given of a parliament, they shall . . . [meet] to point out two fit men to be proposed to the freeholders of the same county to elect, if they please to approve of them, . . . who by them and us shall be so fit."[13]

More frequently, larger counties needed the aid of local institutions. A number of West Country magistrates contended in 1628 that in Devon

[11] Historical Manuscripts Commission Reports, *Manuscripts of the Marquis of Salisbury*, VII, 410.
[12] J. E. Neale, "More Elizabethan Elections," *English Historical Review*, 61 (1946), pp. 32–44. See also Chapter 4 of this book.
[13] Folger Library Mss., Scudamore Papers, Vb 2 (21). This system continued to operate efficiently through the selections to the Long Parliament. For 1626, see British Library Loan, 29/123/39i; for the Long Parliament, Historical Manuscripts Commission *14th Report*, Appendix II (Portland Manuscripts, vol. III), p. 65. Sir Robert Harley and Fitzwilliam Coningsby to the Earl of Essex, October 9, 1640: "We have been invited by divers gentlemen of the best quality in this county to be Knights of the Shire at the next parliament." There is no evidence of a contest for the Short Parliament seats. Cf. D. Hirst, *The Representative of the People?* (1975), p. 219. I am indebted to Jacqueline Levy for the 1621 and 1626 references and for much helpful discussion on Herefordshire. See her "Perceptions and Beliefs: The Harleys of Brampton Bryan and the Origins and Outbreak of the First Civil War," unpublished Ph.D. dissertation, London University (1983).

and Cornwall "it is usual . . . for the deputy lieutenants and justices to assemble for easing the country and avoiding faction to agree which among them shall stand."[14] Benjamin Lovell recalled "whilst I lived in Warwickshire we were wont to advise together about the choice of knights of the shire."[15] Writs that traversed periods in which quarter sessions met allowed the magistrates opportunity for either formal agreements or informal soundings. In 1628 the Staffordshire high constables were directed "to bring in the freeholders to the county town and to entreat them to attend and give their voices for such gentlemen as shall be agreed upon by the more part of the magistrates."[16] Dorsetshire gentry traditionally met before the county day to determine their two candidates. Presence at sessions relieved many of the responsibility of attendance at the selection, as Sir Nathaniel Napper learned to his cost in the Dorsetshire election of 1624 when his supporters failed to appear and he was ousted from his place.[17] In 1624 the magistrates of Cheshire met on the county day and nominated William Booth and William Brereton to be knights of the shire. The sheriff, Sir Richard Grosvenor, announced their decision to the freeholders, urging their support "as you see us respect your good and cast behind us all private respects."[18]

Counties with settled national institutions such as councils and resident bishops, or with the seats of great officers of state or peers of the realm, were able to take their lead without relying upon informal and inefficient local communications.[19] The Earl of Huntingdon, Lord Lieu-

---

[14] PRO SP 16/471/69. I am grateful to Conrad Russell for providing me with a photocopy of this document. It unquestionably relates to the 1628 Cornish selection, which led to recriminations and to the ultimate imprisonment of some of those who attempted to nominate candidates. It does not appear, however, that there was an electoral contest. Cf. Harold Hulme, *The Life of Sir John Eliot* (1957), pp. 176–181; D. Hirst, *Representative of the People?*, p. 217. The J.P.'s of Somerset similarly attempted nominations for the 1624 Parliament, though without success. Farnham, "Somerset Election of 1614," *English Historical Review*, 46 (1931), p. 584.

[15] Huntington Library, Temple–Stowe Mss., STT 1436.

[16] J. C. Wedgewood, "Parliamentary History of Staffordshire," *Historical Collections of Staffordshire*, II (1922), 34. Similarly, in 1593 letters were sent to Norfolk constables in the name of "the greatest part of the justices" on behalf of Sir Edward Coke. Norfolk and Norwich Record Office, Aylsham Manuscripts 16.

[17] British Library, Egerton Mss., 784, fol. 38.

[18] Eaton Hall, Grosvenor Mss., item 25, fol. 14. See also R. Cust and P. G. Lake, "Sir Richard Grosvenor and the Rhetoric of Magistracy," *Bulletin of the Institute of Historical Research*, 54, no. 129 (1981), pp. 40–53. I am indebted to Richard Cust for providing a photocopy of this document. There can be no question of a contest at this selection. Cf. D. Hirst, *Representative of the People?*, p. 217.

[19] Only the power of Sir Robert Cecil prevented a contest in Hertfordshire in 1587. As Rowland Lytton reported, "If it had pleased Sir Edward Denny the younger to have accepted it, he knows I and all my friends would have stood firm for him; but on

tenant of Rutland, wrote to the principal gentlemen of the county before the 1624 Parliament: "I have thought good (out of my love and care of that county whereof his Majesty hath given me that charge) to recommend Sir William Bulstrode and Sir Guy Palmes. . . . So shall I take it as an assurance of your loves and respects towards me."[20] Spencers and Montagues were active in organizing seventeenth-century Northamptonshire selections, sharing the seats between themselves and their clients. In 1603 Sir Edward Montague circulated the news to his dependents: "Sir Robert Spencer and myself having joined ourselves in love for the good of our country and desire that they would again make known their loves to us in putting us in trust for them before any others." Just prior to the selection Spencer wrote in confirmation of their success: "I do heartily thank you that you have performed all promises on your part touching voices for the parliament."[21]

The process of soliciting or pledging support began with news that a writ was to be issued for a meeting on the next county day. This could come informally to individual gentlemen from their regular correspondents in London or from the sheriff once he had received the legal documents. Given the uncertainty of both the summons and the arrival of the writs there was generally little time for even rudimentary communication among the principal gentlemen. Before the 1628 Shropshire selection, "on Thursday last the gentlemen met to consider of parliament men and there resolved when the writs came to choose Sir Richard Newport and Sir Andrew Corbet."[22] In the Norfolk selection of 1586 the writ arrived only two days before the next meeting of the county court; the sheriff sent messengers to those he believed chiefly concerned and relied upon the presence of others who had business to conduct on

his refusal I thought fit best to leave it to a voluntary choice; and so I did not stir until I heard of great labor for others, and that even my own neighbors were not aware of my nomination." Historical Manuscripts Commission Reports, *Manuscripts of the Marquis of Salisbury*, VII, 396. See also the recommendation of the lord president of the Council of the North in the Yorkshire county selection of 1604. J. P. Cooper, ed., *The Wentworth Papers, 1597–1628* (Camden Society, fourth series, 1973), pp. 47–48.

20 Huntington Library, Hastings Mss., HA 5480. He used the same device in Leicestershire at the Short Parliament selections. HA 5550.

21 Northamptonshire Record Office, Montague Mss., 33, B 2.8. Sir Edward Montague to (?); Montague Mss. 9, 25. Robert Lord Spencer to Sir Edward Montague. Spencer nominated his "cousin Sir Valentine Knightly" and advised Montague "to be respective that (according to the late proclamation) you raise as small numbers as can be for your elections, perceiving none to oppose you." Hirst's contention that there was a contest at this selection is based on a document from the previous year. *Representative of the People?*, p. 220.

22 British Library, Loan 29/202/fol. 237. I owe this reference to Jacqueline Levy.

the day of the court.[23] Such a procedure strengthened the social ordering among the gentry, for it reinforced the status of those individuals who were the first to be informed of the receipt of the writ. Lacking time and information, an aspirant for a seat would evaluate his own chances by observng the actions of those whom he believed had the best claim to the place. The factors that elevated individuals above their peers varied: Lineage, office, the possession of great estates, and unique combinations of these and other qualities were recognized within local societies, and their ineffability does not diminish their importance. The inclination of a natural leader to take his seat often resolved many doubts.

On some occasions a gentleman desiring a place might begin by offering his support to someone with an equal or better claim to the honor. This was generally done with the hope that a reciprocal arrangement would follow and that the combined strength of the two would resolve the issue for any other seekers. Thus did Sir Robert Harley write to Sir Walter Pye in 1626, "that I may be sure to reserve my voices to be at your command as I desire the favor of yours."[24] After Beville Grenville and John Arundell had determined to join together for the selection in Cornwall in 1621, Arundell sent Nicholas Burton "to sound how William Coryton would stand towards him." Although Coryton had designs of his own, he immediately agreed that "he would sit down and throw all his voices upon his said kinsman. J[ohn] A[rundell] that would not be behind in courtesy, the next day made him the like offer which he refused and they both agreed that J[ohn] A[rundell] should stand."[25]

This was a common pattern, as was that by which a number of gentlemen would approach their agreed choice and request that he stand for the place. "It pleased the gentlemen of our county at London where I was this term to hold me worthy (I thank them) to be one of those who should stand for Knight of the Shire for the county of Norfolk." Dru Drury wrote to Sir William de Grey to enlist his support in the 1621 selection.[26] Except in the most confused or contentious local societies such a groundswell assured selection, for it meant that a larger network of communication had cleared the way of potential competitors. Either method could result in the candidate being convinced of his right to proceed in requesting support from his kin and neighbors. Once begun, the gathering of voices rippled in ever wider circles. "I am to desire you in Sir William Drury's behalf as well as at my own entreaty

[23] J. Glanville, *Reports of Certain Cases* (1775), lii.
[24] British Library, Loan 29/123/39.
[25] PRO SP 14/117/55.
[26] Norfolk and Norwich Record Office, Walsingham Manuscripts, xvii (2).

that you will procure all your freeholders in Suffolk," Anthony Gaudy wrote to his brother Bassingbourne in 1584, adding, "I myself will acknowledge you to deal brotherly with me in pleasuring my good friend so much."[27]

This initial process of tentative advances and retreats had the object of allowing superfluous aspirants to withdraw without loss of honor and give their support to the surviving candidates. "For my part in Flintshire," Sir Roger Mosteyn wrote to Sir John Wynn in 1625, "it goeth on according to the last choice of Sir John Trevor, whereunto I and all the friends I had had given consent, and to make a show to seek it and fail were a greater disgrace than the benefit thereof would be to him that had it."[28] Like every other aspect of the process, "standing down" worked to narrow the field. By the time a candidate or his supporters began making requests for the commitment of voices it was nearly certain that the outcome had been determined.

Thus the subtle distinction between sounding out and canvassing was displayed in the cautious letters with which most selections began. "I know my own private credit is not such in the shire ... as of myself I can clearly carry away so great a matter," Henry Cocke wrote to Charles Morison in 1584, asking either for "your good help in it or else that you would forebear to hinder me."[29] It was not in the interests of the candidate to announce his intentions too early, for then his withdrawal would be dishonorable. It was not in the interests of his friends and relations to commit themselves too soon, for once made, a commitment was binding and the rejection of a candidate was a rejection of those whose support he had garnered. A pledge was not lightly given and could not ordinarily be withdrawn. The practice of revolting – of switching from one side to the other – was universally despised and gave rise to ugly accusations of dishonor and shamefulness, which suggests that the pledge of support was similar to an oath. "If your promises be of no better value and your credits so light ... but may be drawn to falsify what you have promised I then must pronounce unto you ... [that] neither shall you make account of me either as your friend or your neighbor," Sir Henry Coningsby replied to a group of freeholders who had written to explain why they had to withdraw their voices.[30] "If they

[27]   British Library, Egerton Mss., 2713, fol. 61.
[28]   National Library of Wales, Wynn of Gwydir Mss., Panton Group 9060 E., fol. 142; quoted in J. D. Thomas, "A General Survey of the Parliamentary Elections of 1625–28," unpublished M.A. thesis, London University (1952), p. 124.
[29]   British Library, Additional Mss., 40,629, fol. 33.
[30]   Hertfordshire selection 1584. The seven freeholders involved owed greater allegiance to Charles Morison, whose letter soliciting their support arrived shortly after they had pledged themselves to Coningsby. British Library, Additional Mss., 40,630, fol. 8.

revolt we will turn them all out of their farms that are our tenants," Lady Hobart wrote as the Norfolk Short Parliament selection threatened to degenerate into a contest.[31] "I hear it was proclaimed yesterday at Taunton that Humphrey Coles was revolted. If it be so I am sorry for his particular and for his name-sake. If it proves so, he that so much dishonored himself to all the world . . . will never recover his credit while he lives."[32]

Beyond issues of oath and honor, adherence to a commitment of voices was essential to the orderly operation of county selections. It inhibited a continued quest by those unlikely to be chosen and ensured candidates of the support on which they had ventured their credit. This meant that the meeting on the county day would not result in a chaotic free-for-all, and even in contests there were rarely, if ever, more than two candidates for a given place.[33] If men could withdraw support from one candidate to another there would be less incentive for candidates to put aside their own claims. There was little concern for being on the winning side: If the preelection sounding was efficient, there would be only winning sides.

III

In boroughs the problem of parliamentary selection fell more directly to corporate government and town officials. This was true without regard to variations in customs, size, or franchise. Indeed, franchise is the least useful category in analyzing borough selections, for it groups together towns whose populations, locations, and wealth exhibit the widest variations; it assumes that changes in franchise affected the methods used to nominate candidates, which was rarely the case; and it places undue emphasis upon the tiny fraction of selections that were contests. In fact, studying the history of individual towns and corporations reveals that squabbles over rates, markets, and outlivers – owners of borough property who were no longer residents – were the real impetus for election contests and disputes, rather than any burgeoning political con-

---

[31] British Library, Egerton Mss., 2722, fol. 90; cited in Hirst, *Representative of the People?*, p. 113. Hirst uses this evidence to support his contention that displacement of tenants was part of the pressure used by landlords in elections. While that point is moot, the question of revolting from a pledge falls into a different category. This Norfolk Short Parliament election aroused particularly strong feelings, which Sir John Holland attempted to ameliorate both directly and by refusing to stand against John Potts in the November selections. See R. W. Ketton-Cremer, *Norfolk in the Civil War* (1970), pp. 116–18.

[32] Somerset Record Office, Sandford Mss., SF/1076.

[33] Generally in county contests there was one candidate for the first place and two for the other. Occasionally there were pairs of candidates, two for each place.

sciousness among the excluded.[34] An understanding of parliamentary selection in boroughs is enhanced by focusing not upon the electorate, but upon the methods by which choices were actually made.

Predominantly, boroughs relied upon a combination of internal customary arrangements and nomination by patrons and neighbors to select their representatives. Boroughs might mirror the procedures worked out for selecting mayors or bailiffs, use a select group to present nominations, or create a procedure that would ensure disinterested nominations. Places were frequently reserved for civic officials, like the recorder, high steward, or manorial lord, and nominees suggested by governmental officials charged with administering the borough or from solicitous neighbors and local luminaries. These sources of selections were as fluid as were those in the counties, and at any given moment they reflected both past practice and present circumstance.

Boroughs that regularly chose their own residents – a distinct minority – might jealously guard this tradition. At Hereford the aldermen had "a special oath not to choose any man but an inhabitant and member of their City" and resisted all ministrations to the contrary. "They affirm that the late Earl of Essex, in his best fortunes and High Stewardship of the City, could not prevail with them"; and the Earl of Salisbury fared no better.[35] But this determination might be abandoned when the stock of suitable denizens had run down. The council of York proclaimed that "it tends much to the dishonor of so ancient a City that any stranger ... should act as a citizen of the same city in parliament," only to accept the nomination of such a stranger at their next selection.[36] Nottingham selected townsmen until 1621, when the need to subsidize the charges paid parliamentary representatives convinced a majority of the corporation to vote to select two "foreigners."[37] The impoverishment of many

---

[34] Hirst's argument that the early seventeenth century witnessed the expansion of political consciousness has much to recommend it, but is not likely to be demonstrated by studying either parliamentary franchises or electoral contests. Only contests in which a wide franchise was involved and in which political choices, as distinct from personal or social ones, were at stake would speak to this thesis. But even they would not speak unambiguously. For the failure of franchise changes to affect methods of selection and the absence of correlation between wider franchises and the selection of residents, see Vivienne Hodges, "The Electoral Influence of the Aristocracy 1604–41," unpublished Ph.D. dissertation, Columbia University (1977), p. 122ff. Hodges's dissertation is the most sophisticated analysis of patronage and representation in the seventeenth century.

[35] Historical Manuscripts Commission Reports, *Manuscripts of the Marquis of Salisbury*, XVII, 360.

[36] York Public Library, Corporation House Book No. 35, fol. 180, quoted in Hodges, "Aristocratic Patronage," p. 133.

[37] Thomas Bailey, *Annals of Nottinghamshire* (1852–55), II, 600. There is no evidence

ancient towns, especially northern and western cloth centers, left the choice of representatives in the hands of men largely unsuited for service. Borough records reveal more gratitude than resentment toward powerful neighbors who came forward to accept seats or to supply nominees at no cost to the community. The notion that these increasingly common nominations represented "borough invasions" derives from preconceptions almost entirely anachronistic and from a conflation of very different relationships between boroughs and patrons.[38] To be sure, there were attempts to enforce choices upon unwilling electors by grasping patrons, just as there were boroughs that steadfastly refused to select "foreigners." But these cases were few in comparison to those that stayed within the web of local social relations.

Corporations with dual chambers generally used their aldermen to nominate the candidates to be presented to the common councilors or freemen. This mirrored the hierarchy of office and responsibility in most boroughs and inhibited any canvassing among the broader groups that might hold the franchise. In closed corporations the process could be accomplished all at once, with the nominations in one chamber reported to the remainder of the corporation. In Chippenham, for example, the incorporated burgesses met in an upper room while the freemen waited below.[39] In Oxford the names of the candidates selected by the mayor's council were read out to the freemen in the Guildhall courtyard, and they were expected to give their assent to the two chosen. At the Short Parliament selection the council of aldermen could not agree among themselves, and four names were proposed to the freemen for an election. This development was sufficiently troubling that an order was issued that, in future selections, if more than two candidates were nominated the tally of votes among the aldermen would be reported to the freemen. Such a procedure may well have been designed to head off disgruntled aldermen who might otherwise insist on nominating a candidate who had no other support within the council.[40] A similar procedure was established in Exeter, where the mayor and Council of Twenty-four presented names to the freemen. In 1628 the freemen selected a townsman not nominated by the corporation, which resulted in the refusal of

---

for a contest at Nottingham in 1626. Cf. Hirst, *Representative of the People?*, p. 220.

[38] This was a view inherent in Neale's *Elizabethan House of Commons*, although like much else in that classic work it was advanced more cautiously there than in the later studies it influenced. J. K. Gruenfelder's *Influence in Early Stuart Elections* (1981) and his numerous articles are dominated by these assumptions.

[39] Glanville, *Reports of Certain Cases*, pp. 50–51.

[40] M. G. Hobson and H. E. Salter, *Oxford Council Acts 1626–1665*, p. 92.

the town government to pay his wages.[41] Gloucester's habitual nomination by the aldermen to the freemen was marred in 1604, when the aldermen could not agree among themselves, but otherwise the practice resulted in harmonious selections.[42]

Such methods were used in corporations with both large and small electorates and were usually the result of similar procedures for the selection of corporate officials. Chipping Wycombe was one of many corporations that issued orders that "no canvassing or persuasion of any sort was to be practiced in favor of any candidate for parliament or for the mayoralty before the actual electoral assembly."[43] Bedford, enforcing the same regulation in 1588, went further and decreed that the choice of M.P.'s was to be made "by the one consent of all the burgesses meeting in the council chamber."[44] Helston, like many other corporations with Elizabethan charters, used its aldermen to nominate two candidates for mayor from whom the freemen selected one.[45] This selection too was largely ceremonial, for many places adopted a rotation in which all of the candidates served in turn.[46] The infrequent difficulties between freemen and aldermen that led to disputes, such as that in Exeter, should not obscure the fact that in most places these relations were harmonious. The difficulties at Warwick in 1621 demonstrate both sides of the story. When the commons were aroused to seek their rights, perhaps by Sir Bartholomew Hales, one of the candidates, "they came to give their voices in the said election if they had any." The charter was produced, and Hales himself deputed to pronounce that the franchise rested with the corporation. After a contest in which a majority choice was made "the whole number reassembled and consented and agreed to that election."[47] Almost all aldermanic benches were recruited from the freemen of the lower house by co-option: The aldermen were former freemen, and the freemen were aspiring aldermen.[48] Intractable

[41] Winifred Taffs, "The Borough Franchise in the First Half of the Seventeenth Century," unpublished M.A. thesis, London University (1927), p. 108.

[42] J. K. Gruenfelder, "Gloucestershire Parliamentary Elections, 1604–40," *Bristol and Gloucestershire Archaeological Society Transactions*, 96 (1979), p. 55ff. Although Gruenfelder characterizes Gloucester's electoral history in the seventeenth century as "bitterly fought," only in 1604 was there a contest, the result of the renegade candidacy of Jones.

[43] L. J. Ashford, *The History of the Borough of High Wycombe* (1960), p. 110.

[44] P. W. Hasler, ed., *House of Commons 1558–1603*, I, 112.

[45] H. S. Toy, *The History of Helston* (1937), p. 515.

[46] See J. Guilding, *Reading Records*, vols. II and III. See also *York Civic Records*, III, 127.

[47] J. Kempe, *The Black Book of Warwick*, pp. 410–11.

[48] These processes were diverse and deserve study. In Ludlow, for example, when a vacancy occurred in the Twenty-five (the town's council) the bailiffs would name

economic issues and irascible individuals occasionally marred corporate bodies, but the procedures by which upper houses nominated and lower houses confirmed were natural within the hierarchical patterns of borough life.

So too was the use of more arcane procedures that developed from the frequent need to select civic officers. The town of Barnstaple in Devonshire rarely needed to create precedents for selecting M.P.'s. One of its seats was owned by the Chichester family, and the nomination of the other was generally granted to the town recorder, an office held by successive Earls of Bath. When the fifth Earl died in 1637 the title passed collaterally to a cousin with no West Country base, leaving Barnstaple to work out a new pattern in 1640. The Short Parliament selections appear to have passed peacefully when Thomas Matthews was "by compact elected" along with George Peard, a member of an ancient Barnstaple family. In the fall of 1640, however, difficulties ensued when four candidates were proposed to the free burgesses. To make the election, the mayor ultimately divided the four into two pairs, with one to be chosen from each. When this method was challenged in Parliament the corporation defended itself with the argument that "it is the ancient custom ... used time out of mind to elect the mayor and other officers by proposing four or more and on the election to set two first, one against another."[49]

Newport in Cornwall used its two vianders to select candidates, "providing they could agree." If not, the choice reverted back to the freeholders, who had selected the vianders. In 1628 the vianders desired to select Sir John Eliot, who already held a seat and who proposed a "neighbor in the country and he for the first place was chosen by the general consent of all."[50] The neighboring borough of Mitchell used its portreeve to set selections in train. He would name two elisors to co-opt twenty-two freemen, who together composed the electorate. They

seventeen townsmen who would choose three of their number, from whom the aldermen and common council would select the one replacement. P. Williams, "Government and Politics in Ludlow 1590–1641," *Transactions of the Shropshire Archaeological Society*, 56 (1957–60), p. 285. There were many similar arrangements.

49 Joseph Gribble, *Memorials of Barnstaple* (1830), pp. 346–50; G.E.C., *The Complete Peerage*, under the entry "Bath"; J. R. Chanter and T. Wainright, eds., *Barnstaple Records* (1900), I, 81. The process employed balls and pots. Two nominees had their names placed on pots, and the electors placed one hand in each pot and dropped a ball into one of the pots. The winner of the first pairing was then matched with the winner of the next pairing. This process prevented open conflict while allowing choice. M. F. Keeler, *The Long Parliament* (1954), p. 42; Hirst provides no evidence to support his contention that a contest took place for the Short Parliament seats. *Representative of the People?*, p. 218.

50 J. Foster, *Sir John Eliot: A Biography* (1864), II, 107.

attested on the indenture that the choice was made with the "unanimous consent and assent of the commonalty."[51] Beverley used its Council of Thirteen to nominate candidates to the mayor and governors with whom affirmation or rejection lay. The Council of Thirteen was a group selected from the twenty-six burgesses of the town by the "whole of brothers" or wardens of the borough's trading companies. Thus the route to both civic and parliamentary choice was a narrowing hierarchical pyramid from the guilds to the burgesses to the Thirteen to the governors and mayor.[52]

More unusual, but of the same kind, were a number of committee systems in which those with the responsibility for choice were themselves chosen and then empowered to act for the community. Great Yarmouth used a method of inquest to select both borough officers and members of Parliament. The corporation consisted of seventy-two members, of whom each year a different half were of the inquest. When municipal or parliamentary selection was necessary the names of these thirty-six were placed into four hats and an illiterate boy was instructed to choose twelve. These twelve then retired to make the community's choice, with a three-quarter plurality needed for agreement.[53] The neutrality and incorruptibility of such a procedure – symbolized by the requirement that the boy be "unlettered" – cannot pass unremarked. The use of lots in choice was not uncommon in the seventeenth century; a number of county selections had lots drawn for various reasons. In fact, the House of Commons considered a procedure much akin to Great Yarmouth's for selecting committees.[54] By removing both nomination and selection to a group whose composition was unknown prior to the day of choice, Great Yarmouth inhibited potential conflict among aspirants. Moreover, by endowing the twelve selectors with the voices of the entire corporation, the body evinced a corporate identity that went beyond even the evocations of corporate harmony found in charters and bylaws – passages that modern historians usually dismiss as cant.

Great Yarmouth was not alone in devising a method by which the actual selection was merely confirmation of the work of a preselected committee. York, which almost always chose civic leaders as its representatives, used variations of its city council to nominate four candidates who were presented to the burgesses. The burgesses were to choose two

---

[51] B. D. Henning, ed., *House of Commons 1660–90*, I, *171*.

[52] J. Dennett, ed., *Beverly Borough Records* (1864), II, 107.

[53] C. J. Palmer, *The History of Great Yarmouth by Henry Manship* (1854–56), II, 55–59. When this system changed in the 1620s, the town was besieged by requests for places from patrons. Ibid., 203.

[54] *Journals of the House of Commons*, I, 172. I owe this reference to Ralph Pugh.

of these, who were then presented at the actual selection some days later. This mirrored the process through which the councilors themselves had been selected; the city's major craft guilds named four candidates, from whom the aldermen picked one. The result, in both civic and parliamentary processes, was to reflect unequal levels of power and responsibility within the corporation and to affirm, on the day of selection, a unified choice.[55] Cambridge organized a similar system to achieve the same result. The mayor and assessors chose one "nominator," the commonalty of the corporation another. The nominators then named eight men who acted as the town's electors. Until 1571 the eight electors made their choice unanimously, and thereafter by majority. In 1621 the choices of the electors were presented at a meeting of the corporation and "all the burgesses assented to the election."[56]

IV

The most common method by which communities allocated parliamentary seats was through the use of patrons. Parliamentary patronage was not a separate genus in the flourishing market of reciprocal exchange; parliamentary patrons were not a breed apart. They did not buy up seats or collect groups of dependent M.P.'s as their eighteenth-century successors would do. Rather, they acted in this capacity as they acted in promoting younger sons and cousins, clerics and lawyers, or aspirants to local and national office. In a society with undeveloped institutional channels, personal patronage served critical functions. It was a training ground for state service and an avenue for social mobility.[57] Because it mirrored the hierarchy – patrons held greater status than did their clients – patronage also served to confirm the social order. Though individuals

[55] Victoria County History, The City of York; D. Palliser, Tudor York (1980); York Civic Records, VII–IX, esp. IX, pp. 8–11. Hirst provides no evidence for the claim that there was a contest at York in 1604 or 1624. Representative of the People?, p. 222. The reference to York in Hawarde's diary relates to Sir Arthur Ingram having been elected for two boroughs and choosing to sit for York. Wiltshire Record Office, John Hawarde's Diary, p. 146.

[56] C. H. Cooper, Annals of Cambridge (1842–53), I, 272, 422; II, 269; III, 136. After 1625 this system was abandoned and the corporation began to accept nominations from patrons connected to the town. Ibid., III, 183, 200, 296.

[57] For a study of the role of patronage in providing officials for the central government see G. E. Aylmer, The King's Servants (1969); for ecclesiastical patronage see B. Donagan, "The Clerical Patronage of Robert Rich, Second Earl of Warwick, 1619–1642," Proceedings of the American Philosophy Society, 120, no. 5 (1976), pp. 388–419; for a general study see G. Lytle and S. Orgel, eds., Patronage in the Renaissance (1982).

might corrupt it, patronage was neither a restrictive form of social control nor an abusive one.

These nominations of county magnates or neighboring gentlemen were part of a symbiotic relationship. Corporations and towns strengthened ties that could lead to charitable and educational bequests, favored treatment in legal matters, and the arbitration of petty disputes. Gentlemen afforded themselves, their sons, and their dependents an opportunity to visit London on personal, local, or national business. The relationship cut both ways. When, in 1621, the borough of Reading offered only a token sum "for the King's majesty's daughter," its high steward, Viscount Wallingford, implored them to give more: "I pray you to let the world know I have some power with you."[58] To view patronage only as a parasitic relationship, or as one of brute power involving superiors and subordinates, is to misunderstand the organic nature of early modern society and to posit class conflict within a social group that actually shared similar interests, needs, and aspirations.[59] The interconnection between a borough and its patron was frequently as inextricable as that between the Earl of Northampton and Bishop's Castle, Shropshire: "For though the election be yours by right, the inheritance of the borough is mine and therefore it cannot be feared that I will not be more careful than any to provide for the public weal of the town."[60] While some patrons nominated by right, particularly Crown officers with little personal connection to the locality, others did so as part of their responsibilities. Thus Lord Holderness, possessor of the grant of the Castle of Scarborough, wrote to that Yorkshire corporation in 1626: "I have therefore seriously to entreat that I may have the nomination of one of them ... and this I do desire the rather if need should be that I may give testimony of my love and care for you whom I expect to be my best neighbors in that place."[61]

---

[58] Historical Manuscripts Commission, *11th Report*, Appendix VII (Reading Corporation Manuscripts), p. 221.

[59] This point is perhaps more easily grasped by historians of the nineteenth century. Writing about early modern Ashburton, Professor Hanham observed that "even patronage, when placed in its context, seems to grow out of the needs of the local situation rather than to represent an alien and essentially anti-democratic imposition upon an unwilling community." H. J. Hanham, "Ashburton as a Parliamentary Borough," *Devonshire Archaeological Record Society*, 98 (1959), p. 206.

[60] Bishop's Castle Borough Records, first minute book, fol. 40, quoted in Historical Manuscripts Commission, *10th Report*, Appendix IV (Bishop's Castle Manuscripts), p. 406. Sir Robert Howard inherited the lordship in 1625 and had himself returned in each subsequent parliament through 1640. *Return of Every Member* (1878).

[61] J. B. Baker, *A History of Scarborough* (1882), pp. 224–5. Similarly, see Lord Zouch's letter to the bailiffs of Shrewsbury in 1601 nominating his son-in-law for the second place: "I did purpose only to make a friendly motion whereby I might offer a test

In perhaps the most common method of selecting members, boroughs used one of their civic officers either to hold a place or to nominate to it. In the sixteenth century mayors and other officials charged with making the election returns were eligible to name themselves, but this practice was disallowed after 1604.[62] More often corporations granted a place to their recorder, who as chief legal officer was best acquainted with the details of borough affairs and who, unlike mayors and bailiffs, usually held office over a long period of time. When the corporation of Wallingford had need to bypass its recorder, who "according to order ... should have been chosen," they "entreated they might that time make good their promise, which the recorder consented to."[63] But in 1628 when Richard Taylor, the recorder of Bedford, was to be passed over he proved less compliant: "I conceived it a right, or at least an inseparable courtesy to the place I hold to be one of your burgesses. I know not of any precedent in the time of the memory of any man when the recorder of this corporation has been passed by without his own consent."[64] Large corporations like London, Reading, Gloucester, Bristol, Exeter, Salisbury, and Norwich as well as many smaller ones regularly selected their recorders to sit in Parliament.[65]

Along with the recorder, the other civic official commonly granted a seat in Parliament was the high steward. Numerous corporations remodeled during the reigns of Elizabeth and James I had provision made in their new charters for a high steward, whose appointment was honorary but whose power and protection were critical to the locality. In 1637 Barnstaple decided to exercise the provision in its 1610 charter allowing the selection of a high steward. Its reasoning was succinct: "We have many heavy burdens laid upon us ... and are yet like to be without remedies unless we may procure the assistance of some great man, who is powerful at the court and council board."[66] The little that is known about the selection of high stewards suggests that in most cases the nobleman chosen had some logical connection to the corporation,

of both my love to you and yours to me." *Shropshire Notes & Queries*, N. S., IV, 103–04.

[62] *Journals of the House of Commons*, I, 464. There remained, as always, exceptions.

[63] J. K. Hedges, *The History of Wallingford*, (1881), II, 200.

[64] G. D. Gilmore, "The Papers of Richard Taylor of Clapham," *Bedfordshire Historical Record Society*, 25 (1947), p. 105. In this case the corporation had received requests for nominations from both the Earls of Bolingbroke and Cleveland. Taylor's protest was successful, and he was returned. See also the refusal of the corporation of Colchester to allow its town clerk to stand aside in 1625. Essex Record Office, Morant Papers, vol. 43, quoted in Hodges, "Aristocratic Patronage," p. 200.

[65] See the excellent analysis in Hodges, "Aristocratic Patronage," pp. 437–54.

[66] J. R. Chanter and T. Wainright, eds., *Barnstaple Records* (1900), I, 102.

through land holding in the town or as possessor of a major county estate. Barnstaple chose the Earl of Dorset because he "hath lately declared himself to be a noble friend unto the town."[67] This was especially true in the early seventeenth century, when the patronage accumulated by Leicester, Cecil, and Essex was dispersed. In Berkshire and Oxfordshire, for example, William Knollys, Viscount Wallingford and first Earl of Banbury, was chosen high steward for Abingdon, Banbury, Oxford, Reading, and Wallingford. These offices supplied him with places for his innumerable male relations. The esteem in which corporations held their high stewards can be seen in the refusal of Reading corporation to accept Banbury's resignation in 1630, when the Earl was eighty-three years old, and in the carefully orchestrated manner in which Oxford selected his successor in 1632: "The mayor proposing an election of a high steward by scrutiny... this house thought fit rather to make the selection otherwise; whereupon the whole house, being in number threescore and twelve did every one of them give their consent that the right honorable Thomas Lord Howard, Earl of Berkshire should succeed."[68] By granting the high steward nomination of a place in Parliament, corporations strengthened their bonds with an official who could direct private bill matters during sessions and protect corporate interests between them.

When a corporation used its high steward to provide a candidate for selection, then, it was turning to a civic official rather than to a patron. "The Steward of Retford recommended... one of their burgesses (which being all the courtesy the town hath been able to afford them) have always been yielded to by the burgesses without contradiction."[69] Unlike the recorder, the high steward was generally a peer and therefore incapable of filling the place himself. His right to nominate a single member was, in essence, a right of substitution. Although his nominee might be a stranger to the corporation, the nomination still came from within.[70]

[67]   Ibid.
[68]   Historical Manuscripts Commission, *11th Report*, Appendix VII (Reading Corporation Manuscripts), p. 222; Hobson and Salter, *Oxford Council Acts 1626–1665*, p. 39. See also H. E. Salter, *Oxford Council Acts 1583–1626* (Oxford Historical Society Publications, 87, 1928), p. 205.
[69]   Nottingham University Library, Clifton Papers, C1 LP 51. I concur with Seddon's judgment that there is no evidence, *pace* Hirst, of a contest at East Retford in 1624. P. R. Seddon, "A Parliamentary Election at East Retford, 1624," *Transactions of the Thoroton Society of Nottinghamshire*, 76 (1972), 26–34. Hirst, *Representative of the People?*, p. 220.
[70]   This view differs substantially from those offered by Gruenfelder and Hodges. Hodges is careful to segregate this form of influence from others but does not regard it differently in her general analysis. Gruenfelder lumps them together as aristocratic patronage. Gruenfelder, *Influence in Early Stuart Elections*, especially Appendix VI.

Perhaps this distinction is best illustrated by two examples in which the nominations of Viscount Wallingford were refused. In 1624 Wallingford sent a letter to a corporation of Reading "for nomination of one of the burgesses and both if it may be." The company accepted his choice of Sir Francis Knollys as that coming from the high steward, but refused his suggestion of Sir Robert Knollys in preference to the traditional choice of their recorder.[71] Similarly, Wallingford attempted to fill two places at Oxford in 1620. "The whole house has elected Sir John Brooke at the instance of the Lord Viscount Wallingford for the first place," but the aldermen were badly split over the selection of their recorder, Thomas Wentworth, who had sat during the period 1604–10 and in 1614; and Sir Francis Blundell, whom Wallingford had suggested if the town was not to select one of its own citizens. Wentworth was ultimately returned after gaining a greater number of voices among the common freemen.[72] Indeed, when the Earl of Dorset attempted both places at Ipswich in 1604 (the second for Sir Francis Bacon), he was asked to have Bacon and Sir Michael Stanhope "agree . . . in the said cause."[73] These instances reveal the difference between the nomination of a corporate official and the solicitation on the part of a neighboring magnate. As Viscount Wallingford was both high steward and an Oxfordshire magnate, his nominees for second place were given weightier consideration than they might have received had they come from other powerful neighbors of the corporation; but their rejection demonstrates the distinctions to be discerned in the roles of a patron.

Many towns and some corporations had their principal lands held by a lord of the manor, who might be either a national magnate or a neighboring gentleman. The circumstances of such relationships varied widely: In some cases the largest part of the town was part of a manor

Obviously from the point of view of aristocratic patronage and "influence" the source of parliamentary places is not as important as their existence. From the point of view of the process, however, the distinction is critical.

[71] J. M. Guilding, *Reading Records* (1895), II, 168–69.

[72] See H. E. Salter, *Oxford Council Acts*, p. 297; Notestein, Simpson, and Relf, *Commons Debates 1621*, V, 444; and especially Oxford City Archives F 5.2 f. 40, cited in *Victoria County History of Oxfordshire*, IV, 155. Unaware that the normal pattern of selection in Oxford – the recorder and the high steward's nominee – had been disturbed by Wallingford's request for a second place, Hirst concluded that this contest resulted from the "corporation's decision to discontinue the practice of electing the recorder" and that it was another skirmish in the war between aldermen and freemen. As Oxford's council continued to nominate the candidates for the freemen to confirm, only Wallingford's intervention changed the otherwise peaceful pattern of selection. *Representative of the People?*, p. 205.

[73] Historical Manuscripts Commission, *9th Report* (Corporation of Ipswich Manuscripts), p. 256.

and the townsmen tenants of the lord; in others a direct holding had been commuted to rents, rights, and fees. At St. Albans the owner of the former abbey lands traditionally exercised a right of nomination, though the abbey had long since been dissolved.[74] At Weobley it was ownership of the Garnstone estate that determined parliamentary patronage both before and after the Revolution.[75] The grant might be held from the Crown as a keeper of a castle or of an honor that impinged on the parliamentary borough; or, in a small number of places, the possession of burgages within the town involved special rights and responsibilities. In all of these cases, for better or worse, the interests of the lord of the manor and those of the town were intertwined.

Many of these boroughs granted the nomination of one or both places to their manorial lord as a matter of course; in fact in some places the writs appear to have been sent to the lord and then sealed later by the civic official. John Hender, who had the right of nomination at Bossiney, sent a blank indenture to the Earl of Salisbury in 1609 along with an appeal that he not be picked sheriff.[76] The manor of Aylesbury was owned by the Packington family in the sixteenth century, and one of its members was always returned. In 1572 the relationship was precisely inscribed on the back of the writ: "I, Dame Dorothy Packington ... lord and owner of the town of Aylesbury ... have chosen, named, and appointed my trusty and well beloved Thomas Litchfield and George Burden esq. to be my burgesses of the said town."[77] The Duckett family were lords of the hundred of Calne and frequent Calne M.P.'s.[78] Newton, Lancashire, and Barnstaple, Devonshire were other boroughs in which owners of a principal manor claimed the right to nominate M.P.'s as part of their inheritance. Indeed, at Barnstaple the Chichester family protected their right of nomination in a deed of sale that transferred the castle manor to the corporation: "That the said Sir John Chichester and his heirs being of the age of 21 years or more to have the nomination of one burgess of the town of Barnstaple at the parliament ... and the said burgess not to take any wages ... and to save the town harmless for not returning of that one of their town a burgess."[79]

[74] H. C. Lansberry, "The Parliamentary History of St. Albans 1660–1832," unpublished Ph.D. thesis, London University (1967).

[75] J. Hillaby, "The Parliamentary Borough of Weobley 1628–1708," *Transactions of the Woolhope Naturalist Club*, 39 (1967), pp. 111–16.

[76] *Calendar of State Papers Domestic Series 1603–10*, p. 551.

[77] Browne Willis, *Notitia Parliamentaria* (1730), I, Appendix I.

[78] A. E. W. March, *A History of the Borough and Town of Calne* (1903).

[79] The manor of Newton was purchased by the Fleetwood family in 1594 along with the right to the "nomination, election, and appointment" of the burgesses. E. and A. Porritt, *The Unreformed House of Commons* (1903), I, 97; J. R. Chanter and T.

There is no reason to suppose that relations between boroughs and manorial lords were always either harmonious or benevolent. The Earl of Montgomery, Constable of Queenborough Castle, was not seeking friends when he wrote: "If you choose not Mr. Pooley . . . I shall consider it a neglect. . . . Therefore when soever your occasions shall need my furtherance I [shall] be found your friend according to your behavior to me."[80] Lords of manors were the source of many of the blank writs passed about to senior governmental officials, like those from Bossiney which "Mr Hender of Bottreaux Castle" sent on to the Earl of Salisbury in 1604.[81] The Luttrells failed to provide a candidate for Minehead in 1601, leaving the burgesses first to panic over having to supply one at their own cost and then to proceed to a confused confrontation with the corporation freemen.[82] When Denbigh had the temerity in 1572 to reject the nominee of the lord of the town (albeit the name was sent in after the corporation had made its choice) the town's magistrates were threatened by an enraged Earl of Leicester, who demanded the revocation of their return: "I cannot but greatly marvel (in respect I am your lord and you my tenants)."[83] Yet whatever the nature of these relations – Leicester reminded Denbigh's leaders of "the many good turns and commodities which I have always been willing to procure you" – lords of manors were not borough invaders.

Nor were the governmental officials whose responsibilities included the administration of affairs within a parliamentary borough. Here the relationships varied both with the personalities of the officials and as the individual boroughs grew more or less appropriate as objects of administrative attention. The most important of these jurisdictions were the Duchy of Lancaster, the Cinque Ports, and the Isle of Wight.[84] The

---

Wainright, eds., *Barnstaple Records*, II, 256. Although the Earl of Bath used the family nomination on occasion, it was the Chichesters of Hall rather than of Youlston who inherited this unusual legacy. See Sir Alexander Chichester, *History of the Family of Chichester* (1871). This was equally true at Gatton, Surrey, where the Catholic Copley family owned the borough. In 1586 this situation came to the attention of the Privy Council – "whereas my Lords of the Council do understand that Mrs. Copley hath the nomination of two burgesses for the town of Gatton being a parcel of her jointure." A. J. Kempe, ed., *The Losely Manuscripts* (1835), pp. 242–43.

[80] C. E. Woodruff, "Notes on the Municipal Records of Queenborough," *Archaeologia Cantiana*, 22 (1897), p. 183.

[81] Winifred Taffs, "The Borough Franchise in the First Half of the Seventeenth Century," Appendix, pp. 38–9.

[82] M. K. Mort, "The Personnel of the House of Commons in 1601," unpublished M.A. thesis, London University (1952), pp. 133–37.

[83] J. Williams, *Ancient and Modern Denbigh* (1856), pp. 98–9. Curiously, the man chosen was also a client of Leicester's. I owe this information to Simon Adams.

[84] Gruenfelder discusses these administrations under the category of governmental patronage in his *Influence in Early Stuart Elections*.

chancellor of the duchy administered a dispersed and diversified territory; only in some boroughs did he serve as a civic official worthy of
receiving nominations. Corporations like Clitheroe regularly provided
a seat to a nominee of the duchy, while others like Thetford did so only
"occasionally."[85] The number of nominations made by a chancellor was
more a product of the industriousness of individuals than of any compelling need for places. When Cecil was chancellor in the 1590s he used
places to satisfy the importunities of dozens of hangers-on, but subsequent chancellors did not have to provide for so many placemen. In
1621 when the chancellor desired places in all of the northern duchy
boroughs, his letters overturned the plans of Sir Richard Beaumont's
agents, who had not anticipated such a high level of duchy activity.[86]

Unlike the chancellor of the duchy, the captain of the Isle of Wight
held patronage in a very compact area comprising the three boroughs
of Newport, Yarmouth, and Newtown. Newport gained its representation by being restored in 1584 through the influence of Sir George
Carey, later Lord Hunsdon, who was guaranteed "that he should nominate one of the two members for the borough during his natural life."
By 1601 Hunsdon directed all six of the island's selections, receiving
blanks from Yarmouth "as heretofore you have done."[87] But this situation changed dramatically when the captain's office was held by an
absentee like Secretary Conway in 1628.[88] Nevertheless, Conway approached his trust in the same terms as had his predecessors. "The good
respects you have showed to me makes me not doubt of your willingness

---

[85] W. S. Weeks, *Clitheroe in the Seventeenth Century*, (n.d.), 205, 222ff. There is no
evidence in Weeks's account that there was a contest in 1621. Cf. Hirst, *Representative
of the People?*, p. 276. For Duchy patronage see Gruenfelder, *Influence in Early
Stuart Elections*, pp. 73–84.

[86] See Historical Manuscripts Commission Reports, *Manuscripts of the Marquis of
Salisbury*, VII, for Cecil; J. J. Cartwright, *Chapters in the History of Yorkshire*
(1872), p. 205. The increased activity of the duchy complicated a number of borough
selections, but it did not necessarily lead to contests. Hirst provides no evidence for
his claim that a contest took place at Aldborough in 1621; the letter cited was written
nearly two weeks before the selection occurred. Hirst, *Representative of the People?*,
p. 222.

[87] Weeks, *Clitheroe in the Seventeenth Century*, p. 223; M. K. Mort, "The Personnel
of the Commons in 1601," p. 168.

[88] See the analysis in J. D. Thomas, "A General Survey of Parliamentary Elections," p.
41. Conway's claims were not helped by his peremptory actions in the 1626 selections
for the Isle. As it was reported, "My lord makes no question of their accepting his
recommendations for one in each town and desires it fairly as a courtesy, pleasing
himself best in that way, so long as he finds an answerable respect, but if they should
neglect him in that fair way of asking, he knows how to make use of his authority."
Calendar of State Papers Domestic Series 1625–49, Addenda, p. 97.

in a request I have now to make, whereby in pleasuring me you shall do yourselves a benefit."[89]

Similar in situation to the Isle of Wight were the boroughs under the protection of the lord warden of the Cinque Ports. As Lord Cobham informed the jurats of New Romney in 1584, "Her Majesty's pleasure was that I should have great care that sufficient, religious, and persons well affected to the present government might be chosen burgesses."[90] The lord warden's responsibilities were to maintain coastal defenses in boroughs most likely to bear the shock of a naval invasion and to protect the economic interests of the townsmen. By 1614 the Earl of Northampton had solidified the practice whereby each of the seven ports granted one nomination to the lord warden. This was confirmed by the Brotherhood of the Ports in 1615 and carried out with few exceptions through 1640.[91] Although the lord warden was an official of the central government, it is hard to sustain the argument that his access to Cinque Port seats was automatic governmental patronage. When Northampton nominated his cousin, George Fane, at Sandwich in 1614, the corporation requested that he withdraw the nomination. "We beseech your Lordship that he be excepted for we know he is so disliked of the most part of our assembly...that at the time of choice he will not be allowed."[92] Northampton acceded to their desire ("I will forbear to obtrude my cousin...upon you as he is so much against your appetites"), a course he could not have followed if Fane had been a governmental rather than a personal nominee.

Most of the appointments made by Lord Zouch and the Duke of Buckingham, who followed Northampton in office, were of personal clients or local men rather than of government officials. Indeed, James's effort in 1621 to have Zouch reserve places for royal candidates was a total failure and Zouch's consternation at the suggestion indicative of the more usual pattern.[93] The lord wardens' responsibilities to the boroughs were at least as great as those they had to the court, and they were frequently found aiding the corporations during their long period

---

[89] PRO SP 16/92/6.

[90] Kent Archives Office, New Romney Records, NR A/ep/32.

[91] G. Wilkes, *The Barons of the Cinque Ports and the Parliamentary Representation of Hythe* (1892), p. 66. For earlier grants of nomination see Lord Cobham's letter to Cecil, Historical Manuscripts Commission Reports, *Manuscripts of the Marquis of Salisbury*, VII, 429.

[92] Kent Archives Office, Sandwich Records, Sa/AC 7/31–32.

[93] British Library, Additional Mss., 37,818, fols. 51–2. For Northampton's patronage see L. L. Peck, "The Earl of Northampton, Merchant Grievances and the Addled Parliament of 1614," *Historical Journal*, 24, 3 (1981), p. 535.

of economic decline. A cynic might doubt the sincerity of the expressions of gratitude made by the ports to the lord wardens for their nominees ("whom it hath pleased your honor in your honorable love and affection to recommend to us"), but when the corporation of Winchelsea was threatened by a contest for their second place in 1621 the mayor had no hesitation in writing to Lord Zouch to arbitrate. "Your honor should free the town of a great deal of perplexity in this business and therefore redress the said abuse of getting voices contrary to due course."[94]

Because the lord warden was a national figure, he could function toward the ports as a high steward could toward a borough. With one seat customarily reserved for him, a lord warden eyed second seats longingly. It is easy to forget the pressure for places placed on patrons from relatives and would-be followers and thus to ascribe their quest for seats to overtly political motives. Cecil's papers are full of correspondence pleading for places, pleas similar to the appeal Richard Boseville sent Lord Zouch after writs were issued for the Parliament of 1621: "I humbly entreat your Lordship (in whose power by office rests the command of many burgessships) to be pleased to esteem me fit to be one and to recommend me to a place."[95] The lords warden were always very clear that their entitlement was to a single place, even when they sought the other: "If you shall for my sake elect him for the burgess of whom yourselves have the sole nomination (reserving to me the place of another for such as I shall appoint) it shall be no prejudice to your privilege in future time."[96] When second candidates nominated by the lord warden were rejected in favor of townsmen or nominees of others, the corporation was turning back the solicitation of a private individual rather than that of their lord.[97]

[94] PRO SP 14/118/9. See a similar statement of thanks and affection from Dover in 1621. SP 14/119/2.
[95] PRO SP 14/117/67.
[96] G. Wilkes, *Barons of the Cinque Ports*, pp. 70–1. British Library, Add. Mss., 37,818, fol. 49. See a similar disavowal from Buckingham in 1625: "I have not been forward to yield to his request in regard you might think that I purpose to gain too much ground on your liberty and freedom." British Library, Add. Mss., 37,819, fol. 11.
[97] Gruenfelder does not admit this distinction in attempting to demonstrate the decline of "court influence" on the part of the lord wardens. J. K. Gruenfelder, "The Lord Wardens and Elections," *Journal of British Studies*, 16 (1976). There is only one documented case of a lord warden's single nominee being rejected – the free-for-all at Dover in 1628. Buckingham's failures in 1626 are wholly explicable by the lateness of his applications. It must be remembered that the lord warden sent down the writs, so that when Buckingham sent writs without nominees it was not unnatural for corporations to proceed to selections at their next meeting. See the letter from the corporation of New Romney to Buckingham: "We then expected your grace's letters for recommendation of some gentlemen to be employed as one of our burgesses ... and stayed our election until Wednesday following." PRO SP 16/18/97.

Corporations did receive requests for places from neighbors or county leaders. Yet even here there might be much more to the relationship than an aggressive seeker and a torpid borough. Sir Thomas Denton introduced a bill in 1614 to fix summer assizes in the town of Buckingham, which he represented; Bassingbourne Gaudy kept quarter sessions in Thetford.[98] In 1625 the corporation of Scarborough appealed to the Duke of Buckingham as lord admiral to settle a town dispute in return for the nomination of one M.P.[99] Sir Henry Vane, Sr., took on important legal work for Hull prior to his son's selection there.[100] Archbishop Laud, Reading's benefactor, who secured the corporation's new charter, was rewarded with the privilege of nominating an M.P. to the Short Parliament.[101] Hedon yielded to the Earl of Salisbury's request for a by-election place in 1610 without much persuasion: "Thinking ourselves greatly blessed... in having a patron so worthy who hath such special care of us and our poor corporation... to supply the place both to the general good of the weal public and the private good of our own selves, so we all with one consent do give our whole voice to your good lordship."[102]

Such examples can be multiplied endlessly and provide texture to the reciprocity of patronage. Past services were rewarded and future favors collected. When Andover chose one of Secretary Conway's sons, he wrote of his gratitude: "When you shall require a proof... [put] anything into my hands that may procure the good of your corporation or your own particulars."[103] Gentlemen chiefly responsible for the restoration of a parliamentary franchise were commonly rewarded by being the town's choice for one of its seats. Even the demands of a great peer with estates perched on a borough's doorstep might be met in a manner mutually beneficial. "Considering ourselves bound to satisfy you," the burgesses of East Retford wrote to the Earl of Rutland in 1586, "in that and any much weightier thing, may it please you therefore to make choice and nominate and we will ratify it. If it pleased you to think well of Mr. Denzil Holles we should be very glad, but if not, as your Lordship pleases."[104] Patronage was embedded in an ongoing social matrix rather

---

[98]   G. Lipscomb, *The History and Antiquities of Buckinghamshire* (1847), II, 577.
[99]   Scarborough Letters, Bundle C–1, cited in Roy Carroll, "The Parliamentary Representation of Yorkshire 1625–60," unpublished Ph.D. dissertation, Vanderbilt University (1964), pp. 52–3.
[100] E. Gillett and K. A. MacMahon, *History of Hull* (1980), p. 160.
[101] J. M. Guilding, *Reading Records*, III, 472.
[102] G. R. Park, *The History of the Ancient Borough of Hedon* (1895), pp. 147–48.
[103] PRO SP 16/93/47.
[104] Historical Manuscripts Commission, *12th Report*, Appendix IV (Manuscripts of the Duke of Rutland), p. 208. Holles was returned.

than enforced by political power. There were small boroughs cowed by powerful neighbors or preyed upon by county magnates, but most disposed of their places with a precise logic.

Boroughs were not afraid to reject the ministrations of the powerful and the well connected. When the Earl of Northumberland attempted to achieve places as lord admiral he was continually rebuffed.[105] The Earl of Rutland was passed over at Grantham in 1584; the bishop of Norwich at Great Yarmouth; the town of Leicester rejected the Earl of Huntingdon in 1597, and Colchester the Earl of Holland in 1640: "Though my entreaties prevailed not with you in the election of your burgesses for the last parliament yet the same occasion now returning, and in hope you may think fit to make me some reparation for the neglect past, I have once more ventured my credit in Colchester."[106] There were many times when an offer could be taken up and many others when it could not. Patronage was an effective means of settling the problem of parliamentary selection that allowed a corporation to cement social and political ties while avoiding contests. The grant of nominations was a most effective safeguard against electoral strivings and, when coupled with an internal selection, eliminated all but those to be chosen. Where there were no competitors, there were no disputes.

Before the Revolution, parliamentary selection centered upon the conferral of honor, the practice of deference, and the confirmation of the social order. Selections in counties mirrored the hierarchical assumptions and practices within local society; selections in boroughs strengthened ties with patrons. In counties and boroughs parliamentary selection helped to distinguish individual members of the elite and thus furthered a process of social differentiation among them. It also spotlighted the role of officeholders, the sheriff, and corporate leaders in an official capacity, and the magistracy in an unofficial one, thus giving form to the symbolic interrelationship between governors and government. Lineage, prestige, and lordship were reconfirmed, and social ordering replicated, in parliamentary selection.

---

[105]   C. J. Palmer, ed., *The History of Great Yarmouth by Henry Manship*, II, 206. Roy Carroll, "Yorkshire Parliamentary Representation 1625–60," p. 55.

[106]   Historical Manuscripts Commission, *12th Report*, Appendix IV (Manuscripts of the Duke of Rutland), p. 170. C. J. Palmer, ed., *The History of Great Yarmouth by Henry Manship*, II, 203; J. Thompson, *The History of Leicester*, p. 300. Essex Record Office, Morant Mss., vol. 43; quoted in Hodges, "Aristocratic Patronage," p. 240. See also Dorchester's rejection of the Earl of Suffolk's nominee. C. H. Mayo, *Municipal Records of Dorchester* (1889), pp. 435–36.

3

Contesting and Composing

I

HAD THE SIXTEENTH century a Hogarth who wished to capture the spirit of an election contest, he could not have done better than to have been with pen and ink in York Castle yard on October 3, 1597. On the left-hand side of his sketch might have been the dominating castle, cut away at the bottom to reveal the archbishop of York and Sir John Saville in earnest conversation, Saville's face implacable, the archbishop's concerned. Near the top of the castle wall, at a window overlooking the yard, crowd the undersheriff and ten "indifferent gentlemen" all gazing at the scene below. The foreground would be occupied by a great swell of men, open-mouthed, some with arms upraised, crying out, "A Saville! A Fairfax!"; and others, "A Stanhope! A Hoby!" At the midground, and rising to the upper limits of the yard, intermingled with horses, dogs, porters carrying wares, and women with children at their skirts, are even larger groups of men, indistinguishable from those at the bottom but less animated. They are divided, one portion against the castle wall, the other, somewhat more numerous and amid greater numbers of onlookers and passers-by, on the hilly rise nearer the outer gate. On the right-hand side, out of proportion and as dominant as the castle on the left, the scene swells to the courtyard gate. There stand the undersheriff and a smaller number of the indifferent gentlemen, their poses and countenances now markedly agitated and in their hands sticks with knives poised over them. The clear sky above the castle gives way, by shading and then in thicker strokes, to low-hanging clouds over the gate, which is closed, the object of all attention.

The story is worth telling.

When the writs for Parliament came to the Council of the North in September 1597, Matthew Hutton, archbishop of York and lord president of the Council of the North, took the lead in seeking out two nominees for the county selection. For the first place, perhaps taking direction from Sir Robert Cecil, he had fixed upon Sir John Stanhope, recently appointed treasurer of the chamber, who, though raised in Nottinghamshire, possessed lands in Yorkshire and served as a member of the Council of the North.[1] For the second seat, Hutton assumed that a prominent Yorkshire gentleman would come forward through the informal channels of the county. Instead, only young Sir Thomas Posthumous Hoby presented himself, leading the archbishop to approach Sir John Saville of Howley to see "if he desired to stand for either of the places."[2]

We can only presume that it was the offer of "either" of the places and the knowledge that the treasurer would have primacy that fueled Saville's refusal, for he surprised the archbishop by professing disinterest. When the dispute began on election day, Saville's complaint was that Stanhope was a "stranger," although it cannot have been lost on those assembled that Saville's own upbringing was in Lincolnshire and his establishment at Howley a recent development.[3] The unsuitability of Hoby, "a gentleman of very great hope" but "not as yet well known," was perceived by all involved.[4] Although Saville continued to protest that he was not a candidate, it was clear that he was, and that he would carry the vote for one of the places.

Nevertheless, Hutton had no choice but to move forward with the normal preelection nomination by the council – which by default fell to Stanhope and Hoby – and hope that the council's authority would master Saville's pique. Hutton made careful preparations on two counts, working both to secure Stanhope's selection and to avoid disorder that might lead to a riot. There is little doubt that he was ready to jettison Hoby and allow the West Riding freeholders to select Saville. The leading gentlemen of the county were cautioned to ensure that the election would be peaceable, and Saville himself was called to a meeting with the archbishop in a final effort to forestall the confrontation.[5]

Saville delayed the interview until the last moment. He had received the summons on the evening of October 2 and waited to respond until

---

[1]   *Dictionary of National Biography*, under the entry "Stanhope, Sir John."
[2]   Historical Manuscripts Commission Reports, *Manuscripts of the Marquis of Salisbury*, VII, 417.
[3]   *D.N.B.* under the entry "Saville, Sir John"; Historical Manuscripts Commission Reports, *Manuscripts of the Marquis of Salisbury*, VII, 414.
[4]   Historical Manuscripts Commission Reports, *Manuscripts of the Marquis of Salisbury*, VII, 436.
[5]   Ibid., 417.

six o'clock on the morning of the third.[6] He held two cards – the vast array of followers he had brought to the city, and the assurance that many gentlemen in previous meetings with Hutton had supported his right to be selected. By posing the threat of an actual election he must have hoped that Hutton had stronger aversion to the manifold dangers of a contest than attachment to Stanhope being named to the first place. That he was not simply opposed, willy-nilly, to the choice of Stanhope must be adduced by the fact that he came unpaired to his meeting with Hutton. This meant that his chances in a poll were weakened – Stanhope would have both his own and Hoby's voices for him – but it also meant that the point of no return had not yet been reached. Saville was still able to throw his support to Stanhope for second place, which he could not have done if he had matched his candidacy to another.

But Hutton held his own aces in the knowledge that the principal gentlemen of the county would support Stanhope and in his control of the form of the contest. He had carefully lobbied among Saville's supporters, who may well have tried to convince the archbishop of Saville's right to primacy, and had found no opposition to Stanhope.[7] He had laboriously instructed the undersheriff, who was to conduct the election, to proceed by single candidates "to choose first one and then the other, no doubt Sir John Stanhope had been the one, for he is generally well thought on in all this country."[8] At the moment of their meeting Hutton had little reason to think that he would be outplayed. If Saville could be persuaded to accept second place, things would go as they had been planned in September; if not, then the contest would be unavoidable but the result the same. Nowhere in the copious public and private correspondence that recounts these events is there even the hint of the suggestion that Sir John Saville should be made to stand down.

What happened next cannot be explained unequivocally. We enter into the half-shadows of men's motives, the grey area between intention and happenstance where plan and purpose intermingle with the spontaneous excitement of the moment. At eight o'clock in the morning, when the writ was read, Sir John Saville did not wait for the undersheriff to ask for nominations and voices. Instead he appealed to his multitude of followers, "Will you have a Fairfax or a Mulleverer?"

---

[6]   Ibid., 412.
[7]   British Library, Microfilm 485, reel 33: Hatfield Mss., vol. 139, fol. 76.
[8]   Historical Manuscripts Commission Reports, *Manuscripts of the Marquis of Salisbury*, VII, 435–36.

The choice was Fairfax, thus creating his pairing on the spot.[9] His decisive and unexpected action not only overthrew the sacrificial Hoby, but Stanhope and all of Hutton's plans as well. Saville no longer stood one against two, odd man out, and the undersheriff would no longer propose one name first and allow the contest for the second place.

By the same token, however, the gentlemen of Yorkshire could not have their own man and that of the archbishop: They would now be forced to choose. Why, then, did Sir John Saville seize control and create his pairing when he did? The answer that came most easily to his opponents was his overweening pride. Saville could not be content with the second place and was willing to challenge the archbishop's authority, Stanhope, and his supporters – and risk the likelihood of an armed confrontation in the castle yard – rather than accept being the county's junior representative.[10] When dealing with the conduct of Sir John Saville of Howley, overweening pride is not an explanation to be dismissed lightly. But is it sufficient?

Certainly Saville wanted pride of place and had reason to think he deserved it over Stanhope, whose connection with Yorkshire was tenuous and whose real power was at court. He also had reasons to believe that he would better serve the interests of the West Riding landholders and their cloth-working tenants, whose livelihoods together had suffered from the depression of trade. All of this explains the gamble of refusing the place offered to him by Hutton in September and the ploy at daybreak on October 3, when he hoped that Hutton would relent. It only explains what followed, however, if Saville also knew what the undersheriff knew – if Saville was aware that Stanhope would be offered to the electors alone and that the second place would be allowed to be contested. For if Saville did not know that, then he had lost more in his bluff of Hutton than the first seat. Unpaired, Saville might not be elected at all. The general shout of "Stanhope and Hoby" might easily hold sway over the solitary shout of "Saville." Unpaired, he risked not only the gamble of second place, but the prospect of dishonoring all of his supporters by having their choice denied.[11]

---

[9]   Ibid., 414.

[10]   British Library, Microfilm 485, reel 33: Hatfield Mss., vol. 139, fol. 76. "4. Sir John Saville, in the time of the election used such words of offense to the gentlemen there and to the disgrace of them all and in so mutinous sort, as might have given great occasion of quarrel and bloodshed."

[11]   Thus Stanhope's supporters complained to their candidate after his defeat, "We count this an indignity to you and a disgrace not only to us ... but also to those who, being absent from sickness or age, sent their heirs and officers with their assent and their freeholders." Historical Manuscripts Commission Reports, *Manuscripts of the Marquis of Salisbury*, VII, 416.

Cries of "Stanhope and Hoby," "Saville and Fairfax" filled the castle yard. The undersheriff had little hope of implementing the archbishop's instructions or of achieving the solution that everyone had expected, the selection of Stanhope and Saville. He was now prisoner of the chaos he was assigned to direct; his only real ambitions at this point must have been to avoid pitched battle and to escape with his life. After two hours of unrelenting shouts the undersheriff could make no determination of who held sway. Therefore he required both sides to name a number of indifferent triers to take the view.[12] Stanhope's supporters were ordered to the castle wall, under the chamber from which the view would be made, and Saville's were directed onto the hill near the gate. By now, close to noontime, the proceedings had swept up not only the participants, but undoubtedly the denizens of the city as well. For when the triers went to their perch to determine which group was larger, all of those uninvolved in the election sought their own vantage points, the best by far being the hill near the gate.[13] When the view was made, all of the triers agreed that the concourse on the hill was thicker than that near the wall. But Stanhope's supporters also pointed out the obvious fact that many of those on the hill had no lawful voice in the election.

Hot debate ensued. Saville, now directing his own defense, was understandably offended by the accusation that his supporters were unworthy men of insufficient means. However the decision had been made that his supporters were to occupy the hill, and whoever had made it, he had not brought women and children to swell his side. He offered to reduce his throng by three hundred and still claimed victory.[14] This was no pretense, for whatever else was to be disputed it

[12] Curiously, the account from Saville's side lists ten triers, while that from Stanhope's fourteen. The discrepancy, though not of great significance, is all the more puzzling as both papers name the triers. Ibid., 412, 414.

[13] The critical information that Saville's supporters occupied the hillside is in the letter of protest sent by Stanhope's partisans. The document, with the exception of one important paragraph, has been printed in Historical Manuscripts Commission Reports, *Manuscripts of the Marquis of Salisbury*, VII, 413–415. It reads: "Sir John Stanhope and Sir Thomas Hoby did think in their conscience that the number of persons standing on the hillside, which was the part and side of the said Sir John Saville and Sir William Fairfax, unto which all strangers did resort for sight of the said election, was so replenished with strangers and with such as had not forty shillings freehold whereof many were also unknown..." British Library, Microfilm 485, reel 33: Hatfield Mss., vol. 139, fol. 74. This explains the perplexing claim that Saville's supporters numbered women and children among them.

[14] It is not at all clear that anyone anticipated the results of placing one side closer to the window and the other on a hill. Although nearly everything else was complained of by someone involved, no one complained of the procedure.

appears certain that Saville and Fairfax held the majority. There was only one thing that would deprive Sir John of his seat, and that was the prospect of a long (and perhaps unscrupulous) poll – a poll for which Stanhope's disconcerted followers now clamored. The undersheriff and some of the triers made their way to the gate, collecting sticks to notch as a means of polling the freeholders, for no more suitable provision had been made against this unlikely outcome. But once at the gate they found Saville adamant against the poll and preparing to escort his followers out of the city. The undersheriff, Saville, and Fairfax adjourned for a discussion that lasted the better part of two hours.[15] Again we lack knowledge of the substance of a meeting. If the undersheriff sought to persuade Fairfax to withdraw, or Saville to a poll, as seem the likeliest purposes of the exercise, his labors went unrewarded. He returned to the castle yard to declare the official return of Saville and Fairfax.

The repercussions of the day's events were immediate. Stanhope's leading supporters, many of them justices of the peace for the county, sent the treasurer their account of the election, in which they emphasized Saville's malevolence and Fairfax's perfidy.[16] They importuned Stanhope to "solicit the Queen and the Lords [of the Privy Council] that we may not by violence and practice have our free election taken from us." Such action proved superfluous the following week, when Sir John was placed in one of Cecil's safe seats at Preston.[17] Hutton, too, sent letters to London, some for public consumption to the Privy Council and others, more frank and shamefaced, to Cecil. To the Council Hutton highlighted the danger that Saville's action precipitated: "The supporters of Sir John Stanhope and Sir Thomas Hoby did obey our instructions and that had they been as willing to take offense as Sir John Saville and his party were to give it, there would have been great hurt and outrage done." To Cecil he blamed the undersheriff, like a schoolboy shifting responsibility for failing at an assignment.[18]

Saville's supporters sent their own colored account, inflating the un-

[15]   Historical Manuscripts Commission Reports, *Manuscripts of the Marquis of Salisbury*, VII, 414.

[16]   "Sir William Fairfax promised his voice the day before to Sir John Stanhope." British Library, Microfilm 485 reel 33: Hatfield Mss., vol. 139, fol. 76.

[17]   Historical Manuscripts Commission Reports, *Manuscripts of the Marquis of Salisbury*, VII, 416. Stanhope's seat at Preston, a borough under the administration of the duchy of Lancaster, reinforces the conclusion that Stanhope was Cecil's candidate, for Cecil was chancellor of the Duchy. The connection between the two families was a long-standing one. I am grateful to Simon Adams for this information.

[18]   Historical Manuscripts Commission Reports, *Manuscripts of the Marquis of Salisbury*, VII, 417, 436.

doubted majority they held and the fair courses which were offered to rectify any inequities among those claiming to be freeholders: "[He] said that if any man would take exception to any person as he should go forth at the castle yard gate, that he would take him sworn according to the statute."[19] In the end, Saville was dressed down before the council and alternate places were found for Stanhope and Hoby. Saville's offense was in abridging the authority of the archbishop, not in carrying off the election, as the Privy Council made clear in a letter to Hutton: "That howsoever her Majesty's meaning [not] to mislike any man to use that freedom for his election what the law doth warrant and discretion requires, yet where her Majesty has established authority in such a nature as yourself...she will not suffer any such precedent of contempt to go unpunished, for warning others in like case."[20]

II

Any discussion of electoral contests in the sixteenth and early seventeenth centuries must begin with the question, "What went wrong?" Communities were not used to contested choices in any sphere of social life and had only the most imperfect means of dealing with them. These involved addressing the problem in such a way that the contestants were not ultimately pitted against each other. No parliamentary selection that threatened to degenerate into a contest was without plans for settling the issue peaceably. These could range from local mediation to appeals to the highest authorities. When Sir Thomas Wentworth heard that the ever-irascible Sir John Saville was likely to interfere with the selection of Wentworth and Sir George Calvert in 1621, he suggested to Calvert that "when Sir Francis Darcy opposed Sir Thomas Lake in a matter of like nature, the Lords of the Council wrote to Sir Francis to desist...a word to [the Lord Chancellor] and such a letter would make an end of all."[21]

Indeed, resort to the Privy Council or to its individual members was not uncommon. The object was not to gain support for an election victory for one candidate or another, but rather to bring pressure to avoid a contest. Sir Richard Molyneux's unexpected candidacy at Lancashire in 1593 resulted in a summons for him to appear before the council and a public apology: "Without seeking his Lordship's [the Earl

---

[19] Ibid., 413.
[20] Ibid., p. 426
[21] William Knowler, ed., *The Letters and Dispatches of the Earl of Strafford* (1739), I, 10.

of Derby] good will and favor and without making him privy thereunto I did labor to be one of the knights of the shire."[22]

In a social system that relied upon hierarchical authority and deference, attempts at composing potential contests were made initially by an appeal to the community's leadership. In many boroughs the mayor or corporate executive held near-autocratic power in resolving disputes. In 1621 the mayor of Pembroke admonished the burgesses "that they were foresworn if they did not give their voices as he did."[23] At Helston the majority was defined as whichever side the mayor was on.[24] When parliamentary selections threatened to degenerate into contests, peers of the realm frequently intervened. The role of Hutton in 1597, and later presidents of the Council of the North, was to ameliorate the preelection process. When Lord Montague of Boughton heard of potential difficulties in the 1624 Northamptonshire selection he wrote directly to Lord Spencer: "Myself and other knights hereabouts have entreated Sir John Isham to acquaint your lordship with our desire for the ancient course to be observed to have one knight on each side for the better service of the country without any opposition."[25] The failure of the informal process of sifting among the gentlemen of Nottinghamshire before the Short Parliament election led the Earl of Kingston to request "a meeting at Mansfield... to confer about an amicable and fit election of Parliament knights, thereby to avoid... contrarieties in our opinions and votes about the business."[26]

The sense of responsibility that the nobility assumed when contests threatened is best illustrated by the predicament of the Earl of Southampton in 1614. Absent from Hampshire during the initial soundings among candidates, he was unaware, as he explained to a number of county gentry who had written to him for support, that three candidates had emerged:

I am very sorry that where so many of you agree I cannot assent but now I must either do that which I did never do yet (nor I hope never shall) which is break my word or I must in this election be severed from you [as I] have already engaged myself.... If I had known how you have been inclined as soon as others did, the desire of so many would easily have moved me to concur. I am sure you never found me so transported by my own will that I urged you to anything against yours. [But] seeing mutual offices of love and kindness are fit to be interchanged among friends... I do desire of you that being yet undetermined which way to go we may not sever but that you will with me concur to favor

22   *Acts of the Privy Council*, vol. 24, p. 256.
23   Somerset Record Office, Phelips Mss., DD/PH 216 fol. 11.
24   H. S. Toy, *The History of Helston* (1936), p. 505.
25   Historical Manuscripts Commission Reports, *Manuscripts of the Duke of Buccleuch and Queensberry*, I, 259.
26   Nottingham University Library, Clifton Papers, Cl C 295.

and further those unto whom I have promised my help as you will expect from me the like part of a friend to assist any of you.[27]

If noblemen or magistrates could not successfully intervene to compose potential conflicts, then the responsibility fell to the returning officer in boroughs and to the sheriff in the counties.

The sheriff's role was central, as Archbishop Hutton realized, because he could control the initiation of the procedure. He was also capable of bringing together two contending parties or of putting pressure upon the one whose continued candidacy would cause the most trouble. Sir Thomas Wentworth's friends sought the encouragement of the sheriff of Yorkshire in 1621 for his selection, which Wentworth acknowledged when he informed him of his intentions nearly a month before the county day.[28] The intervention of Sheriff Maynard in the 1604 Essex county selection, organizing a meeting of the county magistrates and reaching agreement as to who would be asked to withdraw, avoided the certainty of a contest.[29] There was no contemporary presupposition that the sheriff should be impartial in these proceedings; indeed it was frequently assumed that he was the best vehicle for conveying preelection decisions to the freeholders and of making them stand up. Sir Richard Grosvenor's speech to the Cheshire freeholders in 1624 was a model of this behavior. He informed the gathered electors of the importance of their meeting, of the instructions from the Crown, and of the decision reached by the magistrates. He added his own weight to all of these in supporting the candidacies of William Brereton and William Booth and exhorted the freeholders "to join with us" in the choice.[30]

When news of a potential conflict in Sussex reached Lords Buckhurst and Montague in 1584 they wrote immediately to the sheriff, Walter Covert. They both requested that Covert make their choices, Buckhurst's son and Sir Thomas Shirley, known to the electors: "As you friendly offered me your furtherance if need were," Buckhurst recalled, "though I doubt not of any great need, yet would I be glad to use the help of my friends in this cause." Lord Montague informed the sheriff, "I have thought good to signify unto you that both sundry noble men and gentlemen with myself have thought Mr. Robert Sackville and Mr. Thomas Shirley most fit for the same...I pray you to make my wish

---

[27] *Sir Henry Whithed's Letter Book, 1601–1614*, p. 114.

[28] William Knowler, ed., *The Letters and Dispatches of the Earl of Strafford* (1739), I, 8.

[29] British Library, Egerton Mss., 2644, fol. 133. There was no contest at this election. Cf. D. M. Hirst, *The Representative of the People?* (1975), p. 218.

[30] Eaton Hall, Grosvenor Mss., item 25, fol. 14. I am grateful to Richard Cust for providing me with a photocopy of this manuscript.

and desire known to the freeholders there."[31] The timely intervention of the bailiffs of Maldon prevented a contest at their 1605 by-election. Sir John Sammes, a near neighbor of the town, had already been promised the place when the Earl of Suffolk's son, Lord Walden, was nominated. "We were driven to some hard exigent," the bailiffs reported, "and sent for the Knight...desiring him to forbear opposition. Unto which he yielded, as not willing to oppose himself against so worthy a man."[32]

Much has been written about "sheriff's tricks" in sixteenth and early seventeenth century elections, and the informality of the electoral process was tailor-made for those intent upon corrupting it.[33] The legal remedies against returning officers were pitifully inadequate: a fine, set according to fifteenth-century values and savagely eroded by sixteenth-century inflation, and an enforced trip to Westminster, which could be conjoined with the collection or return of writs. From the point of view of those who emphasized such malfeasance, what must be most remarkable is how infrequently it occurred and how incompetently sheriffs abused their powers. There is not a single recorded case of a sheriff simply dispensing with the county court and returning the writs on his own authority, which would be the fastest way of achieving a victory for his preferred candidates. Nor has much come to light of blackmail over ratings or distraints, which were the sheriff's real weapons against his neighbors.

In fact, most instances of sheriff's tricks are culled from episodes of irresolvable conflicts in which deep passions were stirred and the sheriff was left to adjudicate matters to the best of his ability. In each case the stakes were extremely high; there was danger of bloodshed at the county court and of a permanent rent among the county gentlemen. Denbighshire did not have an election in 1601 because a brawl broke out between the supporters of Sir Richard Trevor and those of Sir John Salusbury. Owen Vaughan, the unfortunate sheriff, dissolved the court in disarray without making a return.[34] The sheriff of Carnarvonshire was advised

[31] T. W. Horsefield, *The History, Antiquities, and Topography of the County of Sussex* (1835), II, Appendix 2, p. 23.

[32] Historical Manuscripts Commission Reports, *Manuscripts of the Marquis of Salisbury*, XVII, 455. Sammes was selected at the town's next vacancy in 1610 and again in 1614.

[33] See especially J. E. Neale, "Three Elizabethan Elections," *English Historical Review*, 46 (1931), pp. 209–38.

[34] Thomas Carew, *An Historical Account of the Rights of Elections* (1775), I, 206; J. E. Neale, *The Elizabethan House of Commons* (1949), pp. 120–28. Sir John's jocular observation that "the preparations made for the election were more befitting a civil war" describes a situation that the sheriff cannot have viewed quite so lightheartedly. Although Neale describes Vaughan as a partisan for Trevor, he did not return him on the county court day and in fact returned Salusbury two months later. *Return of*

to take precautions before the 1624 election: "Whereas great contention and grief is like to arise within the county...if factious persons shall be suffered to carry weapons in the town."[35] When the Gloucestershire gentry saw their preelection agreement dissolve into a contest in 1640, one of them reported: "I believe in earnest we shall have but bad blood between the gentry and scarce find for the future otherways than a divided bench of justices."[36]

In every circumstance the cases were hard. Sir Andrew Noel was sheriff of Rutland in 1601 when writs were issued for Parliament. He and Sir John Harington (and the patriarchs of their families before them) traditionally shared the Rutland county seats. As sheriff, Sir Andrew was now ineligible and was forced to devolve his interest prematurely upon his nineteen-year-old son. This Sir John Harington would not have, and Noel was caught among the interests of his family, the long-standing amity between Haringtons and Noels, and the peace of the county. What sheriff's tricks did he use to ensure his son's return? In the first instance he implored Harington to accept the situation and make the best of it. When persuasion failed he presented the dilemma to the county freeholders. They importuned him, despite potential legal problems, to accept the seat himself.[37] This solution, made openly and with Harington's consent, neatly solved the seemingly intractable dispute. The election was made in October; Parliament met in November. If notice of Noel's transgression could be delayed through the opening of the session the county would have a new sheriff, Sir Andrew could be returned on a second writ, and all would be well in Rutland. But the transgression was not overlooked. Sir Andrew Noel's self-return was scrutinized in the House, and it seemed certain that he would be fined and perhaps imprisoned. This was only prevented when Sir John Harington rallied to his defense, informing the House that Noel had been reluctant to agree to the freeholders' demand that he return himself.[38]

Every Member (1878), p. 441. In the Montgomeryshire election of 1588 Jenkin Lloyd, the sheriff, could not keep the contending sides from drawing swords even after a special warning was given to each. Neale, "Three Elizabethan Elections," *English Historical Review*, 46 (1931), p. 231.

[35] Historical Manuscripts Commission Reports, *13th Report*, Appendix IV (Dovaston Manuscripts), p. 260.

[36] Public Record Office, State Papers, 16/448/79.

[37] The unsolved problem in this election is why Harington was so intent upon not having the younger Noel as his partner. The public reason, given in all accounts, was that he was too young. This was often a euphemism for some character defect, although there is no evidence that it was in this case. Another possibility was generational. Harington, over seventy, had not yet relinquished his seat to his progeny, and thus Noel's example, enforced or not, may have been discomforting.

[38] The evidence for the Rutland election is Neale's; the interpretation is my own. It is difficult to avoid the conclusion that Harington was a party to the apparent "solution"

Thomas Herbert found himself in a similar situation in Monmouth-shire when he was forced to execute a writ in 1572 for selection of members to Parliament, one of whom was traditionally a member of his own family. In this selection there was no lack of a third candidate nor any doubt as to who should hold primacy. With Thomas Herbert sheriff, Charles Somerset, son of the Earl of Worcester, would be senior knight. The only question was whether Thomas could keep a Herbert seat, in the person of his son, over the rival claim of the Morgan family. There was little doubt that both families merited the respect and honor of the Monmouthshire gentlemen, and even less doubt that the Morgans saw Herbert's shrievalty as the opportunity to regain the county seat. With two competing and meritorious claimants for one seat the prospect of a peaceable selection dimmed. Thomas Herbert could not see why his family should be penalized for its service in the county's highest admin-istrative office. The Morgans could not see why a parliamentary seat should pass so soon to the next generation of Herberts, why the son of one family should have precedence over the father of another. Had Thomas Herbert simply proceeded to corrupt the election, the power of sheriff's tricks would again be demonstrated. But the actuality was more complex. The Herberts met with Charles Somerset. As the county's unanimous choice for the first place as knight of the shire he was most suited to arbitrate the potential conflict. Together they agreed that both Herberts and Morgans should stand down – an action that would elim-inate the impasse. It was only after Somerset failed to persuade the Morgans of this course that the contest and subsequent Star Chamber dispute ensued.[39]

The assumption that sheriffs were disposed to corrupt elections gains

of Noel's self-return and that it was intended to buy time until January. Neale's version of Harington's intervention in the Commons' debate – "Sir John Harington at once rose in defense and with essential honesty and fairness assured the House that Noel had been an unwilling party to the election"–is lame, especially when set alongside his highly colored account of the second election. There is no evidence to suggest that Noel intended to procure the "annulment of the election" before his term as sheriff had elapsed. Had Noel intended to return his son, the occasion for it would have been the first election, when there was no other candidate to oppose him and no need for sheriff's tricks. J. E. Neale, *The Elizabethan House of Commons* (1949), p. 133. For the full details see Neale, "More Elizabethan Elections," *English Historical Review*, 61 (1946).

[39] Again I find Neale too readily disposed to argue from the result – the election of Herbert's son – rather than from the process. The Star Chamber depositions are irreconcilable on almost every point, as might be expected once things had gotten so far out of hand. The details of this election are too close to the famous intrigues of eighteenth-century sheriffs popularized by Namier to resist the suggestion that Sir Lewis's conclusions influenced Sir John's. J. E. Neale, *Elizabethan House of Commons* (1949), pp. 27–32.

credence from the underlying belief that disputes should have been resolved by counting the number of electors on each side. This seems so
unambiguous according to the modern concept of election, that the
"great reluctance to proceed to a poll" becomes prima facie evidence of
foul play.[40] In fact, communities were not merely reluctant to proceed
to the poll: They were obdurate against it. In contest after contest the
community's leadership, on both sides, sought every imaginable means
to avoid a poll. In 1614 the sheriff of Cambridgeshire absolutely refused
a poll, claiming that the selection was already made without one. The
sheriff of Huntingdonshire, in the same election, avoided the difficulty
by not putting forth the name of a third candidate. The septuagenarian
sheriff of Dorset avoided a poll in 1626 by inventing an oath that
excluded latecomers.[41] In the Montgomeryshire election of 1588 the
sheriff and justices held a long debate on how a poll might be taken,
the only man in the company with direct experience claiming that he
had once seen one in Shropshire.[42]

Reluctance to poll did not stem simply from the complexities of determining forty-shilling freeholders or from disdain for the time and
trouble it would entail. By counting each man as one, the meanest
freeholder equal to the worthiest gentleman, the community violated
every other social norm by which it operated. At an election in Lewes,
a chaotic poll was cut short by "seventeen or twenty gentlemen more
who were not polled because they would not go out as the rest did but
said they would number themselves."[43] Lord Maynard's avowal that he
would attend no more elections "where fellows without shirts challenge
as good a voice as mine," may strike us as unbearable snobbery, but to
him it was the profoundest statement that could be made to describe
the *corruption* of elections.[44] Whether freeholders continued to follow
the lead of their lords blindly or occasionally in complex circumstances

---

[40] J. E. Neale, *Elizabethan House of Commons* (1949), p. 88. The full quotation reads,
"For some reason or another, there was sometimes great reluctance to proceed to a
poll." In discussing the Denbighshire election, Neale observes, "It is difficult to believe
that the sheriff ever intended the poll to be completed." "Three Elizabethan Elections," *English Historical Review*, 46 (1931), p. 236.

[41] Thomas Carew, *An Historical Account of the Rights of Elections*, I, 109, 116. British
Library, Cotton Mss., Julius C III, fol. 115. This was probably the result of a preelection agreement. Hirst provides no evidence for his claim that a contest took place
at this selection. Hirst, *Representative of the People?*, p. 219.

[42] J. E. Neale, *Elizabethan House of Commons* (1949), p. 106. Neale regards the decision
to poll by hundreds as a "sheriff's trick" designed to aid one of the candidates. The
sheriff defended his decision by arguing that this was the method used to determine
the precedence of cases to be heard before the county court.

[43] British Library, Harleian Mss., 2313, fols. 8–9.

[44] British Library, Egerton Mss., 2646, fol. 142.

demurred is largely beside the point. The reality of these unequal relationships is indisputable and is revealed in hundreds of peaceful selections in which gentlemen asked each other for the voices of their tenants and freeholders. However ill-disposed we are to the crushing economic inequalities of early modern England, however alienated from the inflexibilities of its social distinctions, we cannot wish them out of existence.

The lulling simplicity of Neale's description of the progression from the voice, to the view, to the vote by which contests were resolved diverts us from the fact that the steps were not linked, that the passage from one to another was degenerative – a declension from the county's acclamation to its open and undeniable division. Men came to selections to give their voices, to make manifest their assent to the community's choice. The "shout" was celebratory. It lasted for hours on end; it was neither a primitive method of determining majorities nor an indication of the superior aural abilities of an oral culture. An age whose members could compute the Year of the Beast, the movement of the stars across the heavens, and logarithmic values could certainly count a few thousand freeholders if it had any mind to. The "view" was equally useless as a means of fixing size, although it was exceedingly helpful if those taking it wanted to know which candidate had the support of county leaders. Gentlemen and their followers still distinguished themselves by the colors they wore, as tradesmen did by their jerkins. A sea of reds and blues, cloaks with heraldic devices, and festooned horses were what caught the attention of those who took the "view." If the clamor of the "shout" could not dissuade a superfluous candidate, then he would be forced to gaze upon those colors that stood opposed to him. A poll was good for one thing only, and on the rare occasions before 1640 when one was actually completed, it was a somber affair. It was a solution akin to Solomon's judgment – equitable but not efficacious.

III

The failure of a community's informal selection process created the possibility of a contest, but it did not necessitate one. The desire for a "free election," unsullied by dispute and division, with the prize openly given rather than wrested away, was pervasive. "If I had not wholly cast myself for a free election," Thomas Smith wrote in March 1640, "I should certainly have called upon you for aid in this particular. But, truly Sir, I never asked a voice of any of my own kindred."[45] As long

---

[45]   Bristol Record Office, Smyth of Long Ashton Mss., 36,074 (133b).

as this attitude dominated the conduct of candidates and magistrates there was little need for refinement of the haphazard preelection process. Eleventh-hour solutions might be less tidy than those easily achieved at the beginning, but they were no less rewarding. Blood feuds were enriched by bitter parliamentary contests; they were avoided by the amicable public demonstrations of harmonious choice. There was room for considerable brinksmanship, like Sir John Saville's ploy, on the part of candidates who still stopped one step short of open competition.

Similarly, the community's leadership in its various forms had a range of devices at its disposal with which to maneuver aspirants out of the way. In the complicated preelection jockeying prior to the Somerset Short Parliament selection, candidates offered to stand down, pairings were fixed and dissolved, and a fourth candidate withdrew. Finally, in the presence of the county magistracy, the three remaining candidates agreed "to proceed no further in laboring for voices... and promise each to the other that neither of us will be present at the election... nor use any endeavors for the obtaining of that place."[46] Sir John Pickering readily agreed to Lord Montague's proposals for accommodation before the 1626 Northamptonshire selection: "The amity that this course is like to lead in the county is the chief thing that gives me contentment. For I affect the peace of the whole more than the honor or victory of either side, which being strictly stood upon will, upon such occasions as this, be a ground of contention among our posterity perpetual."[47] It was not usually necessary to go as far as the Cheshire magistrates did in 1626 when they conducted an agonizingly slow poll for three consecutive days, finally outlasting one of the candidates who voluntarily withdrew.[48] It was rare for the process to fail and rarer still that the quest for composition did not dominate it.

The problems that arose in Buckinghamshire in 1588 had many causes. The county gentry were beginning to fragment, with one clearly recognizable group interested in religious reform. Personal feuds and Star Chamber suits divided others, none more strongly than Lord Grey of Wilton and Sir John Fortescue, who were deep in litigation over a piece of property.[49] But none of these factors outweighed the assumption that the county would choose its representatives unanimously. Thus when

---

[46] Bristol Record Office, Smyth of Long Ashton Mss., 36,074 (49).
[47] Northamptonshire Record Office, Montague Mss., XIV, fol. 51.
[48] Philip H. Lawson, "Family Memoranda of the Stanleys of Alderly," *Journal of the Chester and North Wales Archaeological and Historic Society*, 24 (1921–22), pp. 81–101.
[49] Linda Peck, "*Goodwin v. Fortescue*: The Local Context of Parliamentary Controversy," *Parliamentary History*, 3 (1985), pp. 33–56.

news of the summoning of the House reached the county, Fortescue hurried into action, writing for the voices of the leading gentry including those most closely connected with Lord Grey. On September 20 he canvassed John Temple requesting that he "bestow your first voice for the place of knight of the shire upon me."[50] Temple agreed to support Fortescue's candidacy and organized some of his friends and neighbors as well. All was proceeding smoothly until news arrived from London that Lord Grey would oppose Fortescue with a candidate of his own. As Temple's first allegiance lay with Grey, he immediately attempted to back away from his promise to Fortescue: "Since you did write to me for my first voice...my Lord Grey hath written unto me for my first voice for Mr. Hampden and hath written to many others to that effect and I see his Lordship to follow the matter very earnestly. Wherefore I desire you to take it in good part in that I shall now bestow my first voice to his Lordship's liking."[51] But Sir John was hardly likely to take it "in good part," and he left no doubt as to the seriousness of Temple's "revolt." "Sir, I hardly would have believed but that you have testified that your promise had been of so little regard, but since you make not better reckoning, I must weigh it accordingly." Fortescue would not accept, as Temple reported to him, that others would also renege on their pledges: "Nor do I doubt that they will regard their word which the credit of gentlemen truly requires to concur with deed."[52]

The oncoming contest now divided the Buckinghamshire gentry as none of their petty squabbles had done before. Forced to choose between lord lieutenant and privy councilor, many found that they had given pledges prematurely.[53] It was thus left for an outsider to mediate between Fortescue and Lord Grey or for the county to suffer the consequences of a contested election and a rupture in social relations. Mediation was not long in coming. Fortescue approached Sir Francis Walsingham with details of his candidacy and support and with an account of Lord Grey's intervention. How closely this narration followed the one Walsingham chose to report to Grey is a matter of conjecture, but the essentials are beyond question: "He feels aggrieved that your Lordship be offended with such gentlemen as promised their voices unto him. He protests that if he had known that your Lordship would have stood therein for any friend of yours he would never have proceeded so far. To have your

---

[50]   Huntington Library, Temple–Stowe Mss., STT 795.
[51]   Huntington Library, STT 1933.
[52]   Huntington Library, STT 797.
[53]   As Sir John Goodwin informed Temple, "Lord Grey doth think much unkindness in such as his Lord took to be his friends that they were so forward in promising their voices...without his privity." Huntington Library, STT 851.

Lordship's good will ... he offers to yield and not to stand in the matter." But Walsingham had a different solution. "Especially seeing the gentlemen your Lordship means to stand for are willing to give place, you will be pleased not to urge him [Fortescue] so far as to yield, but rather to move your friends to confer their voices upon him."[54] This indeed was the result. One month after Temple received the request that he support Fortescue, he received a letter from Lord Grey himself. "Being earnestly solicited by a dear friend ... not to hinder the preferment of Mr. Fortescue [I] have yielded myself to be overruled by him in this matter and not to press any friend of mine to cross Mr. Fortescue."[55]

Most complicated selections arose circumstantially rather than purposefully. Saville and Wentworth in Yorkshire and Phelips and Poulett in Somerset might be willing to square off at the slightest provocation, but generally the persistence of surplus candidates was the result of misunderstood intentions, imperfect communications, or unanticipated developments. When Sir Robert Tracy was too ill to attend the county court at Gloucester in the spring of 1640, a ground swell for Nathaniel Stephens ultimately led to a contest that lasted four days. As the magistrates at the previous assizes had chosen Tracy and Sir Robert Cooke, "it was generally expected that the election should be a matter of ceremony and formality and be both speedily and unanimously dispatched." Such occurrences carried with them the potential for irreconcilable disputes – the contest between Tracy and Stephens quickly descended to social smears and ancestral deprecations ("they have divided the country into Cotteswold-shepherds and Vale-weavers") – but more commonly the ruffled feathers were smoothed once the waters calmed.[56] This is one reason why composition was so frequently left until the actual meeting of the electors. There the circumstances that had brought the aspirants together could be discovered, usually with the aid of a mediating authority, and the giving of voices could cement the resolution.

Things did not go well among the Essex gentry when efforts were made to select the two candidates for the 1604 Parliament. Sir Francis Barrington had sat as the county's junior member in 1601 and, recently knighted, aspired to the first place. This was all the more likely as Sir Henry Maynard, the senior knight in 1601 and Barrington's partner as deputy lieutenant, was serving as sheriff. Barrington's inclinations were supported most vigorously by Lord Rich, one of the county's largest

---

54 Huntington Library, STT 2484.
55 Huntington Library, STT 953.
56 Though there were clearly ideological issues at stake in this contest, Tracy's absence was the opportunity for them to come to the fore. See Chapter 5 of this book. Tracy and Cooke were ultimately elected. PRO SP 16/448/79.

landholders. When his quest began, Barrington was unaware of a potential challenge and directed his efforts to securing the support of the leading gentlemen for himself and Sir Gamaliel Capel, with whom he had paired. The pairing ensured Barrington of senior place until word arrived that Sir Edward Denny, a government official with local influence in both Essex and Hertfordshire, was also seeking support for a seat. Denny's appearance was doubly unfortunate for Barrington: He had already made his pairing – too hastily he now realized – and Denny's standing and offices made him a candidate for the senior shire seat and thus a contender with Barrington rather than Capel. Barrington could not withdraw "without hurt to my reputation" but he was equally "unwilling to contend, especially with a gentleman whom I so much respect."[57] In the weeks before the meeting of the county court he could only hope, as he was encouraged to do by Lord Rich, that Denny might seek a seat elsewhere. As Rich made elaborate plans to frighten off Denny and his supporters, Barrington moved more cautiously, seeking to learn the strength of the sentiment for Denny and searching for options.[58]

Barrington's attitude was also in evidence among the other leaders of county society. They too would be caught in the crossfire if a contest resulted. While Lord Rich plotted against Denny, the county's lord lieutenant, the Earl of Suffolk, worked for him – both in London, where he appears to have secured an order from the Privy Council banning "all factious laboring for the places of knights," and in the county, where he admonished the corporation officials of Saffron Walden for offering support to Barrington. "I cannot but wonder," he wrote to the town leaders "that he would either solicit any of you to that purpose without my privity or you so slightly to regard me as to pass your voices before you knew my pleasure."[59] Sir Thomas Mildmay, *custos rotulorum* of Essex, also sought to distance himself from the oncoming affray. When

---

[57] British Library, Egerton Mss., 2644, fol. 130. Denny had served previously as sheriff of Hertfordshire and was shortly to be elevated to the peerage. *D.N.B.* under the entry "Denny, Sir Anthony."

[58] British Library, Egerton Mss., 2644, fols. 128, 130.

[59] British Library, Egerton Mss., 2644, fol. 138. It is almost certain that Barrington had sought these voices before Denny's candidacy was known. Suffolk's attitude was revealing on two counts. First, he assumed that the townsmen would give their voices as he did and thus was disconcerted to learn that they had already been promised: "As I am Lord of the town and most of you my tenants (if there were no other respect) that you give your *free* consent and voices to my good friend, Sir Edward Denny, Knight, which if you shall not regard what I now make known unto you, I will make the proudest of you all repent it, be you well assured." Second, in writing this letter he believed that he had conformed to the Privy Council's ban on soliciting voices. For Suffolk, laboring for voices must have meant requesting those at the disposal of other gentlemen rather than mobilizing one's own tenants and freeholders.

Barrington asked Mildmay to reiterate his support for him, he was answered by a punctilious statement of neutrality:

Where I had liking to give my voice there I would give it....I am sorry to understand of the extraordinary guises set on in this business which I wish may not end with the discontentment of very many and make this country, that hath in the whole course of my poor service therein ever reputed peaceable and quiet, now to become factious, whereunto you are both bound as good patriots to have a singular regard, all private respects set aside.[60]

By the week before the election day it was clear that a solution had to be found that would not only end the division of the county and resolve the selection, but would also release the county's leading gentlemen from their conflicting loyalties. As always, the selection was a problem for the community rather than for individuals. Even Lord Rich, who believed that Barrington could carry a contest and who was as passionate in denouncing those who were wavering in their support as Suffolk was against those who had given it prematurely, saw the most obvious solution: "The end of this crossing opposite course will be that Sir Gamaliel Capel shall desist and [Barrington] and Sir Edward Denny chosen and so no offense to either side."[61] This indeed was the solution worked out by the Essex magistracy. In an extraordinary meeting called by the sheriff, the justices determined to request that Sir Gamaliel Capel voluntarily stand aside "as a good patriot." Letters from Rich and the county justices were sent to Capel, who acceded immediately to the proposal: "I would be loath to be contradictory to so good a proposition though unhappily I may hereby expose my credit to diverse misconstructions.... [But] hoping it will be an occasion to make an end to the controversy . . . and an ease and satisfaction to the whole country."[62]

With Capel disposed of, only one other problem remained, the vexing question of primacy of place, which was the real ambition of Rich for Barrington — "the ancient name of Barrington for first knight of our shire, whose ancestors, I can aver to be knights before English were in England."[63] This the justices solved in an equally evenhanded and conciliatory manner. As both Denny and Barrington had advanced themselves and garnered their supporters, there could be no question of one or the other standing down. Instead, as the justices explained to the two

---

[60] British Library, Egerton Mss., 2644, fol. 131.

[61] British Library, Egerton Mss., 2644, fol. 149.

[62] British Library, Egerton Mss., 2644, fols. 139, 143. When Denny was elevated to the peerage in October, 1604, the county held a by-election in which Sir Gamaliel Capel was chosen. There are numerous examples of disappointed candidates being selected at the next available opportunity.

[63] British Library, Egerton Mss., 2644, fol. 151.

candidates, "we have bethought ourselves of some mediation therein and such as can be no blemish to either of your reputations to consent unto." They proposed that on the evening before the county day Barrington and Denny meet with the sheriff at Chelmsford and draw lots for the first place. "And by that means fortune to be the director without touch of either of your credit." The justices concluded by reminding all involved that more than seniority was now at stake: "So that every gentleman of reputation engaged in this business may retain the honor done unto him in the performance of his word."[64] Though for a time feelings ran high and the peace of the county was threatened, an amicable and sensible result was finally achieved.

The Essex selection exhibits many of the elements common to the preelection process, relying upon a last-minute resolution of the county gentry to compose the potential contest. At no point were the candidates or their supporters unwilling to seek a solution or to recognize the legitimacy of competing claims. Barrington felt deserving of first place, especially as he was first in the field and had advanced his candidacy after he had tested the waters; but he did not question the merits of Sir Edward Denny. The principal difficulty once Denny's intentions were known was Capel's candidacy, and it is instructive that Rich and Barrington did not directly ask him to withdraw, a request they could not have made honorably. Rather, Capel was informed of the dangers that "a fourth person, perhaps be elected." With the peace of the county, the anticipated cost of a contest, and the prospect of defeat all at stake, Capel's decision was easily made.[65] In this instance it was the timely

[64] British Library, Egerton Mss., 2644, fol. 139. The Essex election has received fuller attention in M. E. Bohannon, "The Essex Election of 1604," *English Historical Review*, 48 (1933), pp. 395–413; and in Christopher Thompson, "The 3rd Lord Rich and the Essex Election of 1604," *Essex Journal*, 14 (1979), pp. 2–6. I am indebted to C. S. R. Russell for lending me a photocopy of this latter essay. I differ from Thompson's judgment that the solution was a defeat for Rich. Rich's strong feelings center upon the collapse of the support he had built for Barrington rather than upon any attachment to Capel. He undoubtedly felt that Barrington should have primacy and was reluctant to concede this point. British Library, Egerton Mss., 2644, fols. 149, 151. Yet this most probably stemmed from his belief that Denny entered the preelection process too late to have been allowed to overthrow the arrangements that had been made. As always, possessing only one side of the correspondence, in this case Barrington's, makes an impartial account difficult. A selection of the correspondence has been printed in G. A. Lowndes, "The History of the Barrington Family," *Transactions of the Essex Archaeological Society*, II (N.S., 1884), pp. 14–22. There can be no question of a contest having occurred. Cf. Hirst, *Representative of the People?*, p. 218.

[65] British Library, Egerton Mss., 2644, fol. 149. Rich wrote to Barrington, "I have on Mr. Sheriff's motion written to Sir Gamaliel to wish him to be firm to us or to desist." Thompson takes this to mean that Rich was still eager for a contest. I think rather

intervention of the sheriff (whose strict neutrality would have resulted in a contest, not prevented one) that saved a difficult situation.

In the 1626 Herefordshire selection it was the candidates themselves who resolved the issue of precedence. At a meeting of the justices at quarter sessions, Sir Walter Pye and Sir Robert Harley were nominated for the county seats, apparently in that order. Harley, who was present at the meeting, related to Sir Walter that he had publicly stated "that I being a Knight of the Bath and Sir Walter Pye a Knight Bachelor, I conceived it would be dishonor to me in this service to have the second place and wished the gentlemen to nominate some other to stand with you." Although Pye saw no merit in Harley's reasoning, he was not unwilling to grant Sir Robert's wish: "I do really and freely desire that you may be first returned and this is done for the love I bear for Sir Robert Harley and his house."[66] Disputes over precedence of place were particularly awkward because they involved men of the highest esteem in their communities. Although Sir Thomas Wentworth was of the opinion that he "would not lose substance for such a toyish ceremony," knowledge that they could not have the first place must have helped keep many from advancing their candidacies at all.[67] It was generally competitions for first place that led to the infrequent appearance of two pairs of candidates. If one or the other of the aspirants for the senior place could not be persuaded to desist or, as Saville could not in 1597, be content with the second seat, then pairing for both was necessary to even the odds.

that it was impossible for Rich to ask Capel to stand down after the pairing, which in all probability Rich had arranged. As Rich's letter appears to have detailed the likelihood of great difficulties if Capel did "stand firm," his meaning was clear enough, and he anticipated Capel's decision. "I think by his letter he will not stand in but give up all." Interestingly, Capel wrote Barrington that he had "received a letter from my Lord Rich wherein his lordship very honorably desiring, no doubt, mutual love and atonement doth join with Sir Henry Maynard in a motion unto me to desist." Ibid., fol. 143. As Rich had signed the agreement made by the justices before writing to Capel, he would have been double-dealing indeed had he encouraged Capel to "stand firm." Christopher Thompson, "The 3rd Lord Rich and the Essex Election of 1604," *Essex Journal*, 14 (1979), pp. 2–6.

[66] British Library, Loan 29/123/39. When Pye refused to acknowledge a right to precedence, Harley conceded the point: "If you please not to acknowledge the right of precedency to belong to my knighthood before yours, you will then give me leave to justify it in such a way as shall maintain my honor and not impair yours."

[67] William Knowler, ed., *The Letters and Dispatches of the Earl of Strafford* (1739), I, 12. This observation was made by Wentworth to Secretary Calvert, with whom he had paired for Yorkshire in 1621. The two of them were being challenged by Sir John Saville, and Calvert was being attacked as a stranger to the county. Wentworth proposed that he would stand for the first place against Saville and then have Calvert's name inserted first in the writ of return. Again, a sheriff was willing to accommodate an unusual but effective procedure.

More commonly, however, a tangled preelection procedure resulted from a surfeit of candidates who felt ready for the junior seat. Here the first object was to gain the favor of those who controlled the selection, and failure to do so could result either in a contest or a stiff rebuke. When Sir John Fitz sought the second seat at Tavistock in 1604 he did so without the blessing of the Earl of Bedford and in the end was forced to withdraw. This did little to assuage Bedford's ire, which was not aroused because Fitz sought the seat to which Bedford had already made a nomination, but because he had sought it on his own. "This irrespective course of his I cannot take in good part ... [If he] had moved me therein for my goodwill beforehand that I might have satisfied one of those whom I named, I should the rather have yielded him my good will."[68] The Leicester selection in 1601 illustrates this point in a different way. The corporation wrote to their lord, the Earl of Huntingdon, asking for his nomination and suggesting two possible candidates. Huntingdon's response was less in favor of the town's choices than it was in opposition to a third candidate. "I hear that Belgrave continues his great practice in laboring to be chosen; I hope from the best of you to the meanest (knowing my dislike of it) you will prevent it and not yield to it." This seemed to have settled the matter and resolved a potential dispute until the morning of the formal selection. Then Belgrave arrived sporting Hastings's colors and informing the corporate leaders that he had been reconciled with the Earl and was now his nominee for a burgess. The corporation cheerfully replaced one of its own choices with Belgrave, delighted that a neighboring gentleman and their noble patron were no longer at odds.[69]

In the selection for Cheshire in 1626 a contest for second place was not avoided although not for lack of effort or ingenuity. Cheshire had traditionally followed the lead of its magistrates in selecting its representatives, but in 1626 the bench did not agree on a candidate for the second place. It looks very much as if there were two contenders for the honor, Sir William Brereton and Peter Daniell, connected to different

---

[68]   Bedford Estate Office Mss., Letters, vol. I, fol. 14, quoted in Hodges, "Aristocratic Patronage," p. 178.

[69]   James Thompson, *The History of Leicester* (1849), p. 316. Needless to say, Belgrave's cloak and story were a ruse, and the corporation, rather than yielding to Huntingdon's wishes, had crossed them. It is instructive, however, that Belgrave's tale of a last-minute reconciliation was easily believable. Huntingdon's letter to the corporation in opposition to Belgrave was unequivocal: "Let them know if they think him a person better able to protect them and their causes when occasion falls out, they may ... free me from showing those kindnesses." Only the expectation that some agreement to avoid the contest would be reached explains how the corporation could have been taken in.

elements of the county's social leadership. For the first place Sir Richard Grosvenor was the agreed choice, and he may well have had a hand in efforts to avoid the contest. As the county day neared, Brereton and Daniell were persuaded to cast lots, and the chance fell to Daniell. But on the day of the selection "there was a very great stir, such as the like was never seen in Cheshire before."[70] Daniell was now challenged by John Minshull, and all ministrations failed to prevent a contest between the two.

As always, the sheriff was exceedingly reluctant to hold a poll. After meetings between the candidates and the leading gentlemen failed to resolve the matter, the sheriff adjourned the court to another location. The polling was soon suspended to the next morning. Again long meetings preceded the actual counting of freeholders, and again the counting was suspended until the following morning. By now the pressure on the candidates must have been unbearable. Those of their supporters who remained, day after day and without any apparent end in sight, were forced to endure great expense, with the constant prospect that one party would lose its choice if the contest was brought to result. The entreaties of the magistrates, twice rejected, became sterner and more threatening as time passed. Thus, on the third day, when the freeholders were called and again witnessed the candidates and magistrates remove to an inner chamber for discussion, the contenders "fell upon some terms of peace and it was mediated by gentlemen on both sides... that Mr. Daniell should in loving terms desire Mr. Minshull to yield unto him ... which Mr. Minshull was persuaded to do."[71]

The need to avoid contests stemmed directly from the inability of early modern society to absorb conflict within its social hierarchy. If not regulated by the informal structures of corporations and county communities, parliamentary selections could become a vehicle for widening local and familial feuds and an open challenge to the magistracy. It makes little difference whether the identity of interests among the governing classes, who dominated parliamentary selection, was more apparent than real: When the preelection process unraveled, the community's leadership combined in extraordinary efforts to repair it. After Sir John Saville carried the Yorkshire contest, Sir John Stanhope's supporters believed they had been denied their election – that their voices had not been given and that the result had not been "free." Casting lots,

[70] P. H. Lawson, "Memoranda of the Stanleys," *Journal of the Chester and North Wales Archaeological and Historic Society*, 24 (1921–22), pp. 99–100. See also V. C. H. *Cheshire*, II, 107.

[71] P. H. Lawson, "Memoranda of the Stanleys," *Journal of the Chester and North Wales Archaeological and Historic Society*, 24 (1921–22), p. 100.

throwing dice, and the various other means by which majority decisions were avoided protected the community as well as the candidates from solutions which, in this social system, were partial. Until assumptions about social participation, and with them the process of parliamentary selection, altered, contested elections and majority choices remained aberrant and abhorrent. Until then, Privy Council, returning officers, local magistrates, and candidates behaved as if they believed that all contests could be composed.

4

Addled Selections

I

CONTESTED ELECTIONS were the failures. Before 1640 elections were held infrequently and randomly. They represented a breakdown in the process of sorting and sifting, and then the failure of mediation. In contested elections the characteristic restraints of unified choices – deference toward social superiors, reciprocity with kin and neighbors, obedience to magistrates – were all removed. Because they bypassed the safeguards designed to prevent them, contests were bitterly fought – on occasion literally fought. They called forth the primal instincts of individuals cut adrift from their communities. If selections were designed to affirm the will of local society, elections asserted the power of the individual against it. Contests were inherently divisive, creating tests of elemental allegiance that necessarily rent the larger networks by which communities were held together. They were truly addled – beginning in muddles over intentions and obligations and ending in all manner of antisocial behavior.

The nature of electoral contests has led to some confusion about their frequency and importance in the Elizabethan and early Stuart periods. Because they aroused deep feelings, elections left their mark upon the locality in ways that more prosaic forms of selection did not. Being unusual, they were worthy of comment. News of them comes to us from London gossips and from court savants. Their details can be found in the archives of local leaders and of national figures who were instrumental in attempting mediation before the contest or effecting reconciliation after it. The papers of participants survive in unexpected profusion. Candidates, victors and vanquished alike, frequently felt compelled to explain and justify their conduct to each other and to leaders within their communities. Contests also led to law suits and appeals to Parliament that generated records of a different kind. All these factors

73

make electoral contests the best-documented aspect of the process of parliamentary selection. Knowledge of them survives out of all proportion to their incidence.

This abundance of information has enticed historians into thinking of electoral contests as the normative element in the system of parliamentary selection. Despite recognition that contests were infrequent and unusual, they have exercised a remarkable lure.[1] Excessive concentration upon elections has occurred both among those describing the process at large and those using it to illustrate other aspects of social and political history.[2] This is especially so when the selection of members of Parliament is taken as an exemplar for the political malaise and social disaffection that led to the Civil War and the Revolution. Such a use of the selection process calls attention to contests where local or familial feuds, religious or political ideologies can be conflated and where a few cases can be gleaned to typify the rest.

One of the more mysterious aspects of parliamentary selections in the early seventeenth century is how they remained immune from the increase in the number of local and national disputes. One likely explanation is that the main ideological divisions that appeared so starkly in selections to Parliament in 1640 were not sufficiently well-defined by 1628 to affect any but a handful of communities. Contests needed contestants, and the appearance of groups or individuals opposed to royal policy could only cause contested elections if they were met by groups or individuals that favored it. The unanimous return of forced loan refusers in 1628 makes a point about community sentiment, but it also makes a point about parliamentary selections. The process contained self-correcting mechanisms that inhibited competition. In circumstances in which government policy and government officials were being challenged, these mechanisms worked against the Crown. County magistrates normally labored to prevent electoral contests because of their potential for disorder, disrespect, and dispute. It was as yet inconceivable that they would initiate contests. Thus when they failed to succeed in nominating candidates through traditional channels they had no recourse but to withdraw.

[1] See especially D. M. Hirst, *The Representative of the People?* (1975).
[2] J. E. Neale, *The Elizabethan House of Commons* (1949); "Three Elizabethan Elections," *English Historical Review*, 46 (1931), pp. 209–38; and "More Elizabethan Elections," *English Historical Review*, 61 (1946), pp. 18–44: J. K. Gruenfelder, *Influence in Early Stuart Elections* (1981); and "Two Midland Parliamentary Elections of 1604," *Midland History*, 3 (1976), where he states: "Little is known of the elections that preceded the first parliament of James I's reign. Yet there were many contests" (p. 241); Vivian Hodges, "The Electoral Patronage of the Aristocracy 1603–40," unpublished Ph.D. dissertation, Columbia University (1977), contains a section (beginning p. 78) entitled "Uncontested Elections."

"There was not any one of us all ... present at the election of the shire knights," a group of Cornish magistrates admitted on examination in 1628. "Neither did any man appear there that gave his voice against Sir John Eliot and Mr. Coryton, but by report there were four or five thousand persons present that gave their voices for them."[3]

While emphasis upon contested elections obviously distorts our understanding of the process of parliamentary selection, it must be recognized that it can equally distort understanding of the quality of social relations within a community. Parliamentary selections are simply not a barometer of social conflict. Familial feuds, religious controversy, factional infighting – all of the wounds, scabbed or bleeding, were widened when parliamentary selections degenerated into contests. If disputes were increasing there was all the more reason to avoid their manifestations and their ramifications.

Unified and harmonious choices can as easily hide a churning of discontent as divisive contests can reveal only a perversely combative individual. In some cases electoral contests are the culmination of slights and slanders well recognized within the locality. As in Norfolk, they can serve as public battlefields in an ongoing war of attrition.[4] But others arose unexpectedly, opening skirmishes in uncharted campaigns. When the aldermen of Gloucester denied John Jones's persistent pleas that he be chosen for the first Jacobean parliament, he initiated not only an electoral contest but a series of Star Chamber suits and countersuits that lasted for decades.[5] Yet there is little reason to think that East Retford suffered from anything more contentious than a surfeit of patrons when its need to replace one of its selected members in 1624 resulted in a particularly unpleasant dispute.[6] Contrarily, it would take an act of considerable faith to believe that the religious divisions that embittered the 1604 Worcestershire election did not persist despite the county's subsequently peaceful selections.[7] In itself, an increase or decrease in the

---

[3]   M. F. Keeler, M. J. Cole, and W. B. Bidwell, eds., *Proceedings in Parliament 1628* (1982), VI, 142. There is no evidence that a contest took place at this selection. Cf. D. M. Hirst, *The Representative of the People?* (1975), p. 217.

[4]   A. Hassell Smith, *County and Court* (1974), pp. 314–32. Yet even in faction-ridden Norfolk, Smith finds several attempts made by county leaders to avoid contests.

[5]   Public Record Office, Star Chamber, 8/207/25 *Jones v. Rich and Machin*; STAC 8/4/8–9 *Rich and Machin v. Jones et. al.*; STAC 8/109/19 *Capell v. Hill and Jones*, 1624.

[6]   P. R. Seddon, "A Parliamentary Election at East Retford, 1624," *Transactions of the Thoroton Society of Nottinghamshire*, 76 (1972), pp. 26–34.

[7]   Public Record Office, STAC 8/201/17; R. H. Silcock, "County Government in Worcestershire," unpublished Ph.D. dissertation, London University (1974); Ian D. Grosvenor, "Catholics and Politics: The Worcestershire Election of 1604," *Recusant History*, 14 (1978), pp. 149–62; J. K. Gruenfelder, "Two Midland Parliamentary Elections of 1604," *Midland History*, 3 (1976). In fact, the by-election of 1609 was

number of contested elections provides little guidance to the social and political changes of the early seventeenth century. Those who count contests inhabit the same sort of dream world as those who counted manors.[8]

For such historians, the common experiences by which communities achieved harmonious choices are relegated to passing mention or, more invidiously, described as uncontested. Their failure to conform to the model of general social and political disintegration must be the result of some corrupting force – repressive oligarchs, domineering patrons, intrusive governmental officials. Compared to lusty electoral battles, uncontested elections are at best unhealthy and at worst corrupt. Without sheriffs' tricks, or borough invasions by government and aristocracy; without the grasping aspirations of the rising gentry, or the greedy self-perpetuation of local magistrates; without the lower instincts of higher authority, parliamentary electors would be free to contest at will.

Uncontested elections – the very language suggests worlds of meaning. By making the presence or absence of contests its defining characteristic, the process of parliamentary selection is inverted. Studying selection by concentrating upon contests is like studying marriage by concentrating on divorce. Indeed, the similarities are striking. Like records of typical parliamentary selections, marriage records are incidental, mostly lists of names and occasional details about the ceremony. People marrying rarely find it necessary to justify the practice or to redefine their cultural categories. Records of divorce, like records of contests, are dominated by justifications and fixated on failure. Yet as both are circumscribed by law, their official records, disputed returns, and writs of dissolution will be far more formulaic than descriptive. Studying marriage by concentrating on divorce might lead to the conclusion that the basic tenets of matrimony are extreme mental and physical cruelty – the equivalent of sheriffs' tricks and the use of unqualified voters. If the records of divorce came to dominate the study of marriage, then married couples would soon come to be considered the undivorced, and explanations of their behavior would be sought within models of hegemony, false consciousness, and ritualism.

Yet the records of elections have much to teach about the process of

so peaceful that it aroused suspicion. Public Record Office, State Papers, 14/49/26. Hirst's contention that a contest took place for the county in 1624 is based on a misreading of the word *Winchelsea*. Hirst, *Representative of the People?*, p. 222. See Wiltshire Record Office, John Hawarde's Diary, p. 194. I am grateful to the archivist for providing me with photocopies and to Dr. Mark Kennedy for his transcriptions and advice.

[8]   See especially C. Hill, "Parliament and People in Seventeenth Century England," *Past and Present*, 93 (1981), pp. 100–25.

selection. By focusing upon what went wrong, they cast indirect light upon the participants' expectations of proper procedure and conduct. In the Dorset election of 1624 Sir Nathaniel Napper had seventy voices fewer than his opponent, Sir George Horsey. But Horsey had achieved this majority by promising Napper "that he should not stand," and in consequence Napper had not mustered his support. In the opinion of William Whiteway, "the contrary faction had such a blot cast upon them for their double dealing that they will not easily wipe it off."[9] Contests also illuminate the inherent tensions and weaknesses in the system of parliamentary selection, while their absence suggests unexpected strengths. We must not extrapolate any more meaning from the absence of difficulty than we can read into its presence. But knowledge of the breaking points, of the types of issues that propelled contests forward, makes us aware of the dangers avoided. The threat of a contest could prove as potent a weapon as the contest itself, a fact that reinforces the extraordinary nature of contested elections in the Elizabethan and early Stuart eras. It is only by decoding the evidence from contests that we can use it productively in describing the process of parliamentary selection. By finding what is unusual and offensive in an election we can learn what is common and proper in a selection.

Like unhappy families, electoral contests were all contested in different ways. They have only one common characteristic: a surplus of candidates at the time of the selection. This is their defining element. In contests, candidates forced the community to make a divisive choice, and they did so willfully. In almost every case in which sufficient evidence survives to assess motives and attitudes, it is clear that the contest was viewed as a catastrophe which had nevertheless to be brought to conclusion.[10] "Our rent county cannot be drawn up, but must be torn more and more," Lord Montague lamented as he surveyed the failure of efforts to compose the Northamptonshire selection of 1626.[11] Thus electoral contests are not simply the last stage in the process of winnowing out excess aspirants. The initial presence of competitors did not generally lead to an election. As there were no formal canvasses or stepped gradations, no rapid communications to eliminate efficiently all but those who would be selected, some jostling was inevitable. Yet the prevailing ethos was that everyone except those who were to be selected would be

[9] British Library, Egerton Mss., 784, William Whiteway's Diary, fol. 38.

[10] Thus in the 1601 Rutland contest it was forecast that if James Harington lost "it would make so great a breach betwixt Sir John Harington and Sir Andrew Noel as they would be sorry for it." Public Record Office, STAC 8/220/32.

[11] Historical Manuscripts Commission Reports, *Manuscripts of the Duke of Buccleuch and Queensberry*, I, 262.

eliminated. When aspiring patrons or doting fathers sent commendatory letters to borough magistrates, they were not proposing electoral contests.[12] The mayor of Grantham informed the Earl of Rutland in 1584 that their places were already provided but that "the gentlemen are such as you may command in any lawful matter."[13] Such discouraging replies were rarely answered by demands that an unsuccessful candidacy should go forward. No matter how close to the edge brinksmanship brought candidates before the selection, carrying the issue to public resolution went beyond the precipice.

Contests differed in kind from all other forms of selection. This is imperceptible only when one focuses on ends rather than means. In the result, it makes little difference that Sir Francis Barrington obtained his Essex seat in 1604 because Sir Gameliel Capel withdrew at the behest of the county magistracy rather than because he won it at the poll. Yet it was not simply to save time and trouble on election day that community leaders were summoned together to head off a potential contest. To them the success of the process was of far greater significance than that of any individual aspirant. When in 1614 Sir Henry Wallop, Sir Richard Tichborne, and Sir William Uvedale all published their intention to stand for Hampshire, an "assembly of divers Knights and gentlemen of the county" was convened. There the candidates were entreated "for the maintenance of love and amity between them that some course might be conceived whereby one of them might be persuaded to desist." Like the Essex magistrates before them, they proposed that the resolution be "by lot or hazard ... or any other equal way."[14] This indifference to outcome can be seen in another common practice whereby those who gave way to smooth one selection were, like Sir Gameliel Capel, rewarded at the next. The issue was less who was chosen than how they were chosen.

Nor was the presence or absence of contested elections determined by calculations of victory and defeat. This is another result-oriented fallacy. As individuals could stand in more than one selection, an effort to secure a seat at any cost would have multiplied contests. Rather, during the preselection period when potential candidates canvassed for support, they were concerned to avoid the "repulse." This was a crucial

[12]   The letters sent to the Mayor of Poole in 1624 by Edward Pitt and his uncle persuaded the corporate leaders to answer others "that they are resolved for the disposing of their places." British Library, Additional Mss., 29,974, fols. 72, 74, 76. There is no evidence of a contest having taken place. Cf. Hirst, *Representative of the People?*, p. 218.

[13]   Historical Manuscripts Commission Reports, *Manuscripts of the Duke of Rutland*, I, 170.

[14]   Public Record Office, STAC 8/293/11. Sir Richard Tichborne's deposition.

factor in eliminating aspirants, for the repulse was not only the failure to achieve a seat, but the inability to gain the consent of the community. "I trust this to your discretion," an early contender for the Short Parliament seat at New Romney wrote, "I would not have the foil. If you can so recommend me as to carry it I shall acknowledge it a very great obligation."[15] Candidates were as willing to fall off from their purpose as to proceed when there was news of potential opposition. There was every reason for Sir John Coke to believe that he could secure a seat at St. Germans in 1625 after he had obtained the wholehearted support of the bishop of Exeter. But he would not make the attempt against the interests of Sir John Eliot.[16] Such considerations, vital to the selection process, did not weigh heavily in elections. In contests the repulse was assured. Not only would someone fail to gain his seat, but those who were elected would receive an open repulse from those who gave voices against them. After the election of 1571 Sir Edward Unton would not take his place on the Berkshire bench next to Sir Henry Norris because Norris and his tenants had withheld their voices from him. The riot at quarter sessions that Sir Edward's servants appear to have provoked could have served as the opening scene of *Romeo and Juliet*.[17] Candidates could not accept the fact that in a contest every yea was implicitly a nay. Edward Hoby struck Matthew Cane "over the face" because "he procured voices against him."[18] Sir Andrew Noel charged that supporters of James Harington had labored for voices against his son, an accusation as commonly made by winners as by losers.[19] More importantly, many contests were pursued in the face of certain defeat. Allowing even for the blatant exaggerations of proponents and detractors, it is surprising how lopsidedly so many polls concluded. The victors at Chester in 1628 had nearly twice the number of voices as had their opponents.[20] Sir Henry Wallop's Hampshire supporters created more terror with the flaming W they paraded about the castle yard than they did by their numbers, which were barely two-thirds of their opponents.[21] Henry

---

[15] Kent Archive Office, New Romney Records, NR/Aep/45.
[16] Historical Manuscripts Commission Reports, *12th Report*, Appendix I (Coke Mss.), p. 251.
[17] Public Record Office, STAC 5/N16/38. Bill of Sir Henry Norris.
[18] J. Bruce, ed., *Notes on Proceedings in the Long Parliament . . . by Sir Ralph Verney*, p. 3.
[19] Public Record Office, STAC 8/220/32. "That they should in no way give consent to the said Edward Noel." Sir William Bulstrode deposed that after the election Sir Edward Noel "seemed discontented and moved with anger toward some of the freeholders that contraried the said election . . . of his son." Public Record Office, STAC 5/N1/32.
[20] British Library, Harleian Mss., 2125, fol. 59.
[21] Public Record Office, STAC 8/293/11. Deposition of Sir Richard Norton.

North lost a poll in Suffolk by seven hundred, though he attributed the size of the defeat to an overnight adjournment by the sheriff. D'Ewes, the sheriff in question, had the more likely explanation: "It is no way very probable that the said Mr. North should be so ill beloved or lightly esteemed by such as appeared for him that seven hundred persons would all depart."[22]

Rather, contests were propelled forward by the individuals involved. The small incidents leading to initial misunderstandings became magnified and then loomed large as blots on honor and worth. It is always difficult to dissect the internal history of a contest because they rarely began purposefully. In many cases the candidates and their supporters were unaware of each other's intentions or even presence until after they had made public declarations. Sir Richard Tichborne approached Sir Henry Wallop for his support before announcing his candidacy to the Hampshire freeholders. Was Wallop's "uncertain and doubtful answer" a clear signal for Tichborne to desist or simply Wallop's irresolution about his own intentions? The misconstrual on both parts led directly to the county's difficulties.[23] In other cases, behavior that was unexceptional in the course of normal selections became the grounds of contention once contests developed. Had Sir Andrew Noel trapped Sir John Harington into accepting Noel's callow son for a county seat when he suggested mutual support for any candidate the two might name? This familiar courtesy by which Rutland seats were settled led to an explosive contest in 1601 between these closely connected kinsmen.[24]

Moreover, once candidates were intent upon an open contest they were willing to place the most damaging constructions upon the conduct of their opponents and the most flattering upon their own. Routine appeals for voices and support came to be viewed as conspiracy and laboring; provisions for food and drink as bribery and malfeasance.[25] John Jones's desire to serve as a Gloucester burgess resulted from his "being carried away with an ambitious humor," claimed Thomas Machin, who "did never oppose himself against the said Jones ... nor labor or entreat any man for his voices."[26] In such circumstances, and at this distance, it is injudicious to attempt to weigh the evidence. Locked doors are inherently suspicious; but so are the riots which they occasion. When Thomas Herbert, sheriff of Monmouth in 1572, moved the county court

---

[22]   British Library, Harleian Mss., 97, fol. 8.
[23]   Public Record Office, STAC 8/293/11. Deposition of Sir Richard Tichborne.
[24]   Public Record Office, STAC 5/N1/32. Deposition of Sir John Harington.
[25]   See, for instance, the details of the 1621 Radnor election, Public Record Office, STAC 8/288/9.
[26]   Public Record Office, STAC 8/207/25.

from the castle to the home of the town bailiff, he did so because the supporters of William Morgan had broken the castle's doors and windows and were rioting in the hall. Such action was necessary, Morgan alleged in his subsequent Star Chamber suit, as all means of entry to the castle had been sealed. Yet the riot began, if riot it was, hours before the court was scheduled to convene or the election to be held. Matters were made no easier in this case by the fact that Morgan's opponent was the sheriff's son.[27]

More interesting than the imprecations individuals invoked against each other is their assumption that the contest resulted from their own behavior. Neither candidates nor leaders of the community recognized the possibility that an electoral contest might take place simply because there was a rough equality of support for two or more aspirants. Contests resulted from the willful acts of the participants, either in slighting each other directly or in engaging in unacceptable conduct. Sir Henry Wallop's supporters cast aspersions upon his character, Sir Richard Tichborne deposed, thus explaining why he did not withdraw or accept the casting of lots proposed by the Hampshire magistrates. He would not have it appear "that the freeholders of the said county had forborne to make election of him in regard to these rumors and reports."[28] The Gloucester alderman, Thomas Machin, could not give way to John Jones after Jones had been refused support by the aldermanic bench and "faithfully promised to surcease and give over his suit."[29] When the Catholic gentry of Worcestershire appeared in unusually large numbers at the county court the month before the selection of 1604, they stirred the bishop of Worcester to organize opposition against them.[30] A failure of the Dorsetshire magistracy to agree on county nominees in 1626 had similar results. On that occasion, Sir John Strangways abruptly withdrew from the meeting at Blandford sessions rather than yield support to John Browne. Browne's initial disinclination for the service was soon overcome by Strangways's highhanded behavior.[31] All of these incidents elevated initial difficulties into irresolvable conflicts of honor.

This helps to explain the unruliness of the events themselves. The dual motives of vindication and revenge were hardly calculated to achieve a

[27] Public Record Office, STAC 5/M31/39; 5/M13/5.
[28] Public Record Office, STAC 8/293/11. Deposition of Sir Richard Tichborne.
[29] Public Record Office, STAC 8/207/25.
[30] Public Record Office, STAC 8/201/17. Ian Grosvenor, "Catholics and Politics," *Recusant History*, 14 (1978), pp. 149–62.
[31] British Library, Egerton Mss., 784, fol. 55; W. M. Barnes, "Election of the Knights of the Shire for Dorset in 1625/26," *Somerset and Dorset Notes and Queries*, 4 (1895), pp. 23–24; J. K. Gruenfelder, "Dorsetshire Elections, 1604–40," *Albion*, 10 (1978), pp. 1–13.

peaceable result. Indeed, the most striking aspect of contested elections is the rudimentary nature of the combat. The actuality of the contest was sufficiently fearsome that there was apparently little need to make elaborate preparations for it. These were, in any case, foreclosed by the brevity of the campaign. Most contests occurred within days of the realization that they could not be avoided. Only those prolonged by the delay of the writ or by an invalidation of the initial return presented any opportunity for tactics. Invariably these were as primitive as the state of communications.

In shire elections candidates used their servants – it is more than anachronistic to style them election agents – to deliver letters to potential supporters requesting that they and their dependents come to the county court. In boroughs, propinquity aided the process; but in either case canvassing was both unsystematic and ineffectual. Responses to such requests, even when offering positive support, were as vague as the inquiries themselves. The crucial question of numbers was seldom mentioned. The few compilations of "callanders" or lists of freeholders were made as frequently on election day or after as during the campaign period, and were as likely to be of the candidates' own tenants and kin as of neutral support. Not surprisingly, candidates arrived at the county court without a glimmer of an idea of the potential electorate or of their likely share of it.[32] If they made calculations at all, it was on the basis of the prestige and standing of their most prominent supporters. Thus when Sir Edward Harewell wrote to Sir William Ligon in 1604 asking that he withdraw his candidacy to avoid both the contest and a probable defeat, Ligon's supporters were emboldened only by the calculation that more Worcestershire justices of the peace were likely to support him than Harewell.[33]

Given such chaotic preparations and the acerbic tinge of personal invective, electoral contests were kindling awaiting conflagration. In contests dishonorable acts were sanctioned to vindicate the honor of the contestants. The inherent illogicality of such situations often served to prevent them, but once contests began it was passion rather than reason that dominated. Every account of an election testifies to the tensions that surrounded it and describes actions that heightened them. Candidates and their supporters openly intimidated and cajoled their oppo-

---

[32] Though historians can calculate the size of the electorate appearing at a poll, it must be remembered that polls were uncommon and likely to draw both a larger crowd and a larger electorate than most selections. Moreover, while we can gain some rough notion of the potential electorate for an impending contest, there is little evidence to suggest that contemporaries could or did.

[33] Public Record Office, STAC 8/201/17. Deposition of Robert Walwyn.

nents' adherents. The great pro-Wallop demonstration in which a flaming banner was carried in advance of a throng of his supporters exudes theatricality rather than terror in a post-hustings age. But in an atmosphere in which a riot or worse was the expected outcome of such a large concourse of people, its intended effect was to cow, if not to incite. The supporters of James Price, who was elected for Radnor in 1621, rang the great bells of the church and then "unlawfully marched together in warlike manner armed with swords and other unlawful weapons and did in most insolent and fearful manner threaten and terrify all... that would pass their voices against James Price."[34]

Again we must be struck more by the inefficiency of the intimidation than by its existence. It most frequently occurred in public view, without attempt at concealment, and has the appearance of pique rather than of strategy. Individual voters might be questioned as to their freeholds or threatened with lengthy attendance at county courts or on juries, but such stratagems were both infrequent and inept. Thomas Maples, the sheriff of Huntingdonshire in 1621, was accused of threatening two voters in this manner.[35] Harington supporters were charged with bidding forty shillings for freeholds of their dependents so that they could swear that their land was so valued. Yet this was a particularly incompetent maneuver in light of the fact that Sir Andrew Noel would be taking the oaths.[36] It was not so much the weak and the innocent who were victimized in elections as it was those to whom the conflict of loyalties was sharpest. As most contests took place between kinsmen and neighbors, they were bound to divide families and close-knit social networks. What was Sir William Kingsmill to do in the contest between Tichborne and Wallop when he received Lady Winchester's entreaty to yield to Sir Richard Tichborne his "very best assistance for the choosing of the Knights of the Shire and... my very good friend Sir Henry Wallop to yield him the like"?[37]

Bitter denunciations between contestants and their supporters were the inevitable result of electoral contests. The divisions they created or helped to widen might take years to repair. The feud between Savilles and Wentworths in Yorkshire is but one well-documented example of the discord that electoral contests brought in their wake.[38] The falling

---

[34] Public Record Office, STAC 8/288/9.
[35] Public Record Office, STAC 8/47/7.
[36] Public Record Office, STAC 8/220/32. Interrogatories of Sir Andrew Noel.
[37] Hampshire Record Office, Jervoise Papers, Box 6/44/M69. Kingsmill was closely connected to the Marquess of Winchester and was a cousin of Wallop. Institute of Historical Research, Kingsmill Family Letters, 1317ff.
[38] J. T. Cliffe, *The Yorkshire Gentry* (1969).

out between Edward Clere and Richard Southwell after the 1572 Norfolk election conveys a sharper sense of the personal tragedy that elections could foster. Though Southwell was well disposed toward his cousin Clere and had publicly spoken well of his candidacy, he had promised his voices before Clere had requested them. Though he had advised Clere of his prior commitment – "whereunto I was very loath to yield, forseeing the inconveniency that follows partial part taking" – Southwell's open support of his opponent at the election proved too much for Clere. "They consent and dissent alike that be in true friendship, the property whereof is unity, the cause of the friend ought to be made your own," Clere wrote toward the end of a series of increasingly pathetic letters in which the two renounced the bonds of familial attachment and then of friendship.[39]

The ramifications of contests affected every aspect of a community's life, from the operation of commerce to the administration of justice. Contests always challenged the power of the magistracy and frequently led to a forcible reassertion of it. The Countess of Devonshire's untimely and persistent intervention into East Retford's second 1624 election forced an unanticipated expansion of the aldermanic bench; John Jones's refusal to accept the will of the Gloucester aldermen led to a challenge by the lower chamber.[40] As many contests were pursued with the aim of gaining revenge rather than a seat in Parliament, there were continued incentives to inflict pain upon one's opponent. Star Chamber suits must have been initiated on this principle as much as any other, for as a remedy at law they were wholly ineffectual.[41] Noels and Haringtons were submitting interrogatories and undergoing examinations three years after the dissolution of the parliament whose election they were disputing.[42] Indeed, the suit that arose out of the 1621 Huntingdonshire election, which also survived more than three years past the parliament,

[39] British Library, Additional Mss., 37,960, fols. 9–10.
[40] P. R. Seddon, "A Parliamentary Election at East Retford, 1624," *Transactions of the Thoroton Society of Nottinghamshire*, 76 (1972), pp. 26–34; Public Record Office, STAC 8/207/25; J. K. Gruenfelder, "Gloucestershire's Parliamentary Elections," *Bristol and Gloucestershire Archaeological Society Transactions*, 96 (1979).
[41] Neale's argument that Star Chamber suits were the chief remedy to election disputes before the Commons secured the right to examine its own elections is speculative. There appear to be as many Star Chamber cases from the early seventeenth century as from the very late Elizabethan period. The last was initiated after the 1621 elections. During that parliament the Radnor Star Chamber dispute was turned over to the Commons as "the Lords of Star Chamber would not determine the case." But the Huntingdonshire dispute, *Bedell v. Maples*, was examined in Star Chamber on the principle that it was "otherwise if it were after the Parliament ended." W. Notestein, H. Simpson, and F. Relf, eds., *Commons Debates 1621*, V, 172 (Belasyse's Diary).
[42] Public Record Office, STAC 8/220/32 (1604).

was brought by a private party who used the contest as an occasion to repay the sheriff for past incivilities.[43] It was in their long-term consequences that the peculiar character of contests can best be measured. It is hardly credible that the desired results of the process of parliamentary selection were blood feuds, diminished magisterial authority, and poisoned personal relations.

II

For want of a letter the county was lost. So it appeared to Sir Maurice Berkeley of Bruton in 1614 as he attempted to undo the mischief caused by the failure of the two candidates for the second Somerset seat to arrange an accommodation. Throughout the preceding half-century, the Somerset gentry had amicably shared the county honors with no single family or individual dominant. With easy access to the deep pool of West Country boroughs, there was ample opportunity for younger sons and lesser houses to satisfy their ambitions. Judging from the returns, the shire seats were rotated among several families, the Berkeleys, Hastings, and Pouletts being the most prominent. After the turn of the century the prospering legal career of Sir Edward Phelips brought a new family into the county elite.

In 1601 Sir Edward sat as junior knight to Sir Maurice Berkeley, and in 1604, when Berkeley shifted to Minehead, junior to Sir Francis Hastings. During the first Jacobean decade Sir Edward's successes multiplied. In 1604 he was selected speaker of the House of Commons. Later he served as justice of common pleas for the duchy of Lancaster, and in 1611, his fiftieth year, he came into his reversion of the mastership of the rolls.[44] His achievements at law added luster to the bright impression he was making on county society. He built a splendid mansion at Montacute to satisfy the requirements of his growing family and to enable him to provide the hospitality expected of a prosperous gentleman. Since 1591 he had taken his place among his neighbors on the bench of justices, and in 1608 he was named county *custus rotulorum*. His heir, Robert, gave every indication of carrying forward the family's achievements, sitting in his first parliament in 1604 at the age of 18 and being knighted on the same day as his father. The Phelips's burgeoning prominence was furthered by the death of one of the county's knights of the shire, Sir

---

[43] Public Record Office, STAC 8/208/15, *Maples v. Bedell*, with the future sheriff accusing Bedell of charging his wife unlawful and exorbitant fees.

[44] *Dictionary of National Biography*, under the entry "Sir Edward Phelips."

Francis Hastings, who was replaced in the parliamentary session of 1610 by John Poulett, the 24-year-old squire of Hinton St. George.[45]

News that another parliament was imminent, which became widespread in the first months of 1614, began the informal process of sifting among the Somerset gentry. Sir Maurice Berkeley, who was inclined to resume his place as senior shire knight, quickly became the object of attention of those interested in the junior seat. In February he received a request from John Poulett to pair together for the county places, a request that posed a dilemma. Though Sir Edward Phelips was not likely to seek a place for himself – in the previous few years his legal affairs had expanded as his health had declined – he might desire one for his son. Prodded by Poulett's letter, which may have expressed concern over Sir Robert's ambitions, Berkeley sought an interview in London to discover Sir Edward's intentions.

Sir Maurice politely offered to stand aside to further the Phelips interest. When Sir Edward refused this courtesy for himself, Berkeley probed to discover whether or not he would set his son forward: "You asked thereupon whether my son would not be the other; I told you I had no such purpose."[46] Berkeley then approached Sir Robert, who like his father initially expressed no interest. "I do well remember at that present I did not intend to have been of the House at all."[47] But when Berkeley revealed the information he had from Poulett, Phelips's game was flushed out. Sir Robert allowed that he would be honored to accept the second seat if Berkeley would pair with him. This Berkeley would not do without risking the danger of a contest or the loss of John Poulett's friendship: "If we three stood for the place of necessity I must lose one of them; that though I love Sir Robert very well, I made not so mean account of Mr. Poulett that I would lose him for such an ambition."[48]

Having now been approached for pairing by both candidates, Berkeley recommended the only practical course. He advised that if Sir Robert became firm in his intention to stand that either he or his father write to Poulett "to entreat his furtherance" – to request, in short, that he withdraw.[49] The interview between Berkeley and Sir Robert Phelips

[45] *Return of Every Member of Parliament* (1878), p. 445.
[46] Somerset Record Office, Phelips Mss., DD/PH 216/84. Sir Maurice Berkeley to Sir Edward Phelips (with Sir Edward's marginal notes), March 13, 1614. The letter from Poulett to Berkeley does not survive but must be inferred from the substance of Berkeley's conversation with Sir Robert Phelips.
[47] Somerset R.O., DD/PH 216/87. Sir Robert Phelips to Sir Maurice Berkeley (n.d.).
[48] Somerset R.O., DD/PH 216/84. Sir Maurice Berkeley to Sir Edward Phelips, March 13, 1614.
[49] Somerset R.O., DD/PH 216/84. Sir Maurice Berkeley to Sir Edward Phelips, March 13, 1614.

ended inconclusively. Berkeley wanted to allow Sir Robert time to consider his alternatives and asked only to be informed once the decision was made. Phelips expected that Berkeley would return for an answer; Berkeley assumed that Phelips would send it in writing. He soon left London for Wiltshire, where he stayed until the first week of March.[50]

At this point Berkeley had cause for self-congratulation. He had established his own candidacy and was assured the support of whoever emerged to occupy the second seat. By hesitating to accept a pairing, he had raised the stakes for both Poulett and Phelips, making it likely either that Phelips would not proceed – it was clearly not his father's ambition – or that if he did, he would ask Poulett to desist. Such a request coming from Sir Edward would surely be requited. One way or the other Berkeley would have maintained good relations all around, obviated further anxiety, and secured his own selection. He need only wait for a letter.

So it appeared to Sir Maurice Berkeley in the middle of February. For Sir Robert Phelips, however, Berkeley's visit inflamed a purpose only half kindled. The conversation revealed that Berkeley was more than willing to give his support to Phelips and that Poulett was more than likely to stand aside. Though Poulett had held the county honors only briefly, he had held them; and it could easily be imagined that if Poulett wanted to sit again it should be in the safe haven of a nearby borough.

On the day after Berkeley called on the Phelipses, father and son met. Sir Robert revealed his ambition and asked his father for his advice and consent. Sir Edward was only lukewarm to the proposal. He had already told Berkeley that he would not exercise his influence to secure the seat for his son. But Sir Robert came armed with the better argument: Berkeley had offered his support of a pairing, and thus little effort, energy, or expenditure would be required. To this urging Sir Edward succumbed. He told his son to inform both Berkeley and Poulett of his resolution.[51] Additionally, he warned him that he could not leave his affairs in London to call upon his own indebted connections. He could do little more than offer the use of his country servants to act as messengers.[52]

[50] Somerset R.O., DD/PH 216/87. Sir Robert Phelips to Sir Maurice Berkeley (n.d.). "Much other speech to this purpose had we and at length in conclusion was that I should consider upon the effect of our discussion and you would be pleased before you departed to repair to me for my resolution in that. Which had you done the great mischief which now is like to follow without doubt had been happily prevented."

[51] Somerset R.O., DD/PH 216/88. Sir Edward Phelips to the knights, justices, etc. of the county of Somerset, March 18, 1614.

[52] Sir Edward's aloofness can be deduced from his assertion to the justices that he had not labored any of them for voices; from John Seward's subsequent affirmation that Sir Edward had not written to anyone for voices; and from Sir Edward's letter to his son – "this cause concerneth little more but you." Somerset R.O., DD/PH 216/88. Sir Edward Phelips to the justices, etc.; Somerset R.O., DD/PH 216/86. John Poulett to Sir Edward Phelips, March 28, 1614; Somerset R.O., DD/PH 224/8. Sir

During the next weeks Sir Robert Phelips began to organize his supporters. Sir Maurice Berkeley had not returned to hear of Sir Robert's
now firm intentions, but there was time enough; news of the ensuing
parliament had preceded the issuance of writs and the nearest county
day was not until March 7. Sir Robert sent his father's servant, John
Seward, to notify his friends of his purpose and to seek out John Poulett
especially to request his support.[53] He also asked Sir Nicholas Halswell
to inform Sir Maurice Berkeley that he had determined to stand, a
message that Sir Robert believed concluded their engagement together.[54]

Seward located Poulett at the end of February and found him forth-
coming and pliant. Seward related that although Poulett had not received
any letters from Sir Robert or his father, "in his respect and love to your
father and you he meant to offer his voices to the disposing of his master,
for you as one and to Sir Maurice Berkeley as another, and that if my
master and you refuse it, he meant to stand for it himself." Poulett was
most concerned to maintain his pledge of support to Berkeley, a pledge
that Phelips's candidacy in no way threatened. Seward concluded his
letter to Sir Robert, "He expected a letter from yourself which I pray
you afford him for confirmation of my message."[55]

At the end of February and during the first days of March Sir Robert's
supporters bruited his candidacy. Squires, freeholders, and tenants were
all solicited and, as no one expected either opposition or difficulty, this
was done without caution or concern. Berkeley supporters, Poulett dependents, and Phelips allies alike were approached with the news that
the writs would come down for the county day at Ilchester on March 7.
All was proceeding smoothly for Sir Robert's selection[56] – or so it appeared to Sir Robert Phelips.

In Wiltshire, Sir Maurice Berkeley continued to believe that Sir Robert
Phelips would not stand for the county, for neither he nor his father
had written to John Poulett to ask that he give way. Nor had Berkeley
received a request to join with Phelips on the county day. When Sir
Nicholas Halswell met with Berkeley he repeated only what Sir Maurice

---

Edward Phelips to Sir Robert Phelips, March 20, 1614. The use of his servants,
however, did convey the impression that Sir Edward was interested in the cause.

[53] Somerset R.O., DD/PH 216/82. John Seward to Sir Robert Phelips, February 24,
1614.

[54] Somerset R.O., DD/PH 216/87. Sir Robert Phelips to Sir Maurice Berkeley (n.d.).

[55] Somerset R.O., DD/PH 216/82. John Seward to Sir Robert Phelips, February 24,
1614.

[56] That the laboring for voices was indiscriminant is seen in both Sir Maurice Berkeley's
letter to Sir Robert Phelips and in Sir Edward's response. Somerset R.O., DD/PH
216/89. Sir Maurice Berkeley to Sir Edward Phelips, March 19, 1614; Public Record
Office, SP 14/159/96. [Sir Edward Phelips] to Sir Maurice Berkeley, March 24, 1614.

had begun to hear himself, that many gentlemen believed that Sir Robert would come forward for knight of the shire. Berkeley viewed this message from Sir Robert as "only a declaration of his purpose but in no sort a demand of my assent."[57] He had made it clear at their meeting that he could not pair with Phelips until Poulett had voluntarily given way. Indeed, Berkeley was disturbed that Phelips appeared to be going on without either his support or Poulett's.[58] As the days passed, Berkeley learned that Sir Robert's friends were approaching his own supporters urging that they be at Ilchester on March 7 and "that divers of those that labored for Sir Robert Phelips were also labored against me."[59] Moreover, news of the activities of Phelips's supporters had also reached Hinton St. George, where John Poulett waited in vain for his letters from the Phelipses.[60]

Poulett too had begun to wonder whether the stirrings for Phelips were genuine and if Sir Robert had decided to continue alone: "I did imagine that either Sir Robert would not stand, or else was unwilling to have either of us joined with him."[61] He sought out Sir Edward Phelips's servant Seward and questioned him closely, satisfying himself that Sir Edward had no part in laboring for voices for his son.[62] Though perplexing, Seward's information was reassuring, for Poulett was particularly concerned to give no possible offense to Sir Edward.[63] On the morning of the day of the county court, Poulett gathered his supporters together and informed them that he had not yet taken resolution to stand for one of the knightships. He had pledged his support to Sir Maurice Berkeley, and he hoped that all who rode with him that morning would help him perform that trust. As for the second seat, he could only promise "that they would know my mind more plainly when I came to the county

---

[57] Somerset R.O., DD/PH 216/89. Sir Maurice Berkeley to Sir Edward Phelips, March 19, 1614.

[58] Somerset R.O., DD/PH 216/84. Sir Maurice Berkeley to Sir Edward Phelips, March 13, 1614.

[59] Somerset R.O., DD/PH 216/84. Sir Maurice Berkeley to Sir Edward Phelips, March 13, 1614.

[60] Somerset R.O., DD/PH 216/83. John Poulett to Sir Edward Phelips, March 12, 1614. "All this while I imagined my letters had the ill hap to miscarry."

[61] Somerset R.O., DD/PH 216/83. John Poulett to Sir Edward Phelips, March 12, 1614.

[62] Somerset R.O., DD/PH 216/86. John Poulett to Sir Edward Phelips, March 28, 1614.

[63] We can only speculate on the relationship between Poulett and the Phelipses. In both of his letters Poulett signed himself "your son" and in the first iterated: "You have long done me the honor to profess yourself my father." Somerset R.O., DD/PH 216/83. John Poulett to Sir Edward Phelips, March 12, 1614. Poulett's father died when he was fourteen, leaving open as one possibility that Sir Edward had acquired the wardship. No record of this, however, survives in the papers of the Court of Wards. Sir Edward might also have served as Poulett's godfather.

court and then desired them to give their voices as I gave mine."[64] On the morning of March 7, Poulett still intended that if Sir Robert asked for them, Poulett's voices would be his.[65]

On that morning Poulett and his followers from Hinton, Sir Maurice Berkeley and his company from Wiltshire, all descended upon Ilchester. Neither had received the sheriff's summons for the election. They proceeded only on the rumor of the event: "I was brought thither by hearsay," Poulett abashedly recalled.[66] Like Poulett, Berkeley approached Ilchester uneasily, for he too had no intimation of Phelips's plans. He still hoped to effect an accommodation between the two young aspirants, and he still believed that his position as senior shire knight was unassailable. "[I took] horse that morning with a full resolution to have persuaded Mr. Poulett or to have desisted myself upon the least motion either from yourself or Sir Robert," he attested to Sir Edward Phelips two weeks later.[67]

But no such motion met either Berkeley or Poulett that morning. When they arrived at the county court they found neither Sir Robert Phelips nor the writ for the election of knights. Sir Robert's absence, along with his inexplicable conduct, gave rise to dark thoughts of false play and chicanery.[68] Berkeley and Poulett reassured themselves that neither had had direct word from Phelips, and they repeated what they knew of the behavior of Sir Robert's industrious supporters. Amid the clamor of their followers, they pledged support for each other when the election was held.[69] Then before they departed Poulett and Berkeley agreed to write separately to Sir Edward informing him not only of their decision to join together, but of all their prior dealings with his son.

The letters sent to Sir Edward Phelips had several common themes. Now that Berkeley and Poulett had paired together and effectively ex-

[64] Somerset R.O., DD/PH 216/86. John Poulett to Sir Edward Phelips, March 28, 1614.
[65] Somerset R.O., DD/PH 216/86. John Poulett to Sir Edward Phelips, March 28, 1614. "I went out of my doors that morning (as I hope to be saved) with a resolution that if either I had met Sir Robert or any letter from him, to have entreated all my voices to cry out for him."
[66] Somerset R.O., DD/PH 216/86. John Poulett to Sir Edward Phelips, March 28, 1614.
[67] Somerset R.O., DD/PH 216/89. Sir Maurice Berkeley to Sir Edward Phelips, March 19, 1614.
[68] Berkeley wrote in his letter that the absence of the writ "will hardly be imputed to accident or negligence." Somerset R.O., DD/PH 216/84. Both Sir Robert and Sir Edward vigorously denied any involvement in the delay of the writ. On March 22 Sir Edward wrote to his son that "it is public said here that you kept back the writ of election. You must endeavor to satisfy the country of the villainy of that report." Somerset R.O., DD/PH 228/19. Sir Edward Phelips to Sir Robert Phelips, March 22, 1614.
[69] Somerset R.O., DD/PH 216/86. John Poulett to Sir Edward Phelips, March 28, 1614.

cluded his son, both felt an obligation to justify their actions. Each provided clear accounts of those events in which they had been involved, reiterating their eagerness to accommodate what they knew of Sir Robert's desires. Berkeley told of seeking him out even after Sir Edward had played down the prospect of his candidacy: "I resolved I would leave nothing undone which might be thought convenient." Poulett recounted his various efforts to discover if letters to him had failed in their delivery.[70] For both, the turning point had come with the news of lobbying on Sir Robert's behalf. Berkeley complained both that Phelips's supporters busied themselves among his friends and allies and that they did so in Sir Robert's name only. Poulett protested "finding myself much less esteemed by him than I may well challenge to have merited."[71] Nevertheless, neither had resolved to proceed in his own candidacy until the county day, when they had intended to meet with Sir Robert and adjudicate the matter. It was Sir Robert's absence and his mysterious behavior that had led to the pairing, which they were now both sworn to maintain at the election to be held on April 4.

Yet the letters penned by Poulett and Berkeley in the week following the county court had deeper purposes than their bare narratives might reveal. The skeleton of events they recounted was already known to Sir Edward, and they could assume that he would flesh it out with details and explanations from his son. Exculpatory accounts were doubly insufficient: They were not likely to please Sir Edward, and they did not do justice to the depth of emotion that the electoral contretemps had inspired. Poulett lamented his "unhappiness to have this occasion to hazard your favor" and he and Berkeley were quick to assess the danger of winning a place in Parliament and losing the esteem of friends and neighbors.[72] Berkeley poignantly summarized this bittersweet sentiment: "For though to be Knight of the Shire be a thing I much desire and even the highest mark of my ambition, yet I would be loath to purchase it with the loss of . . . a friend."[73] The tangle of misunderstood intentions and lost opportunities now became occasion for reflection upon past courtesies and obligations. This was especially difficult for Poulett, who had enjoyed close personal relations with Sir Edward — "you have long done me the honor to profess yourself my father" — and who had received

[70] Somerset R.O., DD/PH 216/84. Sir Maurice Berkeley to Sir Edward Phelips, March 13, 1614; Somerset R.O., DD/PH 216/83. John Poulett to Sir Edward Phelips, March 12, 1614.
[71] Somerset R.O., DD/PH 216/83. John Poulett to Sir Edward Phelips, March 12, 1614.
[72] Somerset R.O., DD/PH 216/83. John Poulett to Sir Edward Phelips, March 12, 1614.
[73] Somerset R.O., DD/PH 216/89. Sir Maurice Berkeley to Sir Edward Phelips, March 19, 1614.

from him a letter full of good cheer and confidences written at the same time that he was making his pairing with Berkeley.[74] Whatever else might happen, it was necessary to assure Sir Edward that their conduct had been above reproach.

The danger existed on two levels – that the peace of the county would be shattered by hostility among three of its leading families, and that one or all of the individuals involved would suffer a loss of honor and reputation. "I see some go about to make apparent factions within the country," Poulett reported to Sir Edward, cautioning him that they were equally at risk for "they do labor in this kind rather to set divisions between us than to express any true affection towards either part."[75] Both he and Berkeley began their accounts with attestations of their care for the quiet of the county, its "universal and long continued good agreement," which they hoped would not be jeopardized.[76] At stake in any disruption of the county was the prospect that their own behavior would be questioned. If it were necessary to raise allies and call out freeholders, it would be impossible to avoid calumny and recrimination. Thus Poulett and Berkeley emphasized their belief that they had adhered to the implicit code of neighborly conduct. "If I have swerved [but] a hair's breadth from the strictest rule either of friendship, or of honesty, or of discretion, let me know your censure," Berkeley concluded his appeal to Phelips, using language similar to that used by Poulett.[77]

The failure of Berkeley and Poulett to achieve their selection harmoniously required explanation. Though both believed that by pairing together they had effectively settled the selection of knights of the shire, neither saw this as an end in itself. They were compelled to satisfy Sir Edward of the propriety of their deportment. Thus they wrote forthrightly to him, explaining what had happened, admitting their anger at some of his son's behavior, yet still relying upon Sir Edward to evaluate their conduct fairly. Poulett declared himself "willing to have no other judge for my part but yourself," and ready to do "what you shall command me as far as my credit and honesty will give me leave; farther I know you will not press me."[78] They appealed for Sir Edward's understanding, if not his approbation, and there is little hint that either ex-

---

[74] Somerset R.O., DD/PH 216/83. John Poulett to Sir Edward Phelips, March 12, 1614. Sir Edward's letter also contained news of the birth of his last child.
[75] Somerset R.O., DD/PH 216/83. John Poulett to Sir Edward Phelips, March 12, 1614.
[76] Somerset R.O., DD/PH 216/84. Sir Maurice Berkeley to Sir Edward Phelips, March 13, 1614.
[77] Somerset R.O., DD/PH 216/84. Sir Maurice Berkeley to Sir Edward Phelips, March 13, 1614.
[78] Somerset R.O., DD/PH 216/83. John Poulett to Sir Edward Phelips, March 12, 1614.

pected the matter would involve more than temporary discomfort. As the meeting of assizes followed the county court, there was ready opportunity to smooth things over and gain the approval – both of their candidacy and of their conduct – of the county justices.

Although they were not to have their intended effect, the letters sent by Sir Maurice Berkeley and John Poulett to Sir Edward Phelips are critical for an understanding of the contest for the shire seats in Somerset. They plainly reveal the conceptual framework in which all of the contestants operated. Despite the irreconcilable differences that would ultimately emerge, the electoral contest took place within a common set of assumptions. There was nothing intended about the difficulties that arose. Though both Berkeley and Poulett wished to be selected as shire knights, neither sought to do so at the hazard of an electoral contest. Nor did Phelips anticipate such a result before March 7. Sir Robert believed that he had been enjoined to stand with Sir Maurice Berkeley and that John Poulett had consented to the arrangement. His father had explicitly told him that "if they both desired to be [knights of the shire] that then he should forbear it."[79] As Berkeley had informed Sir Edward and his son of his plans, so Sir Robert was to inform him and Poulett. It was assumed by all that open communication was the only acceptable mode of behavior.

Nor did any of the aspirants approach the county day with the notion of securing an electoral victory. Neither Berkeley nor Poulett did much to further his cause. When they felt they could no longer ignore the strength of rumors that the writ had arrived, they merely gathered together nearby groups of friends and kin. Like Sir Robert, both spent much of the time before the county day out of Somerset.[80] The clamor of Sir Robert's supporters was far too indiscriminate to have been an effort at acquiring great support. "Myself and many others had never been moved for him until the Thursday in our assize week," John Symes recalled.[81] Once the contest got under way in earnest, they would all exhibit great resourcefulness.

The response from London came as a thunderclap. News of the events at Ilchester on March 7 outpaced the letters sent to Sir Edward by Berkeley and Poulett. Already he had heard his son's account of what

---

[79] Somerset R.O., DD/PH 216/88. Sir Edward Phelips to the knights and justices of Somerset, March 18, 1614.

[80] According to Poulett, Sir Robert Phelips did not arrive back in Somerset until March 13. The first letter addressed to him by his father was dated March 20. Somerset Record Office, Sanford Mss., SF/1076/39. John Poulett to Richard Weekes, March 21, 1614.

[81] Somerset R.O., DD/PH 216/81. John Symes to Sir Edward Phelips, April 17, 1614.

Sir Robert believed had transpired; his servant Seward's relation of his meeting with Poulett; and Sir Nicholas Halswell's narration of his interview with Berkeley. Sir Edward Phelips was mortified. Though he had not encouraged his son initially in his ambition, he believed that Berkeley's offer of support was a further mark of honor for the Phelips family. The shame he now experienced was all the greater for being unexpected. He had always regarded Berkeley and Poulett as worthy friends, and their actions implied not only hard dealing but rejection and betrayal – "to cast the unworthy blemish upon the family of him who they know have better deserved of them."[82]

By the time Sir Edward received Berkeley's letter he had already decided that the pairing with Poulett was an organized conspiracy against his son. Thus he rejected all suggestion that the outcome had resulted from a series of blunders. In the margin next to Berkeley's assertion that he had "discharged the duty of an obliged friend" in seeking out Sir Robert, Sir Edward Phelips scrawled "a fair mask for a false face."[83] He placed blame for his son's rebuff squarely on Berkeley. Berkeley had made the original approach to the Phelipses; Berkeley had suggested Sir Robert's fitness as a candidate; Berkeley had promised Sir Robert his support; and then Berkeley had publicly embraced Poulett. After having enticed Phelips into the fray, Berkeley had deserted him at the critical moment. In electoral behavior nothing was as despicable as revolting from one's pledge.[84]

Having savagely annotated Berkeley's letter, Sir Edward gave it over to his son for response.[85] Sir Robert too was apoplectic. He castigated Berkeley for having failed to return for an answer before leaving London, "which had you done the great mischief which now is like to follow had without doubt been happily prevented." Without an opportunity for a personal meeting, Phelips took what he considered the next best course, sending his answer to him "by a gentleman . . . of worth." Berkeley's denial of the importance of Sir Nicholas Halswell's message left Sir Robert dumbfounded. "I cannot sufficiently wonder that by this you

[82] Somerset R.O., DD/PH 216/88. Sir Edward Phelips to the knights and justices of Somerset, March 18, 1614.
[83] Somerset R.O., DD/PH 216/84. Sir Maurice Berkeley to Sir Edward Phelips, March 13, 1614.
[84] When Poulett heard that one of his pledged supporters had revolted he wrote that "he will never recover his credit." Somerset R.O., Sanford Mss., SF/1076/36. John Poulett to Richard Weekes, March 27, 1614.
[85] Poulett had still not received a reply by March 21. "Our letters have no answer. Our messengers went three times for it but was never spoken with, by which you may guess of the rift." Somerset R.O., Sanford Mss., SF/1076/39. John Poulett to Richard Weekes, March 21, 1614.

should find cause to except against me and to accuse me of neglect and too much shifting." Berkeley's explanations of events bore no relation to reality. Phelips could only conclude that they were inventions designed to obscure his perfidious conduct, and he left no doubt as to the consequences, describing his letter as "the last that will ever pass from me to you."[86]

Sir Robert's rancor and Sir Edward's fury – "he will set up his rest and follow the matter with might and main," Chamberlain reported – were tempered only by the gravity of the situation in which they found themselves.[87] Sir Robert vowed himself "ready and resolved to meet your opposition," but to do so meant an open electoral contest that would inevitably divide the county.[88] For Sir Edward, such a course presented a multitude of dangers. Foremost was the issue of honor and reputation. In Sir Edward's view it was this that Berkeley had sullied by his reprehensible conduct, and it was this that must be exonerated, "finding this unkind proceeding to touch me in point of reputation."[89] Yet there was no immediate prospect for vindication. A vexatious electoral contest could foster accusations that the Phelipses were simply ambitious and factious, that they were using their Court connections to intrude themselves within county society – imputations that would do more to damage their honor than had the indignity already suffered. Additionally, vindication in an electoral contest generally implied victory, and with Berkeley and Poulett paired and already in the field, the chances of winning were remote.[90]

Yet beyond their own reputations there was, in two very different senses, the peace of the country to be considered. Like the family feud to which it was now akin, an electoral contest would divide county society into warring groups; such a duel could only leave disfiguring

---

[86] Somerset R.O., DD/PH 216/87. Sir Robert Phelips to Sir Maurice Berkeley (n.d.).
[87] N. E. McClure, *The Letters of John Chamberlain*, I, 518.
[88] Somerset R.O., DD/PH 216/7. Sir Robert Phelips to Sir Maurice Berkeley (n.d.).
[89] Somerset R.O., DD/PH 216/87. Sir Edward Phelips to the knights and justices of Somerset, March 18, 1614.
[90] Many must have been in the position of John Symes, who had promised his support to Berkeley and Poulett before he was approached for Phelips, "at what time first I perceived myself reduced to one of these extremes: either dishonestly to violate my promise made to these gentlemen or else to hazard the love of my honorable friend." Somerset R.O., DD/PH 216/81. John Symes to Sir Edward Phelips, April 17, 1614. Poulett related that when Phelips finally began his campaign he was forced to "hunt after single voices on both sides, and when he is told it is promised to me he seems well contented that I should join with him and when of Sir Maurice Berkeley's side, the like. So [he] means to take a voice from every one of our side. But we will prevent him well enough." Somerset R.O., Sanford Mss., SF/1076/39. John Poulett to Richard Weekes, March 21, 1614.

scars. To cast down this gauntlet was to place high value on family honor, for the innocent would be victimized with the guilty. Moreover, for Sir Edward Phelips, master of the rolls, the peace of the country also meant the peace of the realm. An electoral contest might become an occasion for sedition and treason, an opportunity for plotters and conspirators. As a servant of the Crown, Sir Edward could not fling himself into a private quarrel without regard for its public consequences, could not "pluck up drowned honor by the locks."

Thus in the weeks that followed the March county court, Sir Edward Phelips prepared for both conflict and resolution. He could not hold his own disgrace above the peace of the county or of the country without first appealing to county and country for his right to vindicate it. The means to do both were ready at hand. In Somerset the county leadership was drawn together at Chard for the court of assizes, a meeting that traditionally confirmed the county candidates when the two events coincided. At Westminster Sir Edward could appeal directly to the Earl of Somerset, the King's principal secretary and favorite, who could bring a matter of private concern to public consideration.[91]

On March 18, Sir Edward wrote to the county justices. His purpose was both to justify his own and his son's actions and to entreat the county leaders to find a resolution between Sir Robert and the "combined confederates." Sir Edward renounced any "disposition either to raise or nourish dissension in my country" and pointedly reminded the magistrates of his own inactivity: "To you my worthy friends nor to the least freeholder of the shire I neither wrote letter nor sent message of request for your aid."[92] Though his son had suffered most unfairly at the hands of his opponents, he and Sir Edward were resolved to allow the magistracy to mediate the matter "without dividing the county or putting it to the public question whereby love may continue and sedition be prevented."[93] In the week following this appeal, Sir Edward informed the Earl of Somerset of the circumstances of the dispute and offered "in respect of him to have his son forbear the contest."[94]

Neither county magistrates nor privy councilors instructed the Phelipses to desist from pursuing exoneration. No responses from the mag-

[91]   The Earl of Somerset had some reason to wish to gratify the Phelipses, as Sir Robert had given up the rights to a lease of part of the forefeited Raleigh estates in favor of Somerset. *Calendar of State Papers Domestic Series 1611–18*, pp. 200, 211.

[92]   Somerset R.O., DD/PH 216/88. Sir Edward Phelips to the knights and justices of Somerset, March 18, 1614.

[93]   Somerset R.O., DD/PH 216/88. Sir Edward Phelips to the knights and justices of Somerset, March 18, 1614.

[94]   Somerset R.O., DD/PH 216/91. Robert, Viscount Lisle to Sir Edward Phelips, March 28, 1614.

istracy survives to provide a guide to their deliberations. With both Berkeley and Poulett among them to present their own compelling accounts of events, the problem proved intractable. It was more than just Phelips honor that was now at issue. As Berkeley and Poulett had publicly professed mutual support, they could no longer give way gracefully. Indeed, it may well have been the county magistrates who proposed that all three candidates withdraw. Poulett reported "that two messengers have been sent to us that if Sir Maurice and myself would suffer two others to be chosen, Sir Robert would be very willing unto it and be content to go to London without it." But such proposals only firmed their intentions: "The case is so clear of our side."[95]

Nor did the Earl of Somerset intervene. He did not reply to Phelips's missive, and it was some days before Sir Edward heard indirectly from Viscount Lisle that Somerset would not move him "to do a thing which but for your respect to him you would not willingly do." Although Lisle himself urged Phelips to consider the more moderate course – "you shall by this means restore quiet to your neighbors ... exempt your son from hazard and trouble, and the cause of strife being taken away" – it was clear that the issue of family honor had been recognized at court.[96]

Indeed, during the next weeks support for Sir Edward and his son strengthened their intentions. "I understand within this hour of a fine trick played upon your son," James Montague, bishop of Bath and Wells, wrote to Sir Edward. "By my faith I cannot endure to hear you should be so used in Somersetshire." He promised the support of all of his tenantry "or they shall smart for it."[97] The tenants of the Prince of Wales were engaged in the Phelips's cause, as were those of the Lord Cavendish. The ubiquitous family of the late Chief Justice Popham were called into the fray. "The Court here is well satisfied of the wrong offered you," Sir Edward reported to his son on March 28, adding that "you may easily perceive by my often writing of letters how much I am distempered."[98]

As the days drew the county court nearer, Sir Edward and Sir Robert

95 Somerset R.O., Sanford Mss., SF/1076/37. John Poulett to Richard Weekes (n.d. ?March 28, 1614).

96 Somerset R.O., DD/PH 216/91. Robert, Viscount Lisle to Sir Edward Phelips, March 28, 1614.

97 Somerset R.O., DD/PH 216/92. Bishop of Bath and Wells to Sir Edward Phelips, ?March 19, 1614. "Our noble and worthy bishop ... has written to all of his tenants and friends to stand for you with as great zeal as if it concerned his own honor," Sir Edward informed his son. Somerset R.O., DD/PH 224/8. Sir Edward Phelips to Sir Robert Phelips, March 20, 1614.

98 Somerset R.O., DD/PH 224/8. Sir Edward Phelips to Sir Robert Phelips, March 20, 1614; Somerset R.O., DD/PH 224/9. Sir Edward Phelips to Sir Robert Phelips, March 28, 1614.

plotted an energetic strategy to inflict the most pain upon Berkeley and Poulett. "I would not have you yield any place to either of them," Sir Edward instructed his son, "let them win it and wear it."[99] County honors would not be freely given, and their selection would not represent the will of the entire community. Knowing that his son's opponents had little stomach for the contest, he played upon that weakness brutally. "All care, diligence, and industry is to be observed against two such dispirited adversaries."[100] Poulett was upbraided for his conduct in a letter from the bishop of Bath and Wells. Berkeley was subjected to Sir Edward's own wrath: "How unworthily you have requited me the most barbarous man can easily judge."[101]

Their tactics were normal ones within the anarchic context of electoral contests. All the codes by which honor and merit were usually preserved were now stripped away. One gave as good as one got and expected the worst from one's opponents. Poulett was told of rumors that "new" freeholders might be brought forward on the election day. He was ready to counter this by making all who gave voices as freeholders liable for jury duty.[102] Sir Edward advised the taking up of the inns at Ilchester; the listing of names of faithful and faithless dependents; the canvassing of freeholders; and all of the other articles that were stock in trade.[103]

But the chief problem for the Phelipses centered upon combating the pairing. Together, Berkeley and Poulett were too strong for Phelips alone, and it is indicative of the personal nature of the quarrel that no fourth candidate could be found to pair with Sir Robert. Thus the first danger was that Sir Robert's own supporters would provide, with their second voices, the majority against him. Though there were few rules for the conduct of an electoral contest, it was evident that polling procedures had been brought to the attention of the lawyers. William Hakewill had recently propounded that the most equitable method was for each voter to be polled for both of his voices at once and that the two candidates with the highest number be chosen.[104]

---

[99]   Somerset R.O., DD/PH 224/8. Sir Edward Phelips to Sir Robert Phelips, March 20, 1614.

[100] Somerset R.O., DD/PH 224/8. Sir Edward Phelips to Sir Robert Phelips, March 20, 1614.

[101] Somerset R.O., DD/PH 224/8. Sir Edward Phelips to Sir Robert Phelips, March 20, 1614; Public Record Office, SP 14/159/96. Sir Edward Phelips to Sir Maurice Berkeley, March 24, 1614.

[102] Somerset R.O., Sanford Mss., SF/1076/37. John Poulett to Richard Weekes, March 27, 1614.

[103] Somerset R.O., DD/PH 224/8. Sir Edward Phelips to Sir Robert Phelips, March 20, 1614.

[104] Somerset R.O., DD/PH 224/8. Sir Edward Phelips to Sir Robert Phelips, March 20, 1614.

This was precisely the result Sir Edward set out to avoid.[105] In the first instance, his strategy was to settle the contest by the view, with the hope that Sir Robert's supporters would be more numerous than those of one of the other two. If the electorate were divided into three companies there would be no second voices. If the view proved inconclusive, as was likely in such a close contest, Sir Robert's next best chance was to insist upon the selection of the senior knight first. This would again have the effect of eliminating second voices. Berkeley's supporters would then have to choose between Phelips, Poulett, or their homeward journey, and many might defect in one way or another. The course of least advantage was to allow a poll of the freeholders. If that were to happen, Sir Robert's only hope was to have his opponents' companies polled first. Some might fall off to Phelips for second place, while in his own company "for the second they must be instructed to name any other gentleman."[106]

Nor were Sir Edward's stratagems aimed only at polling procedures. On the day of the election he had briefed lawyers to assert that the writ was to be interpreted so that knights were to be chosen before esquires and therefore "that Mr. Poulett was not eligible."[107] He had also ensured an immediate petition to the lord chancellor against the result. This alleged that the sheriff had refused to name Sir Robert after his company proved superior during the shout and that he had rejected the views of the lawyers that Poulett was ineligible.[108] To strengthen prospects on appeal – the "aftergame," as Sir Edward dubbed it – Sir Robert's company refused to be examined on the poll. Thomas Hughes reported that the shout was "so great and violent for three quarters of an hour at least, that at the cross and all about it, I heard no other sound but 'A Phelips,' " and he thought that Sir Robert might have carried it at the poll.[109] But Sir Francis Popham and the other leaders of Sir Robert's cause knew the futility of a poll once they failed to eliminate second

---

[105] There is no evidence to suggest that the sheriff, Sir John Horner, did anything other than conduct the election fairly. He refused contentions on both sides to disable an opponent; he proceeded with as much dispatch as was likely to conduct the poll; and he refused to allow any type of poll other than by examination of freeholders. Cf. E. Farnham, "The Somerset Election of 1614," *English Historical Review*, 46 (1931), p. 595; Thomas Barnes, *Somerset 1625–40* (1961), p. 133.

[106] Somerset R.O., DD/PH 224/9. Sir Edward Phelips to Sir Robert Phelips, March 28, 1614.

[107] Somerset R.O., DD/PH 216/115. Thomas Hughes to Sir Edward Phelips, April 9, 1614.

[108] Somerset R.O., DD/PH 216/95. Supporters of Sir Robert Phelips to the lord chancellor, April 4, 1614.

[109] Somerset R.O., DD/PH 216/115. Thomas Hughes to Sir Edward Phelips, April 9, 1614.

voices. Probably acting on instructions from Sir Edward, they drew off the company before their turn came to be counted. Thus they could contend, as they did both in their petition to Chancellor Ellesmere and to all who would listen, that Phelips had not been rejected by the electorate but was the victim of corruption. In the end, Berkeley and Poulett were returned.

It is not known whether the contest for the shire seats satisfactorily removed the stain of dishonor from the Phelips family name. The "aftergame" was pursued with as much diligence as had been the gathering of freeholders before the contest. Along with the petition to the lord chancellor, a case for a dispute in the House of Commons was readied. Phelips's agents industriously scoured the country to take subscriptions from those who claimed to have been present to support Sir Robert at Ilchester. They hoped to controvert the claim that Berkeley and Poulett held a majority.[110] In the autumn the two shire knights were summoned before the Privy Council, a further annoyance and reminder of the partiality of their election.[111] Whether all this gratified Sir Edward remains imponderable. The commotion and ill feelings cannot have improved his deteriorating health. "This aftergame must be won with providence, care, and industry . . . for mine own part I can spare neither."[112] In less than six months he would be dead.

Yet for the county the legacy was enduring. Friends and neighbors who divided in 1614 would remain divided over the succeeding decades. The contest for allegiance drew the lines of social obligation sharply. When Richard Weekes, an active Poulett supporter, discovered that his brother had pledged his voice to Phelips, he suggested to Poulett that he ask for the second voice. "To write for a second voice," Poulett replied, "I need it not, nay I scorn it."[113] Many, like John Symes, who penned a fulsome self-justification to Sir Edward Phelips, had been caught in the middle and could only wait until after the election to attempt to wriggle free. Others, like Humphrey Coles, who changed sides in the middle, had longer to wait: "He hath so much dishonored himself to all the world as he will never recover his credit whilst he

---

[110]   Somerset R.O., DD/PH 216/116. Thomas Warr to Sir Edward Phelips, April 28, 1614.

[111]   *Acts of the Privy Council, 1613–14*, p. 611.

[112]   Somerset R.O., DD/PH 228/19. Sir Edward Phelips to Sir Robert Phelips, March 27, 1614.

[113]   Somerset R.O., Sanford Mss., SF/1076/37. John Poulett to Richard Weekes (n.d. ?March 25, 1614).

lives."[114] The two surviving principals, Sir Robert Phelips and John Baron Poulett became uncompromising enemies whose personal feud helped define county politics in Somerset in the years before the Civil War. For want of a letter the county was lost.

[114] Somerset R.O., DD/PH 216/81. John Symes to Sir Edward Phelips, April 17, 1614; Somerset R.O., Sanford Mss., SF/1076/36. John Poulett to Richard Weekes, March 27, 1614.

PART II

Elections and Political Choice

The more opposition, the greater is the glory to carry it.
From the Buckingham election of 1685

5

The Transition

I

HISTORY PREFERS the incipient to the vestigial. Any study of the growth of institutions and ideas quite naturally stresses the thriving members of the social organism. The atrophied lose their interest along with their function. The time-lapse photography that historians practice magnifies change and compresses its pace; and photographic technique possesses many other advantages. By freezing the frames appropriately it throws into relief transformations which might otherwise be imperceptible. By isolating shifts in attitudes and practices it examines them more precisely and better predicts their impact upon the larger system. In short, it gives innovation its proper shape and importance.

Yet the drawbacks can be equally potent. Anachronism and inevitability are constant dangers. In analysis the result defines the intermediate points of interest; in reality the process unfolds in the opposite direction. Thus historians endow participants with foreknowledge and emphasize those who tread along preordained paths. All too frequently the formative period is given characteristics that only subsequently appear. The result becomes the only possible result. The durability of past practices is minimized and their impact on the emergence of new ones undervalued. The contrast between before and after attenuates the periods of coexistence – periods which are fundamental in shaping both change and a society's reaction to it.

The problem admits of no easy solution. Blurring the lines of change eases the dilemma of the society that has experienced it. It replaces interaction and choice with the triumph of irresistible forces. Hardening the contours gives the process a confrontational quality. It creates a battle between old and new in which both sides are fully armed and aware of their enemy. Between Scylla and Charybdis there must be a moderate course. Yet by avoiding the extremes we risk the danger of underestimating both the resiliency of political values and practices and the transforming power of radical ideas and methods. We also make it difficult to pinpoint the interrelationship. Change moves unevenly in both time and space. Perceptions of change, no less than reactions to it, are initially colored by old attitudes and beliefs. Old and new coexist and, for a time, may even be mutually reinforcing if resistance is provoked. Simple recognition of these difficulties is insufficient, for there is no midpoint at which historical reality lies. Perhaps the best approach to a transitional period is to detail as fully as possible the forces both impelling and impeding change. Thus their interaction and its unpredictable results will appear at the points of contact.

During the course of the seventeenth century the process of parliamentary selection underwent a profound transformation. The guiding convictions that had dominated men's behavior until the Civil War were eroded and redefined. Under successive waves of political, military, and ideological pressure, enduring patterns of selection disintegrated. Customs and practices that had begun to solidify with the frequency of selections in the 1620s gave way before the urgent political decision making that consumed the parliaments of the 1640s and 1650s. Even the dictates of law were temporarily altered as the Cromwellian Protectorate created new rules for the conduct of selections. Everywhere was confusion and disarray. A process characterized by social constraints gave way to one dominated by political considerations. Into the conflagration of the midcentury were cast hierarchical deference, magisterial leadership, the code of personal conduct, even the bonds of kinship and neighborliness. By the Restoration all were melted and misshapen. So too were both the ideal and the reality of unified choice.

Yet there was more arrayed against these changes, confronting them and altering their path, than just the force of habit; though not even the explosive power of the Revolution could overcome all the inertia of tradition. But the persistence of older values owed more to efficacy than to inertia. For many, consensus was a principle of greater urgency in the face of political turmoil. Because unity could give as much strength to the achievement of reform as to its obstruction, it maintained a broad appeal. The defense of local powers and interests united communities against Cromwell as it had against Charles I. Moreover, many of the emerging practices were incompatible with surviving social and political realities. The local magistracy, neighboring gentry, and officers of central government frequently served community interests. The reforms introduced by the Instrument of Government, not unintentionally, reinforced the role of these common parliamentary patrons. Finally, the Restoration brought a conscious retrenchment against the innovations of the Revolution. Traditional patterns of behavior returned along with the monarchy. Tradition, conservatism, and reaction all played their parts in slowing and shaping change.

To this mixture must be added the volatile elements of the revolutionary decades. The period of transition in the process of parliamentary selection had its own dynamic. It coincided with upheaval in every aspect of political life and suffered from the aftershocks. Civil strife hastened the replacement of dominant groups and individuals in some places and stabilized their position in others. Competing theories of political participation focused upon parliamentary selection and initiated successive reforms in its formal and informal regulation. Parliament itself took on a new meaning, and membership in it a new importance. The pattern of sessions regulated the pace of change. The two selections in 1640 were followed by a long hiatus punctuated only by the sporadic recruitment of the Long Parliament. The Cromwellian elections presaged a return to regularity, but with a new franchise and changed constituencies. The three parliaments in the three years that ended the Revolution altered the rhythm again. Moreover, each cluster had a different atmosphere. The fervor of reform that fueled the Short and Long Parliaments was spent by the 1650s. Elections to Oliver Cromwell's parliaments were governed by the need to impose order and stability. The selections of 1659, 1660, and 1661 were stoked by the conflict of loyalties among supporters of Commonwealth, Protectorate, and monarchy. In all of the sessions of the Revolution the process of selection was forged in the crucible of political crisis. By the general election of 1678 the transformation was complete. An entire generation knew no other mode of parliamentary selection than that practiced during the revolutionary decades. A half-century separated the Petition of Right from the Exclusion Crisis.

II

A process at once as diffuse and complex as that of early modern parliamentary selection was in a constant state of evolution. No sooner were patterns established and customs recognized than social circumstances or individual personalities conspire to change them. An irregular event at uncertain intervals governed by arcane practices resists precise description. Though we can set out its main lines in the period before the political turmoil of the midcentury, these must be in the nature of general contours rather than of distinct features. From place to place and parliament to parliament selections had less rather than more in common. The process remained unsystematic, the product handcrafted rather than machined. Communities sought to honor distinguished denizens, placate powerful patrons, and avoid cost and commotion. In guiding the process, magistrates weighed a mixture of social deference, enlightened self-interest, and the implicit code of personal conduct. The varied compounds that resulted – unmixed in some places, finely blended in others – shared only the principle that choice should be united. The benefits to be derived from bestowing honor on a worthy inhabitant, gratifying the requests of a munificent neighbor, or establishing ties to a well-connected patron were benefits to be derived by all. Placid communities made united choices easily; divided ones labored more strenuously, and on occasion failed. But before the Revolution the quest for unified choices underlay the process of parliamentary selection.

It was during the revolutionary period that the nature of parliamentary selection was decisively transformed. Whether the English Revolution initiated or simply accelerated radical change, it had a profound impact upon the organization of political life. Nowhere was this more marked than its effect on the role of Parliament itself. By 1640 Parliament had come to be regarded as an institution of critical significance to the nation, endowing its members with unprecedented importance. Parliament could no longer be viewed as an event. In the 1640s it was contesting with the Crown, and in the 1650s it was the repository of sovereignty in the nation. The attention of the governing classes was now riveted to its actions, and appreciation of its overarching political significance was shared by its opponents and supporters alike. Competition for seats or for influence on them was not limited to the lawyers, court aspirants, and discontented country gentlemen who had intrigued for places in the 1620s. The choices for the two parliaments of 1640 were different from any that had gone before when judged by the activities of candidates, the interest of electors, and the difficulties in attaining unified selections. The selections of the 1650s added other fresh elements, for they were made on a new franchise in reformed constituencies. Nor could the restoration of the prerevolutionary format for the selections in 1659 and 1660 halt the progress of change.

The elevation of the political significance of parliament also increased the interest individuals and communities had in parliamentary membership. This was manifested most clearly in the quest for seats. Before 1640 parliamentary service was rarely seen as a goal in itself. Selection as knight of the shire confirmed honor and standing and was generally sought for its prestige. It could be distributed indifferently through rotational patterns, the *cursus honorum*, or a seniority system. Service to boroughs was more a mixed blessing. Most men who applied from outside the borough did so to conduct private business or state service.

Internal candidates were chosen largely from local magistrates and legal officers. Even patronage was loosely organized around natural connections. Contests were normally affairs of honor involving a third candidate and only occasionally extended to two pairs of contestants. The issues that generated them rarely went beyond the bounds of personal and local dispute.

The crisis of the midcentury altered these patterns. Never before had communities been so aggressively divided and never before had the results of parliamentary selections been so critical: "Every man laid about him as if his all was at stake."[1] In 1628 the triumphant return to Parliament of men imprisoned for resistance to the forced loan was achieved within the context of unified choice. Thousands appeared at county courts in places as disparate as Essex and Cornwall to voice unanimous approval for their knights of the shire. Even efforts to produce less provocative candidates remained within traditional channels and yielded to community sentiment.[2] In 1640 magistrates faced the cleft stick of provoking division by following the largely apolitical practices of the past or encouraging it by allowing ideological dispute into the process. When Barnstaple experienced its first contest at the Long Parliament selection, its mayor attempted to apply the traditional methods of pairing used in borough elections. This only widened the dispute.[3] Edward Phelips predicted that the Short Parliament elections were "like to produce great factions in all parts," and the wounds opened in the spring were still fresh when a second parliament was summoned in the fall.[4] In the political turbulence of 1640 contested and disputed elections multiplied.

The result was an explosion of potential candidates. Beginning in 1640 counties and boroughs were besieged with nominations. Sandwich, a cinque port under the patronage of the lord warden, was faced with six rivals in the spring of 1640. The six London members elected in the reformed constituency of 1654 were chosen from forty-seven nominees.[5] The expansion of county seats in the reforms initiated by the Instrument of Government exacerbated this tendency. Slates of candidates were put forward by opposing groups. In 1656 the West Riding of Yorkshire

[1] T. Birch, ed., *Thurloe State Papers* (1742), V, 328.

[2] R. Johnson et al., eds., *Proceedings in Parliament 1628*, v. 6, pp. 138–42; 146–48; J. Birch, *Court and Times of Charles I*, I, 325. In both places, efforts by justices of the peace to propose alternative candidates failed, and there is no evidence that either selection was contested.

[3] Joseph Gribble, *Memorials of Barnstaple* (1830), pp. 346–50.

[4] Bristol Record Office, Ac/c58/9.

[5] Kent Archive Office, Sandwich Records, Sa/Ac 7, fols. 365–67; British Library, Additional Manuscripts, 33,512, fol. 40; British Library, Harleian Manuscripts, 6810, fols. 164–65.

alone had eleven candidates.[6] Men searched frantically for marginal connections in places where they had remote associations. Henry Oxinden's unsuccessful interest at Hythe in 1659 was first made by his wife's cousin's son-in-law.[7]

Additionally, individual aspirants had to contend with powerfully supported opponents. Government officials were coming to grasp the importance of establishing political connections with parliamentary boroughs and of providing seats for like-minded colleagues. This was a new type of patronage. Among the six Sandwich candidates, one was proposed by the lord warden, one by the lord admiral, and a third by the lord keeper.[8] The Earl of Northumberland was particularly active in 1640, circularizing ports with letters claiming a nomination as lord admiral. His successes were limited. Many places, like Hull, were perplexed by his assertion, for "this not appearing in any of our memorials."[9] Indeed, many of Northumberland's entreaties served only to complicate borough choices and led, as in Great Yarmouth, to the rejection of the nominees of more traditional patrons.[10] Nor was he alone in creating this kind of confusion. At Carlisle, in the spring of 1640, the Queen, through her council and her household, recommended two men for the same seat.[11] Increased interest in official nominations led slowly to their coordination, a process which would tie Cromwell's Major-Generals to Danby and the Duke of York.

The injection of issues and ideologies deadened the comfortable routines of the past. In the struggle between those to whom selection was an honor and those to whom it was a necessity, there could be little doubt of the eventual outcome. Gratification of rank and standing or deference to a powerful outsider now had to compete with matters that roused deep emotions both locally and nationally. The unexpected contest at the Gloucestershire Short Parliament election came with the nomination of "Mr Stephens of Eastington for the opposing of Ship Money ... and with an opinion of much zeal for the zealous."[12] The oft-quoted couplet from the Lincoln election, "Choose no Ship Sheriff nor Court Atheist/No Fen Drainer, Nor Court Papist," was actually an appeal for the selection of two locally connected candidates, the town recorder and the bishop of Lincoln's chancellor. "But if you'd scour the Pope's Ar-

6   *Mercurius Politicus*, no. 324, August 1656.
7   Dorothy Gardiner, ed., *The Oxinden and Peyton Letters*, p. 225.
8   Kent A.O., Sa/Ac 7, fols. 365–67.
9   *Calendar of State Papers Domestic Series 1639–40*, p. 568.
10   C. J. Palmer, ed., *The History of Great Yarmouth by Henry Manship*, II, 206.
11   Cumberland Record Office, Carlisle City Records, CA/2/120/17; CA/2/120/22.
12   Public Record Office, State Papers, 16/448/79.

mory/Choose Dallison and Dr. Farmery."[13] The Kent contest, in the spring of 1640, was exacerbated by Sir Edward Dering's conviction that "in times so desperate I would contribute no help to any privy councilor or deputy lieutenant."[14] The selections in 1656 were seen by the Major-Generals as nothing less than the struggle between darkness and light. Hezekiah Haynes reported that all of his efforts in Norfolk were for the selection of Lord Deputy Fleetwood "that the honest party may have someone to address themselves to."[15] In Suffolk he despaired that "the honest men...will be compelled to take in with the presbyterians to keep out the malignants."[16]

These concerns led directly to the development of criteria for the choice of candidates based upon specific qualifications. The growing fragmentation of political life, both in terms of ideology and experience, placed a severe strain on concepts like the "community of the realm" and what later came to be called virtual representation. There was, of course, always an element of particularism in parliamentary selections, especially when local interests were involved. But this only touched individual members in generic categories like freemanship, residency, or legal training. In the past particular individuals had occasionally been seen as inappropriate members of Parliament, like young Sir Edward Noel, on the basis of individual characteristics. Less commonly were men enabled by some peculiar quality or gift. Invocations for the choice of wise and discreet men rarely descended to particulars. The formula by which many boroughs granted nominations on the expectation that the nominee would serve the borough's interests suggested that no specific talent was required to perform the service.

More than ever before, the revolutionary decades called forth adherence to programs or policies as criteria for selectors and selected. Those who found themselves leeward to the ever shifting winds suffered at elections. Edward Nicholas's defeat in the Short Parliament election at Sandwich was attributed to rumors that he was a papist.[17] Sir Henry Oxinden was opposed at Hythe in 1659 because he supported the royalists in the second civil war. He combated this contention with an affidavit attesting to his "fidelity and affection to the public cause."[18] The sequence of election petitions to the Council of State in the 1650s

[13] British Library, Additional Manuscripts, 11,045, fol. 99.
[14] F. W. Jessup, "The Kentish Election of March 1640," *Archaeologia Cantiana*, 86 (1971), p. 2
[15] T. Birch, ed., *Thurloe State Papers*, V, 311.
[16] Ibid., 230.
[17] *Calendar of State Papers Domestic Series 1639–40*, p. 561.
[18] Dorothy Gardiner, ed., *The Oxinden and Peyton Letters*, p. 227.

all centered upon the qualifications of individuals. Robert Wood, chosen for Surrey in 1654, "is a derider of the people of God, a profane swearer [who] refused assistance in sending forces to Worcester," his opponents declared. Wood defended himself by presenting receipts for expenses in raising horses and arms and a testimonial of his godliness subscribed by nine ministers.[19] Bennett Hoskins could mount no such defense against those who protested his selection for Hereford in the same parliament. They submitted copies of royal commissions naming him and depositions of those upon whom they were executed.[20] Perhaps the most remarkable complaint was made by the "well-affected" of Tiverton. They protested that they were "overpowered by numbers" and thus could not secure the election of a godly candidate.[21]

Only the franchise and constituency reforms of the Instrument of Government can be said to have broadened participation in parliamentary selections. In most respects the Instrument continued the process of narrowing based upon political principle or wartime loyalty. Since the 1640s royalists and other classes of parliamentary opponents were barred both from giving voices and from being selected. These restrictions continued during the Protectorate. Loyalty oaths, to the government and to the Protector, were imposed upon members of Oliver Cromwell's parliaments. They deterred many from seeking seats and, in 1656, disabled many who had attained them. Public figures like Judge Bradshaw, Sir Arthur Hasilrig, and Sir Henry Vane, Jr., were reviled in efforts to prevent their elections.[22] After the borough of Chipping Wycombe returned Cromwell's bugbear, Thomas Scott, its corporation was remodeled and its leading magistrates replaced.[23] In Northamptonshire Major-General Boteler secured the unanimous return of his slate of candidates in 1656 by instructing the sheriff to ignore the large party of gentry who had come to nominate others.[24] Even the elections in 1660 proscribed candidates whose fathers had been in armed opposition to Parliament. In Somerset John Ashburnham told Hugh Smith "that the

[19] *Calendar of State Papers Domestic Series 1654*, p. 314.
[20] Ibid., p. 312.
[21] Ibid., pp. 279–80. The details of their charges against Robert Shapcote are equally interesting: "He is a great promoter of gaming, frequents alehouse and taverns, blowing and cock matches, and draws malignants together to them."
[22] T. Birch, ed., *Thurloe State Papers*, V, 313. Paul Pinckney, "A Cromwellian Parliament: The Elections and Personnel of 1656," unpublished Ph.D. dissertation, Vanderbilt University (1962), pp. 166–68.
[23] S. R. Gardiner, *The History of the Commonwealth and Protectorate*, v. 4, pp. 54–55.
[24] Paul Hardacre, "William Boteler: A Cromwellian Oligarch," *Huntington Library Quarterly*, 11 (1947), p. 8.

proviso in the act for dissolving the Parliament renders you incapable
...by reason of your father's being at Sherborne." This did not deter
Smith, who was elected. Nor did it inhibit those like Sir Edward Dering
who believed that if Parliament voted to restore the King the prohibition
would be voided.[25]

These new political dimensions focused attention not only upon candidates but upon the selection itself. As men found enhanced value in
Parliament and places in it, their attitudes toward the process altered.
Membership in Parliament came to carry political import and allowed
participation in great affairs of state at a moment when affairs of state
had an unusual immediacy. Whether one hoped to promote reform or
proclaim the millennium, to protest taxes or to protect self-interest,
entering Parliament was suddenly imperative. "Much ado there hath
been about the elections here," Thurloe reported in 1656. "Every faction
hath bestirred themselves with all their might."[26] If it was becoming
worthy to aspire to a seat in the Commons, to plan and labor for it,
and even to expend large sums to attain it, then it could not be long
before merit would attach to the effort as well as to the end. Thus was
initiated a profound conceptual shift in which the dishonor of receiving
a rebuff was transmuted into the credit of making the running.

No longer could men be expected to give way to the aspirations of
others. "I could not be taken off but by the major vote of the country."
Robert Eyre proclaimed in responding to requests that he yield to Sir
John Curzon in the 1660 Derbyshire election. "By God's grace I am
resolved to try it out...I am engaged; I will never shrink."[27] In the
politicized atmosphere of the revolutionary decades there was less concern that the actions of individuals might further divide the community.
Edward Phelips saw no prospect of John Coventry withdrawing as a
candidate for the Somerset seat in the autumn of 1640: "I believe he
doth not think the disgrace of losing it to be so great."[28] Sir Thomas
Peyton had expressed the same attitude in the spring. He informed the
chief jurat of Sandwich that "if in following the press into your town
for the baronship I be overthrown, it is the hap that many man finds in
a multitude."[29] Peyton freely admitted that the confusion engendered by
so many nominees might enable him to scrape by, a calculation well

[25] Bristol Record Office, Smyth of Ashton Court, AC/c74/11; M. Bond, ed., *The Diaries and Papers of Sir Edward Dering*, p. 110. For the general qualifications see M. W. Helms, "The Convention Parliament of 1660," unpublished Ph.D. dissertation, Bryn Mawr College (1963).

[26] T. Birch, ed., *Thurloe State Papers*, V, 349.

[27] British Library, Stowe Manuscripts, 185, fol. 145.

[28] Bristol R.O., AC/c58/5.

[29] British Library, Additional Manuscripts, 44,846, fol. 2.

suited to his insouciance about losing. Fear of the foil had been an integral part of the winnowing process; it had acted like a nerve signaling pain. Numbing that nerve could lead to irreparable injury. By the time of the Restoration, Samuel Gott could regard the election itself as the process of arbitration. He informed the mayor of Rye that he had advanced himself not knowing of the presence of another candidate. But "as elections ought to be free, I shall most freely leave it to yourselves to arbitrate between us in this present competition."[30]

The ramifications of this simple inversion of values spread widely. Men who clung to the ideas of the past found themselves challenged by determined resistance. "I am sorry that you should meet with such a requital from some of the gentry of this county as to oppose your election," Robert Breton wrote to Colonel Edward Harley in 1660.[31] Those who continued to seek unified choices were overmatched by those willing to form opposition. Consensual agreements by magistrates and aldermanic benches proved unenforceable among those immune to the discipline of unanimity. "It was among the better sort of people so well understood that there was little doubt of it," John Philpot wrote of Secretary Nicholas's election at Sandwich. "But the factious non-conformists [have] . . . so crossed this business as we fear much what the success shall be."[32] The mayor of Bedford assured Bulstrode Whitelocke that his supporters in a contested election "exceed[ed] the other party not only in quantity but in quality."[33] A meeting of the Lincolnshire gentry fixed upon colonels Hatcher and Rossiter as the shire representatives in 1660 but also met strong opposition from "a third party (who agreed not with us in our declaration.)" Rather than foreclosing an electoral campaign, their agreement constituted its first step.[34]

While some were bypassed by the change in attitudes and assumptions, others found them a convenient excuse to abandon participation altogether. This was especially so in the 1650s, when the vicissitudes of politics proved dangerous for the cautious country gentleman and the profit-minded businessman. The public humiliation that Lord Maynard believed he had suffered in the Essex Short Parliament election, when "the rude vulgar people . . . would neither make place for me upon the bench nor show any respect unto me as I passed through," led him to

[30]   Historical Manuscripts Commission Reports, *13th Report*, Appendix IV (Rye Corporation Mss.), p. 243.
[31]   Historical Manuscripts Commission Reports, *Manuscripts of the Duke of Portland*, III, p. 220.
[32]   *Calendar of State Papers Domestic Series 1639–40*, p. 561.
[33]   Longleat Manuscripts, Whitelocke Papers, vol. 16, fol. 69.
[34]   Andrew Trollope, "Hatcher Correspondence Relating to Parliamentary Elections," *Associated Architectural and Archaeological Societies' Reports*, 23 (1895–6), p. 135.

resolve to spurn further attendance at "popular assemblies."[35] Perhaps it was memories of these events that kept Essex freeholders from the poll twenty years later. "It was a very pitiful appearance," Sir John Bramston recollected of the 1659 election. "I think the most was but one hundred and fifty voices upon the poll."[36] Disqualification and self-exclusion had a narrowing effect upon the process of selection. It allowed groups bound together by adherence to issues or beliefs to dominate selections. By 1660 correspondents could identify candidates by their affiliations. "In [Worcestershire] we have two proper young gentlemen ...but they are arrant cavaliers.... But we have a precious man, one Mr. Foley which opposes them."[37] The shifting fortunes of political regimes gave most of these interest groups an opportunity to enforce their will upon the larger community.

The impact of change was as great upon those who caught the tide as on those swept away by the eddies. Determination to secure a place meant application to the process of selection. The demure, self-effacing attitudes that succeeded in the past now left their possessors in the backwaters. Preparations for selection were undertaken with the aggressive efficiency that was coming to be applied to estate management or the outfitting of a merchantman. Candidates were quick to take sail, making their presence known by personal appeal and personal appearance. Nominations from patrons were followed up by self-commendatory letters that quickly shed their initial awkwardness. "It is not unknown to you that the Lord Warden (to whom you usually express respect in this kind) hath recommended me to be one of your burgesses," Sir John Manwood wrote to the mayor and jurats of Sandwich three months before their election. His own letter was to depict his especial qualifications, "I being a Sandwich man in blood and affection also."[38] Agents were sent on circuits of counties or shipped into boroughs with precise instructions as to whom to count upon and whom to cultivate. Sir Edward Nicholas dispatched John Philpot to follow his affairs in the port of Sandwich while his patron, the Earl of Northumberland, ferried in Sir John Pennington for the same purpose.[39] Information streamed back to the aspirants in the form of pledges and predictions and forward to the agents and key men in the localities, filling the letterbooks of usually indifferent correspondents. The weeks before a selection were awash with activity.

[35] British Library, Egerton Mss., 2646, fol. 142.
[36] P. Braybrooke, ed., *The Autobiography of Sir John Bramston*, p. 162.
[37] Historical Manuscripts Commission Reports, *Manuscripts of David Laing*, I, 311.
[38] Kent A.O., Sa/C1/13.
[39] *Calendar of State Papers Domestic Series 1639–40*, pp. 561, 569.

Preparations were made to amass support to drive off potential opponents, or to muster it for their defeat. Henry Oxinden was informed on his first inquiry at Hythe that "the bigger vote are already fixed for other men."[40] One Captain Fisher made such elaborate preparations for the selections at the Isle of Ely in 1656 that he stood ready to challenge Secretary Thurloe if necessary: "He would not recede by any means, yea so violent is he that your own interest seemed to be called into question."[41] Indeed, the reform of constituencies in the 1650s necessitated planning if a free-for-all were to be avoided on the county day. The county commissioners, the grand juries, and in 1656 the Major-Generals all took a hand in efforts to slate candidates. "I have consulted with the honest people of every county as I came along," Major-General Desborough reported of his west country progress. "With them I agreed upon names and I have set them at work for the improvement of their interest."[42] Slating was but the first step, for as one side organized, so did the other. "I know not how it will succeed," Major-General Bridges informed Cromwell, "the other gentlemen having made their party strong, having been any time this month about it."[43] Even polls were anticipated and plans made to maximize support. Though Worcestershire had not had an electoral contest in three decades, William Russell was not daunted by one in the fall of 1640. He arrayed his supporters "to dispatch those of our side first in whom I had least interest, for fear they should slip from us, reserving my nearest friends for the last."[44]

Internal divisions within a community became the toehold for rival candidacies. Bulstrode Whitelocke was solicited to stand at Great Marlow by those who sought to defy the corporation's leadership. His influence within the Long Parliament Committee of Elections secured the freemen their franchise and him his place.[45] The freemen of Great Yarmouth, imitating a practice much in vogue during the elections of 1640, held an election separate from that of the corporation in 1654.[46] Candidates openly, even apologetically, provoked franchise disputes, offer-

[40]   Dorothy Gardiner, ed., *The Oxinden and Peyton Letters*, p. 225.
[41]   T. Birch, ed., *Thurloe State Papers*, V, 353.
[42]   Ibid., 303.
[43]   Ibid., 313.
[44]   Worcestershire Record Office, Berrington Papers, 705/24/623 (30), quoted in R. H. Silcock, "County Government in Worcestershire," unpublished Ph.D. dissertation, London University (1974), p. 203.
[45]   M. F. Keeler, "The Election at Great Marlow in 1640," *Journal of Modern History*, 14 (1942), 433–48.
[46]   *Calendar of State Papers Domestic Series 1654*, p. 285, "Other freemen of the place who are dissatisfied with its present government proceeded in a popular way to elect two other burgesses."

ing inhabitants and outdwellers the opportunity of gaining voices. Sir Thomas Peyton implored the chief jurat of Sandwich to understand that his campaign among the commons of the town resulted from his late entry into the contest. "That you would not think that out of a neglect or slighting of your bench I endeavor to wind myself into the favor of the commons or use one power against the other."[47] Such behavior left various Committees of Elections the task of establishing unitary rules in the place of variegated customs.

Indeed, many aspirants seemed more willing to take their chances with the committee of elections than with the electors. "I am likewise cast out," Edward Phelips bitterly related to Thomas Smith after the Ilchester Long Parliament election, "so that I am left to play an aftergame by bringing it to a dispute in Parliament."[48] Overt competition highlighted an aspect of the official return of members to Parliament that had not been in view before – the slackness of the legal processes involved. A writ was delivered to the sheriff for selections within the county. This he kept to be read at the county court and sent precepts directed to the returning officers in the boroughs. These were much less formal documents. They were sent back either to the sheriff or to chancery, usually with the signature of the returning officer or some other official mark of the community. Thus it was possible for there to be more than one precept for a borough election, as John Pyne discovered when the seat Edward Phelips did secure in the "aftergame" was vacant again in 1646. Unable to dissuade the town magistrates from their pledge to another candidate, Pyne attempted to prevent the election by confiscating the sheriff's precept. This did little to forestall the mayor, who simply requested another copy from the sheriff, who obligingly sent two.[49] Beginning in 1640, the adjudication of double returns – the return of more than one precept naming different individuals to the same seat – became the main business of the Committee of Elections. By 1659 double returns were already identified as a structural problem. "There is great prejudice from double returns which sheriffs make for fear of actions. They know not what to do in some places and in others there are petty designings."[50]

The double return was a creative response to the changing conditions of parliamentary selection. Even with the increasing efficiency of the Committee of Elections, cases brought before it were time-consuming and expensive. In a franchise dispute, those petitioning for their rights

[47] British Library, Additional Manuscripts, 44,846, fol. 2.
[48] Bristol R.O., AC/c58/8.
[49] David Underdown, "The Ilchester Election, February 1646," *Proceedings of the Somerset Architectural and Natural History Society*, 110 (1966), p. 46.
[50] J. T. Rutt, ed., *The Diary of Thomas Burton*, III, 55.

had to hire counsel, secure legal documents, and provide witnesses to prove malfeasance at the election. The magistracy faced the same costs in defending itself, along with the implicit challenge to its authority. If the disputants were successful within the life of the parliament, another election would be ordered and the candidates would be put to the trouble of a second campaign. The petitioners could ensure success neither at the committee nor at the second poll, though they were certain to bear the charges of both. The double return cut a swath through these complexities. The chosen members stood as a proxy for the rights of the electors and the magistrates. They personified the issues, could testify to events, and had an interest in the decision. Their presence at Westminster initiated the dispute, and they bore the brunt of the contest and its costs. Double returns were heard quickly by the Committee of Elections, for they involved the representation of the constituency rather than the merits of individual elections.[51] Moreover, the resolution of the case brought immediate remedy with the seating of the successful candidates. Perhaps most advantageously, the struggle took place at Westminster rather than in the locality. Candidates, electors, magistrates, eventually even the Committee of Elections all came to benefit from the use of the double return.[52]

By removing some of the bitterness in arguments over authority and rights, double returns lowered social costs as well as financial ones. This, rather than any demonstrable upsurge in class conflict, helps to account for the escalation of franchise disputes after 1640. The irregularity of past practices and the jumble of ancient precedents by which most boroughs conducted their affairs meant that both magistrates and citizens could mount impressive legal cases. Many franchise disputes elicited observations similar to that made by John Hampden in the Short Par-

[51] It is clear that the Committee of Elections was baffled by the emergence of the double return. When the Short Parliament committee decided to refuse seating to all involved in double returns it was flooded with requests for exceptions. The more sensible rule, adopted by the Long Parliament committee, that individuals named on both returns would be seated, eliminated some inequities but continued to make possible the submission of a wholly spurious return that would deny an individual his seat. By 1660 the committee had worked through the problem to arrive at the most equitable solution: Those who were returned by the "proper" returning officer were to be seated unless more than one for each seat were so returned. This led to the establishment of a list of duly constituted returning officers, a significant advance on accumulating knowledge about the process as a whole. For this development see M. Bond, ed., *The Diaries and Papers of Sir Edward Dering*, pp. 36–7.

[52] It was the double return that allowed the Short and Long Parliament Committees of Elections to choose between individual M.P.'s and thus to infuse a political element into such choice.

liament's examination of Great Bedwin. There was "no certainty appearing who ought to be the choosers, being never any competition had before."[53] When the magistrates of Shaftesbury were challenged over their corporation franchise, they produced the town's Jacobean charter with its explicit definition of the electorate. The issue was not merely political: Members of the corporation took an oath to uphold the prescriptions of the charter.[54] Yet, as many borough officials came to discover, even explicit stipulations might be overturned by one committee of elections and upheld by another. Thus franchise disputes were rarely resolved: Once begun they gyrated between precedents and principles, fueled by the prospect of successful appeals. When Colchester's Protectorate charter disenfranchised the town's free burgesses, they held a counterelection in 1656. Their appeal was disallowed. Undeterred, they held another counterelection in 1659 and won their case.[55] The common burgesses of King's Lynn were even more persistent. They lost appeals in three successive disputes before the Cavalier Parliament recognized their rights.[56]

Double returns could also be used as proxies for contests, both by candidates attempting to avoid defeat and by communities attempting to avoid divisions. In Short Parliament elections such as at East Grinstead and Blechingly, disappointed candidates used the double return as earlier disputants had used the election petition. These were familiar three-cornered contests in which one competitor had the assent of the electors while support for two others was divided. The advantage of this procedure lay in cases where one of the two candidates was selected for more than one constituency. He would choose his undisputed seat, and the candidate named in the double return could avoid a new election when his opponent failed to defend the case.[57] Although double returns

---

[53] The Short Parliament journal of Sir Thomas Aston, fol. 200. I am grateful to Judith Maltby for providing me with a transcript of this material.

[54] C. H. Mayo, *The Municipal Records of the Borough of Shaftesbury* (1889), p. 65.

[55] J. H. Round, "Colchester During the Commonwealth," *English Historical Review*, 15 (1900), pp. 641–64.

[56] Historical Manuscripts Commission Reports, *11th Report*, Appendix III (King's Lynn Corporation Mss.), pp. 184–85.

[57] At East Grinstead one of the candidates, Mr. White, was returned for another constituency. *Journals of the House of Commons*, II, 10; W. H. Hills, *The History of East Grinstead* (1906), p. 34. For Blechingly, *C. J.*, II, 4; E. Cope, ed., *Proceedings of the Short Parliament of 1640*, p. 144. At the Long Parliament election for Norwich, the sheriff returned two indentures informing the Committee of Elections that one of those returned was not a freeman and that if he were to be disabled the third man named should have the seat. M. F. Keeler, *The Long Parliament* (1954), p. 56.

at Minehead and Reigate suggest that they were used to avoid contests, they could also, as in Great Bedwin, be the result of separate elections.[58]

The creative possibilities of double returns are best illustrated in the Short Parliament elections at Bere Alston and Plympton Erle. At the initial meeting of the Bere Alston electorate, three candidates – Strode, Slanning, and Wise – presented themselves. "The question was put to the burgesses if any of them had a voice for any but one of them three. They answered no."[59] It was then agreed by all present that Strode would be chosen in the borough's senior place if either Slanning, who had already been selected at Plympton Erle, or Wise were named knights of the shire. The completion of the election was delayed until after county candidates had been named. When Wise secured one of the Devon seats, the Bere Alston electors reconvened. But now two new candidates appeared and challenged the arrangement made by Strode, Slanning, and Wise. They forced a new election in which the unfortunate Strode, the only one of the original three not yet elected, was placed last. Vexed by Slanning's behavior and determined to secure a seat, Strode adopted the expedient of the double return. He returned himself, on his own precept, not for Bere Alston but for Plympton Erle, in opposition to Slanning, although he had never contested the seat there.[60]

All of these practices were beginning to congeal into the distinctive late seventeenth-century occupation of "making an interest." With competition more certain, information more accessible, and preparations more elaborate, securing a seat in Parliament absorbed the attention of men who sought a place in political life. Making an interest entailed not only good management and strong allies, but for the first time specific knowledge about the electorate and the powerful influences upon it. When Lord Willoughby de Eresby assessed his brother's chances at the 1661 Stamford selection, he calculated that "it will be easy for him to make my Lords Exeter's and Campden's interest."[61] Aspirants began to gauge their campaigns less by the prominence of their supporters and more by the realities of where the voices lay and how many there were. The interest of men like Lords Exeter and Campden was not the general influence that their names commanded, but rather a specific number of electors pledged to support their candidates. It was this rivalry of can-

[58] The Short Parliament journal of Sir Thomas Aston, fol. 201; C. J., II, 15; Aston, fols. 198–99.
[59] The Short Parliament journal of Sir Thomas Aston, fol. 203.
[60] The Short Parliament journal of Sir Thomas Aston, fols. 203–4; C. J., II, 7, 14. "Whether the third indenture of Sir Richard Strode was delivered in to the clerk of the crown by the sheriff, or his deputy, or Sir Richard Strode himself."
[61] Andrew Trollope, "Hatcher Correspondence Relating to Parliamentary Elections," Associated Architectural and Archaeological Societies' Reports, 23 (1895–6), p. 135.

didates that "expanded" the electorate. Without men eager to stand against each other, the electorate was only a theoretical entity; with vigorous competition it gained substance. That substance proved malleable to those who sought an interest and to those who sought a seat.

With the supply of seats constant and demand for them high, the cost of parliamentary selection inevitably rose. This was another unanticipated consequence of the changes of the revolutionary period. In the past, optional postelection feasts had been the principal financial outlay of an election. These celebratory dinners served the dual purpose of expressing gratitude to the electors and maintaining traditional hospitality. They thus involved a kind of expense that might be incurred in other contexts. The beneficent Earl of Salisbury feted nearly nine hundred of his countrymen in 1628 at a cost of three hundred and fifty pounds.[62] Trifling sums for messengers and gratuities to servants, perhaps a journey to the borough to be sworn a freeman – these outlays added little to the bill. Contests, especially at the county level, were costlier. The expense of feeding and housing a larger number of supporters could fall upon the candidates, though it might be partially absorbed by the gentlemen who brought their freeholders and tenants in train. When Sir Henry Wallop requested that his cousin Sir Henry Whithed attend the Hampshire election in 1614, he also asked that Whithed bring with him "for the mending of our diet... some of your good carps."[63] Borough contests were cheaper still, as the electors were fewer and could provide for their own maintenance.

By the Restoration the cost of elections was staggering. Contesting a county could require an outlay equal to the annual income of most gentlemen. Nicholas Lechmere recorded that the Worcestershire election of 1659 "was very costly." The expense of inns alone amounted to six hundred and fourteen pounds, "which we paid to the penny."[64] Making an interest meant constant application to wavering supporters, and maintaining it could require blandishments during the years between elections as well. Care for the needs of the community could be manifested in well-publicized contributions to the institutions of social welfare. Robert Read, during his campaign for the Short Parliament seat, offered the borough of Hastings twenty pounds for the town's paupers and an

[62] L. M. Munby, "The Early History of Parliamentary Politics in Hertfordshire," *Transactions of the East Hertfordshire Archaeological Society for 1955–61* (1964), p. 72. The Essex Short Parliament election cost Sir Thomas Barrington only forty-two pounds. F. W. Galpin, "The Household Expenses of Sir Thomas Barrington," *Transactions of the Essex Archaeological Society*, N.S., 12 (1913), p. 211.

[63] *The Letterbook of Sir Henry Whithed*, p. 115.

[64] Historical Manuscripts Commission Reports, *5th Report* (Journal of Nicholas Lechmere), pp. 299–300.

annuity of ten pounds while he lived.[65] More spectacular demonstrations of devotion to local well-being appeared as well. Lavish spending on parliamentary elections can be seen as but one element of a widespread revival of conspicuous consumption. The ability to bear the costs of an election soon became another qualification for a seat.[66]

III

Old values die hard. Political transformations rarely do more than subsume traditional practices and beliefs. Their persistence is one of the less tidy aspects of historical change, and not even brisk sweeping with new brooms will scatter them to the winds. Embedded in the fabric of assumptions and actions, they cling tenaciously and, like dust, resettle when stirred. The alterations in the process of parliamentary selection during the revolutionary era took place alongside the survival of customary arrangements. In some places they hardly penetrated at all, while in others they produced curious hybrids. Across the nation and throughout the Interregnum the characteristic elements of the traditional selection process can be discerned. The social component of selection, expressed in the code of honor and worth, retreated with the radical drift of the Revolution but was never entirely eliminated. The importance of patrons and of patronage, in all its symbiotic ramifications, continued to be recognized. The use of the local magistracy for slating and vetting candidates flourished. Compacts, both to mediate disputes and to foreclose them, sealed Caroline as well as Cromwellian selections. The ideal of unified choices, even when challenged by the manifest divisiveness of civil war, endured.

Though they coexisted uneasily with the new attitudes, questions of merit and worth continued to figure prominently in the elections to the Short and Long Parliaments. Sir John Stawell advised Thomas Smith to "rely wholly upon your merit and virtue" in seeking one of the Somerset knightships in the spring.[67] Smith's attitudes were entirely conventional. He considered his candidacy a draft from well-wishers in the county and resisted organizing a campaign or even writing to his own kinsmen for support. When the machinations of Sir Ralph Hopton, one of his potential opponents, were made known, Smith voiced dismay but pur-

---

[65] *Calendar of State Papers Domestic Series 1639–40*, pp. 565–66.

[66] Thus Baynham Throckmorton wrote to John Smyth before the 1661 Gloucestershire election that he could not afford the cost of standing for the county. Historical Manuscripts Commission Reports, *5th Report* (Chomondeley Manuscripts), p. 345.

[67] Bristol Record Office, 36,074 (146).

sued the honorable course. "I am too far engaged into [my candidacy] to decline the fiery trial, although for peace sake and respect unto Sir Ralph Hopton, within this few days I made an offer to sit down unto his election and Mr. A[lexander] P[opham]."[68] The result was a compact entered into by the three candidates, in the presence of the county magistracy, to free their supporters from all pledges of support "and to leave them at liberty to choose such gentlemen of worth as they shall think fit."[69] Sir Thomas Peyton's candidacy at Sandwich was in almost every way a gloss upon the new attitudes toward securing a seat. Yet after the spring election was concluded he wrote to one of his opponents, Sir Thomas Palmer, to defend "the motives to bring me on." "I proceeded with such a respect to you in it that where I found you had possession, I think no man will say I offered the least intrusion ... Being tender of the least disunion between our families, I desired to give you this satisfaction."[70]

That such attitudes appear less frequently in the records of Cromwellian elections is not altogether surprising. The Civil War gave a political complexion to officeholding of all kinds, driving out of service wave after wave of former participants. Even without the expansion of county seats, which necessarily diluted their prestige, few members of the local elite were willing to advance themselves as candidates and fewer still were under the illusion that election represented the assent of the whole community. Robert Wilton appealed to John Buxton to attend the Norfolk election in 1656 for "the country ... have made choice of you as one of their representatives ... The adverse party are and will be hard at work plotting and contriving their game how to play it for their own advantage."[71] In 1654 only three out of eighteen Suffolk candidates were knights, and in 1656 only two out of twenty-two. After the surge of electoral interest before the civil wars, participation at the elections of the Protectorate receded. By a rough calculation, less than half the number of Suffolk freeholders that attended the Long Parliament contest appeared in 1654, while the twenty-two candidates of 1656 could only manage 80 percent of the number that three had achieved in 1640.[72]

---

[68] Bristol R.O., 36,074 (133b).

[69] Bristol R.O., 36,074 (49).

[70] British Library, Additional Manuscripts, 44,846, fol. 2.

[71] Historical Manuscripts Commission Reports, *Manuscripts in Various Collections*, II (Buxton Mss.), p. 270.

[72] Suffolk Record Office (Ipswich), GC 17/755. Aggregate poll figures are difficult to work with, especially for comparative purposes. One rough measure is the total votes cast divided by the number of "ballots" each voter had – two in 1640, ten in 1654 and 1656. This will underestimate the total of voters, especially in a three-cornered contest, if each voter does not use all his ballots. I owe this reference to P. J. Pinckney.

Thirty years after fifteen thousand men were reported to have attended an Essex county selection, Sir John Bramston recorded the meager appearance of a few hundred in 1659.[73]

Still, when Herbert Morley was informed by the corporation of Rye that he had been selected there in 1654, he accepted enthusiastically. "I do acknowledge it a great honor... without my seeking or solicitation, overruling Providence hath by your free election devolved upon me."[74] Bulstrode Whitelocke described his nomination for a Buckingham county seat in 1654 in traditional language: "I understand from several of my friends in Buckinghamshire of their intentions of honor and respect to me, to name me for one of the knights."[75] Indeed, it might be argued that the return of so many new members enhanced their own sense of merit and worth even if traditional candidates did not seek seats. For what it is worth, every knight who stood for a Suffolk county seat between 1640 and 1660 achieved it, as did all four of those who stood for Norfolk in 1656.[76] Throughout the Interregnum, London continued to nominate and elect corporate leaders. How deeply these attitudes were ingrained can be measured by their reappearance in 1660. "Mr Thorneton, who stood for Cambridgeshire, knowing that his rival was a person of greater quality and estate, told him that he would withdraw if the other would engage for the restoration of King and Church."[77] Surely the town of King's Lynn took the opportunity to honor a representative of the social elite that had not previously existed. In its 1649 by-election to fill a vacancy to the Long Parliament it chose the Earl of Salisbury as a member of the House of Commons and received "an open and free acknowledgement from me of your kind and good affections."[78]

Salisbury's selection at King's Lynn reminds us that the symbiotic patronage relations of the early seventeenth century continued to operate during the revolutionary period. Communities sought out those who could preserve their interests amid the changing circumstances at Westminster, while successive governments hunted for places for faithful

[73] P. Braybrooke, ed., *The Autobiography of Sir John Bramston*, p. 162.
[74] Historical Manuscripts Commission Reports, *13th Report*, Appendix IV (Rye Corporation Mss.), p. 223.
[75] Longleat Manuscripts, Whitelocke Papers, vol. 16, fol. 74.
[76] Suffolk R.O. (Ipswich), GC 17/75; *Norfolk Archaeology*, I (1847), p. 67.
[77] O. Ogle et al., eds., *Clarendon State Papers*, IV, 657.
[78] H. Gurney, "Extracts from the Proceedings of the Corporation of Lynn Regis," *Archaeologia*, 24 (1832), p. 328. It is beginning in 1650 that the phrase Member of Parliament obtained its modern meaning as synonymous with membership in the lower house. S. R. Gardiner, "The Use of Member of Parliament," *English Historical Review*, 8 (1893), p. 525.

adherents. The activities of the court in 1640 have already been noted.[79] But while applications increased, the relationships that were exploited remained those based upon natural affiliations. Northumberland's failure to build an admiralty interest (an endeavor at which the Duke of York would soon succeed) should not obscure the nature of his appeals. The Protectorate was no less active in offering well-connected officials to serve communities. The correspondence preserved by Secretary Thurloe shows how he acted as a clearinghouse for electoral information.[80] Nor were the Cromwellians any better rewarded – despite military presence, the disabling of royalists, and the reshaping of the electorate – when they attempted to introduce outsiders.[81] The survival of borough constituencies under the Instrument of Government was tacit recognition of the importance of patronage relationships. Borough franchises were not reformed, and it was not required that borough elections be held on the national polling day.[82] This left them as capable as ever of drawing upon local benefactors or national figures. Few expressed their needs better than the magistrates of Bedford to Bulstrode Whitelocke: "What remains then but that we quietly repose under so happy a shelter and that your Lordship deign to receive us into your patronage."[83]

There was also change among those capable of providing services and protection to communities during the revolutionary decades. Many natural ties were, of course, loosened by the exclusion of the King's active supporters. Manorial lords, high stewards – the bulk of the peerage in general – were unable to perform their traditional roles. In their absence came other members of the same classes, as well as new men whose offices absorbed these functions. The civil wars had created political

---

[79] See also J. K. Gruenfelder, "The Election to the Short Parliament, 1640," in H. Reinmuth, ed., *Early Stuart Studies* (1970), pp. 180–230.

[80] Thurloe acted as conduit for the electoral activities of the Major-Generals in 1656. This is not to say that the government was conducting a coordinated campaign from the center, but it was clearly monitoring local activity. There is every reason to believe that these preelection reports were subsequently used by the Council of State in excluding elected members from their seats.

[81] Thus at Rye in 1656 Major-General Thomas Kelsey's nominee was unsuccessful in a contest against a nominee of Herbert Morley, the parliamentarian head of a prominent Sussex family. Historical Manuscripts Commission Reports, *13th Report*, Appendix IV (Rye Corporation Mss.), p. 228.

[82] The Instrument of Government is silent on these points. Article eleven specifies that county elections are to be held on the fifth Wednesday after the issuance of writs. The date of borough elections is to be announced by the returning officers. Article eighteen established the two-hundred-pound estate qualification for county electors but does not regulate those in boroughs. C. H. Firth and S. Rait, *Acts and Ordinances of the Interregnum*, II, 816–18.

[83] Longleat Manuscripts, Whitelocke Papers, vol. 16, fol. 69.

figures of national reputation. Many were military men who had made their mark on the battlefield and who were celebrated in the national press. After the political intervention of the New Model Army, senior officers began to be recruited into the Long Parliament.[84] During the Commonwealth, Fleetwood, Lambert, and Desborough among others were catapulted into prominence. "For the town of Nottingham," Major-General Whalley wrote to Cromwell in 1656, "I have a great influence on it, they will not choose any without my advice."[85]

Yet others who assumed the role of patron were but revolutionary analogues for their Stuart predecessors. These were garrison commanders, local militia colonels, and, after 1655, members of the regional military establishments of the Major-Generals. It is easy to overlook the role of military men in traditional patronage. The lord warden, lord admiral, lieutenant of the Isle of Wight, and a host of other officials were essentially military men. So too were the lords lieutenant. Military commanders were important figures in fortified coastal and border garrisons, and their parliamentary patronage was but one part of reciprocal (though not always harmonious) relations. When Sir John Conyers was appointed governor of Berwick in 1640, "I was informed that formerly the governors had the choice of one burgess."[86] Thus the importance of military men as patrons and as members in Cromwellian parliaments is not so great a departure from previous practice as it sometimes appears.

As they had before, communities made use of their magistracy and local leadership in organizing parliamentary selections. The expansion of county members required more, rather than less, preelectoral planning. This enlarged the role of county institutions, whether the magistracy or the Major-Generals, and enhanced their influence. The old notion that the Major-Generals acted as election bosses has been refuted in all but a handful of instances.[87] Rather, they performed functions akin to those of lords lieutenant or resident peers. Elections to both of Oliver Cromwell's parliaments coincided with summer assizes, and the bench and grand jury took an active role in slating candidates. "I now begin to fear Suffolk finding so malignant a grand jury, who will have a great advantage to possess the country," Major-General Haynes wrote, assessing electoral prospects in East Anglia.[88] In Hampshire, Colonel

[84] D. E. Underdown, "Party Management and the Recruiter Elections, 1645–1648," *English Historical Review*, 83 (1968), p. 243.

[85] T. Birch, ed., *Thurloe State Papers*, V, 299.

[86] *Calendar of State Papers Domestic Series*, 1640-41, p. 258.

[87] Paul J. Pinckney, "A Cromwellian Parliament," unpublished Ph.D. dissertation, Vanderbilt University, 1962.

[88] T. Birch, ed., *Thurloe State Papers*, V, 230.

Richard Norton was made foreman of the grand jury prior to the 1656 elections. He prepared one slate of candidates, while Richard Cromwell, Oliver's heir but also a local resident who had married into a Hampshire family, formed another. Major-General Goffe proposed "that my Lord Richard Cromwell and Colonel Norton should debate and agree their men before the day of choice; and certainly they would carry it without dispute."[89] This appears to have been the result, as Cromwell, Norton, and Goffe were among those chosen. In Norfolk the "country" gentlemen slated candidates and allowed little by way of compromise, even leaving Fleetwood off their list.[90]

These differing attitudes toward compromise and conflict are suggestive of the coexistence of values during the revolutionary period. The desire to achieve unified choices was not simply washed away by successive waves of military and ideological conflict. The increase in electoral contests was matched by a determination to avoid them. Throughout the 1640s and 1650s constituencies selected their members consensually if they could. King's Lynn's choice of the Earl of Salisbury in 1649 was made unanimously.[91] "I was by the inhabitants of Bewdley, *nullo contradicente*, chosen burgess to Parliament," Sir Nicholas Lechmere recorded in his diary for 1648.[92] The corporation of Rye informed Lord Warden Fleetwood in 1659 "that they have unanimously elected William Hay and Mark Thomas."[93] At Reading, in the same year, the two members were "unanimously elected burgesses in Parliament by near 1,000 persons" after a remarkable demonstration of the unity of the corporate freeman.[94] From London, Alderman Robinson reported to Charles II that the members to the convention parliament had been chosen without dispute.[95] Despite political polarization, communities

[89] Ibid., 215, 329.
[90] Historical Manuscripts Commission Reports, *Manuscripts in Various Collections*, II (Buxton Mss.), p. 270.
[91] H. Gurney, "Extracts from the Proceedings of the Corporation of Lynn Regis," *Archaeologia*, 24 (1832), p. 328.
[92] Historical Manuscripts Commission Reports, *5th Report*, p. 299.
[93] Historical Manuscripts Commission Reports, *13th Report*, Appendix IV (Rye Corporation Mss.), p. 233.
[94] Historical Manuscripts Commission Reports, *11th Report*, Appendix VII (Corporation of Reading Mss.), p. 193. This was at the second election held by the mayor who had been deposed by the corporate burgesses after he ruled that all freemen could exercise the franchise. J. T. Rutt, *The Diary of Thomas Burton*, III, pp. 16–17. It was reported to Clarendon that "when the mayor of Reading proposed a person for election to Parliament not acceptable to the burgesses . . . they took from him his gown and mace, elected a new mayor and such a burgess as pleased them." O. Ogle et al., eds., *Clarendon State Papers*, IV, 126.
[95] O. Ogle et al., eds., *Clarendon State Papers*, IV, 630.

continued to achieve agreement over selections. The cry "no swordsmen, no decimators" was an appeal for the unity of the locality against the intrusion of government, as many Major-Generals disconsolately discovered.

The expanded county constituencies of the Protectorate necessarily made unified choice more difficult. The problems involved in multiple selections overwhelmed the traditional process of sifting candidates. Even without the competitive slating that took place in some counties, disputes and contests were bound to arise. Yet unity could still be expressed in the selection of individual candidates. John Lambert's selection for the West Riding of Yorkshire in 1656 was much like that of a senior shire knight before the revolution: "My Lord Lambert was agreed on by all parties and chosen at first . . . the rest had competitors."[96] This was also the manner in which it had been intended to choose Colonel Charles Cocke at Norwich in 1654; but a dispute over the second place resulted in a three-way poll.[97] Cocke's experience at Norwich illustrates the fact that candidates acclaimed by the electors had to have their supporters polled to resolve other contests. Sir John Hobart's selection at Norfolk in 1656 can hardly be described as contested. He secured the voices of over 90 percent of the assembled voters and had over a thousand voices more than the last successful candidate.[98] In Suffolk, Henry North was similarly acclaimed; but the last man elected in this contest failed even to secure a majority.[99] Thus contests for the bottom places in county representation often obscured the unanimity achieved by those at the top.

The desire to achieve unified choices could be seen more clearly at the time of the Restoration. The electoral reforms brought in by the Instrument of Government collapsed after 1656. The Humble Petition and Advice had removed the power of scrutinizing returns from the council to the parliament and, after the death of Oliver Cromwell, there was widespread desire to restore some semblance of normality.[100] The 1659 elections were a hodgepodge of old and new, aptly summarized by the experience of Leominster: "Here is a very great division and much seeking. . . . They are so compounded and so divided . . . that it is the more

[96]   *Mercurious Politicus*, no. 324, August, 1656.
[97]   *Calendar of State Papers Domestic Series 1654*, pp. 278–79. See also J. T. Evans, *Seventeenth Century Norwich*, pp. 206–8.
[98]   H. Gurney, "Norfolk," *Norfolk Archaeology*, I (1847), p. 67. Hobart polled 2,781; Colonel Woods, who was tenth, polled 1,692. The smallest number of votes was garnered by Captain Cocke, 609.
[99]   Suffolk R.O. (Ipswich), GC 17/755. These calculations are subject to the same cautions as above, n. 72.
[100] C. H. Firth and R. Rait, *Acts and Ordinances of the Interregnum*, II, 1049–50.

uncertain that the best of my wits invites me not to beg, hunt, or crave much enthusiasm."[101] With the prospect of reestablishing old forms – and not only in the process of selection – community leaders began to reassert their roles. In Shropshire Sir Richard Leveson was informed "that Sir Francis Lawly and Sir Richard Ottley are thought the two fittest persons to be Knights of the Shire."[102] At Derby John Milward "met many of the gentlemen of our county. We have, without any contradiction, fixed upon my Lord Cavendish and Mr. Frescheville to be Knights."[103] The 1661 election at Kent fell on "Sir Thomas Peyton by the full consent of the whole field, *nemine contra*"; while the dispute for the second place was between Sir John Tufton and Sir Roger Twysden, who "having not at all solicited for the employment hardly owned a thought of it five days before."[104]

Yet nowhere was there greater desire to turn the electoral clock back to before the revolution than in Herefordshire. There, in 1621, the county leadership had made a compact to avoid disputes and electoral contests, a compact which had held together until the by-elections to the Long Parliament. The return of the King provided opportunity to reestablish this amity. "It is now above forty years since upon debate and consent of the gentry, met upon like occasion as this, it was agreed that the Sheriff... should give notice to the gentry to meet to agree upon such persons as they would jointly present to the freeholders," Viscount Scudamore recalled to the assembled county elite in 1661. That first compact had followed from a falling out among the gentry, and its success had created "union and agreement."[105] Now, following an even greater breach among them, it was necessary for the county leaders to subscribe again, "each man submitting to the opinion of the major part then present."[106] Such a compact, Scudamore assured both gentlemen and freeholders, would be as pleasing to the Lord as to the county. "It is the order which the wisdom of the creator... hath thought good to fix in nature, namely that inferiors are to receive from their superiors that participation of knowledge and light by which their resolutions and actions are to be guided."[107] On this occasion, the unity of the Here-

---

[101] Historical Manuscripts Commission Reports, *13th Report*, Appendix IV (Loder–Symonds Mss.), p. 392.

[102] Historical Manuscripts Commission Reports, *5th Report* (Duke of Sutherland Mss.), p. 148.

[103] British Library, Additional Manuscripts, 34,306, fol. 11.

[104] Huntington Library, Hastings Mss., HM 41536, fol. 74.

[105] British Library, Additional Manuscripts, 11,044, fol. 253.

[106] Ibid., fol. 227.

[107] Ibid., fol. 253.

fordshire gentry would last only until the first by-election of the Cavalier Parliament.

IV

The continuities and contrasts in the changing system of parliamentary selection are aptly illustrated by the experiences of the county of Kent in choosing members to Parliament in 1640. In the spring, Sir Roger Twysden and Sir Edward Dering, kinsmen and close friends, found themselves opposing each other for the senior shire seat. Their unexpected contest resulted from a combination of political principle and personal misadventure. When news of the summoning of the long-awaited assembly reached Dering he wrote to Twysden to encourage him to accept a seat. "I were guilty of a weak friendship if I did not let you know that ... I did with some eastern friends name you for a Knights' service to the House, which was received with a cheerful desire."[108] Dering's promotion of Twysden was in part a manifestation of his opposition to the selection of Sir Henry Vane, secretary of state and treasurer of the King's household, who had the backing of the lord lieutenant of Kent, the Earl of Pembroke.[109] But, as Dering learned from his cousin, Vane also had the support of Twysden, who had written for him and for Norton Knatchbull, the accepted choice for the junior seat.[110] Dering importuned Twysden to stand in Vane's stead, and Twysden labored equally hard to convince Dering to back Vane.[111] He invited him to Roydon for an extended visit "and I doubt not but to give you such reasons for the Treasurer's election as shall with willingness persuade you to interest all your friends."[112]

[108] L. B. Larking, ed., *Proceedings Principally in the County of Kent*, p. 1.
[109] Pembroke had also asked the deputy lieutenants to support Vane "that there should be no clashing amongst ourselves." British Library, Stowe Manuscripts, 743, fol. 136. Sir George Sondes and Sir Thomas Walsingham had agreed "both to sit down rather than Mr. Secretary fail of the place," though Sir George desired a seat to defend his actions both as a ship money sheriff and as a deputy lieutenant.
[110] Twysden's support for Vane is a useful caution against the lockstep assumptions of a court/country split in the elections of 1640. Twysden was an early opponent of ship money and had refused to pay it on constitutional grounds. This did not prevent him from supporting Vane even though he recognized that anti-Vane sentiment centered on this issue: "Truly the common people had been so bitten by ship money that they were very averse from a courtier." L. B. Larking, ed., *Proceedings Principally in the County of Kent*, p. 6.
[111] Dering stated his reasons for refusing support quite concisely: "In times so desperate I would contribute no help to any privy councilor or deputy-lieutenant." F. W. Jessup, "The Kentish Election of March 1640," *Archaeologia Cantiana*, 86 (1971), p. 2.
[112] L. B. Larking, ed., *Proceedings Principally in the County of Kent*, p. 4.

What passed at this meeting between old friends was a subject for disagreement. Twysden believed that he had convinced Dering to support the candidacy of Vane; Dering believed that he had demurred and maintained his reservations. When the gentry of Kent gathered for assizes, Dering made it plain that he would not give his support to Vane and discovered that others were opposed to the treasurer's candidacy as well. In the face of this opposition, Vane withdrew. In his place, Dering was prevailed upon to stand, though without the acquiescence of Vane's backers.[113] Rather than settling matters peaceably, the meeting at assizes served only to restir the muddied waters. With Vane's candidacy abandoned, two of the county deputy lieutenants, Sir George Sondes and Sir Thomas Walsingham, were freed from their pledges to abjure their own pretensions.[114] More decisively, Sir Roger Twysden took Dering's action as a personal affront, and he too declared himself a candidate. "The truth is I took it very unkindly to see Sir Edward Dering from whom I had hoped (and had good reason to do so) assistance...should be erected only to make a stop in the business," Twysden wrote to Dering in an emotional letter. The irony for Dering was that he now stood out against his own first choice.[115]

Despite the potent political issues bubbling under the surface of this election – the rejection of a courtier and the specter of religious divisiveness being the most obvious – feelings ran higher between the candidates than among their supporters. On election day "the sheriff offered to draw lots...and the clerk offered in the afternoon to cast dice."[116] All composition was refused. When neither sheriff, clerk, nor magistrates could prevent the contest, the county electors voted with their feet. They shared the opinion of Sir Francis Barnham "that the county need not trouble themselves for this election since they could not choose amiss

---

[113] As Twysden remarked: "Sir I fear you will see that they not least love you that at the assizes wished you not to begin." British Library, Stowe Manuscripts, 184, fol. 10.

[114] Sir Edward Hales presumed that the withdrawal of Vane meant that Sondes would now go forward, and he informed Dering: "It is true that at the assizes I was for Sir Henry Vane, but I was first for Sir George Sondes, so now...I am constant where I was at first." British Library, Stowe Manuscripts, 743, fol. 142. On Dering's account, Sondes remained in the contest until the day of the poll. Jessup, "The Kentish Election of March 1640," p. 3.

[115] British Library, Stowe Manuscripts, 184, fol. 10. He concluded "[I] was as sorry to see him for such a toy contract such potent enemies."

[116] Jessup, "The Kentish Election of March 1640," p. 3. Dering's initial opposition to Vane is not a sufficient explanation for his persistence in the contest. In fact, once Vane had withdrawn, Dering's initial desire, the selection of Knatchbull and Twysden, had been achieved. But during the campaign Dering's character and honor had been maligned.

between two gentlemen both so worthy."[117] Nearly four of every five freeholders who had given voices for Norton Knatchbull retired from the court before the poll that elected Sir Roger Twysden.[118]

There was little of accident in the campaign of Sir Edward Dering for a seat in the Long Parliament. His defeat in the spring was galling, and he brooded over it. He composed a list of the imputations made against him and sketched a self-justifying narrative of events.[119] He even went so far as to attempt a rough calculation of the support he had received, compiling a parochial calendar of the county for this purpose. Whether Dering's dreams were nightmares of the past or fantasies of the future, he could hardly imagine how soon he would have an opportunity for vindication. Upon news of the summoning of the fall session, Dering bounded into action. He did not await a draft from friends or pause to discover who might enter the lists against him. Instead he wrote far and wide, to kinsmen and neighbors, to friends and local worthies, proclaiming his candidacy.[120] From all he asked their own voices and those of their sons and dependents. "I conceive you do yourself a great deal of right in resuming your pretension," George Strode responded to one of these missives.[121]

Sir Edward's energetic behavior was matched by shrewd electioneering. His prompt proclamation of his intentions ultimately dissuaded several other candidates from pursuing initial inclinations.[122] His agents were busily at work in the towns of eastern Kent, lining up support at Dover, where Sir Edward had been lieutenant of the Castle, and in Canterbury, where John Craign found "the yeomen about us wonderfully desirous to choose you."[123] At Surrenden, Lady Dering coordinated agents and correspondents alike. Sir Edward did not eschew moderation altogether. He may not have followed Sir Edward Hales's advice to

[117]   Jessup, "The Kentish Election of March 1640," p. 4. This was also the opinion of Sir Edward Hales: "I could wish, as I said, that this trouble might be spared." British Library, Stowe Manuscripts, 743, fol. 142.

[118]   Jessup, "The Kentish Election of March 1640," p. 4.

[119]   Ibid., p. 4. He was accused, simultaneously, of being a papist and a Puritan, a country oppositionist and a supporter of ship money and distraint of knighthood.

[120]   "In this election, there was no social link, no friendship, and no family relationship which Dering and his supporters did not turn to good use." A. Everitt, The Community of Kent and the Great Rebellion (1966), p. 77.

[121]   Larking, Proceedings in Kent, pp. 8ff.

[122]   Richard Spencer and Sir Robert Mansell were the two most serious rivals. Mansell's withdrawal was reported to Dering by Sir John Culpepper on October 19. British Library, Stowe Manuscripts, 743, fol. 158.

[123]   British Library, Stowe Manuscripts, 743, fols. 153, 155.

"crave my Lord Chamberlain's [the Earl of Pembroke] favor and furtherance," but he certainly approached Twysden in an effort at reconciliation.[124] Yet his campaign relied more upon active recruitment than
upon passive acquiescence.

To bolster his cause in the western part of the county he entered into
a marriage of convenience with Sir John Culpepper. The two pledged
to solicit voices for each other to deter a third candidate from pursuing
a contest.[125] Actually, there was little enthusiasm for Culpepper among
Dering's supporters. Edward Kempe, Dering's agent in Dover, went so
far as to pronounce to the electors there "that you join not with Sir
John Culpepper."[126] The two partners left the question of senior honors
unresolved, and Dering professed himself too busy to meet Culpepper
before the election. For his part, Culpepper was chiefly concerned with
finding the least expensive way of showing appreciation to their common
supporters. He lamented the mustering of support necessitated by the
oncoming contest and recommended self-catering rather than use of the
overpriced Maidstone hostelries.[127]

Dering's tactics might well have produced a routine selection but for
the divisive events of the spring. The Kentish tradition by which men
chosen for the county in one Parliament did not offer themselves for
selection to the next had precluded Twysden. But it did not prevent him
from vigorously promoting a third candidate, Richard Browne. Browne
was brought in on Twysden's support and his enthusiasts, said to be
most numerous among the county's Puritans, labored for him among
those who opposed either of the precariously paired partners. "I do not
hear of any but comes singly into the field and I think it much the better,
for I find the country in many parts desirous of their freedom in placing
voices," Twysden warned Dering.[128] Though Culpepper had hope that
their combined strength would finally discourage Browne, Dering knew
that his candidacy was aimed to show defiance rather than to inflict
defeat. On the day of the county court Dering and Culpepper secured
an easy triumph. The matter did not rest there, however, as Browne's
supporters carried their case to the House of Commons.[129]

---

[124] Ibid., fol. 147; British Library, Stowe Manuscripts, 184, fol. 17.

[125] British Library, Stowe Manuscripts, 743, fol. 156.

[126] Ibid., fol. 153.

[127] Ibid., fols. 149, 156.

[128] Everitt, *The Community of Kent*, p. 76; British Library, Stowe Manuscripts, 184,
fol. 17.

[129] British Library, Stowe Manuscripts, 743, fol. 157; W. Notestein, ed., *The Diary of
Sir Symonds D'Ewes*, p. 107. The petition against this election was apparently not
delivered to the Committee of Elections. When it was reported on the floor of the

As these experiences in Kent suggest, the transition in the process of parliamentary selection, though unmistakable, was rough and uneven. Personal and public codes of conduct continued to shape the selection process and the frequency of contests within it. They were not simply overwhelmed by the infusion of ideological or political issues. Indeed, the mixture of the two was particularly potent. In the spring, Dering's political outlook overmatched his personal loyalties; but it was personal rather than political motives that led to his clash with Twysden. The efforts of the county magistrates to compose the dispute indifferently tied the Short Parliament election securely to past practices. In the fall, ideology was subsumed under the vindication of Dering's honor. The advent of new attitudes toward the process is easily perceived in the contrast between the accidental contest in the spring and the purposeful one in the autumn. The informal sifting, the use of the lord lieutenant and the meeting of assizes for winnowing, characterized the early stages of the spring campaign. Dering's candidacy in the fall displayed all of the zeal that the new politicization was bringing to the process. The array of stratagems, the single-minded quest for victory – these were uppermost. Nor was Dering alone in shedding the cloak of moderation. The willingness of Browne and his supporters to hold out against certain defeat and their initiation of an electoral dispute in the Commons were coats cut from the same cloth.

Yet the greatest transformation in the process of parliamentary selection was its dominance by contested elections. The emphasis upon qualification, the shift in values, the intensity of preparations, and the increase in costs all intersected to make contests an accepted and anticipated part of the selection process. They emerged in response to nearly every other change in attitudes and practices. Franchise disputes occasioned contests; religious controversy occasioned contests; political programs, governmental intervention, constituency reform, careerist aspirations all occasioned contests.

Not only did contests multiply and cover the land, they changed in nature and shape as well. They no longer originated in muddles of misunderstanding and mistaken intention that could be sorted out by mediating authorities. Nor were they mainly affairs of honor that developed from feuds and slights. Men did not oppose each other, they sought a seat in the house. This depersonalization of the process enabled

---

Footnote *129 cont.*
Commons it was moved that the many members of the House who had been present at the election be allowed to testify that there was no question as to where the majority lay. This extraordinary resolution indicated the difficulties over elections experienced by the Long Parliament.

the loosening of ties of kinship and neighborliness. Thus contests lost their intensity, and with their social significance they shed much of their divisive quality. Sir Edward Dering recorded matter-of-factly the events of the 1660 election in Kent. "Sir John Tufton and myself having the assistance of all the royalists and moderate men in the county and Colonel Weldon and Mr. Boys of Westhanger being set up against us...we had it by so vast a disparity...that it was yielded without polling and all over in two hours' time."[130] There was now little advantage for community leaders in preventing elections, and much advantage for local merchants, shopkeepers, and electors in encouraging them. Contesting and winning was the keynote of the new process of parliamentary selection.[131]

[130]   M. Bond, ed., *The Diaries and Papers of Sir Edward Dering*, p. 110.
[131]   See Chapter 7 of this book.

6

Counties and Boroughs

I

"WE CAN TALK of nothing but the elections," one of George Treby's correspondents wrote in the winter of 1679.[1] One enduring consequence of the English Revolution was the importance of Parliament and its members ever after. Whatever view successive generations adopted toward the "Good Old Cause" or the "Late Usurpation," they shared a perception of the preeminence of the House of Commons. Lessons and legacy were plain. In the space of twenty years Parliament had removed the crown from one monarch and restored it to another; it had become the key to prosperity or penury by confiscating and redistributing wealth; it had become the source of authority in the nation by assuming the responsibilities of government. In the space of twenty years Parliament had revealed a power – and a potential for power – unimagined by seer or sage. Thereafter, the English governing classes, marrying prudence with ambition, pursued seats in Parliament headlong. "Our measures now at court are so taken that it is essential to a man's succeeding there to be of the Parliament."[2]

Interest led to study; and study, mastery. Assiduous candidates and patrons reformed the haphazard parliamentary selection process. Anticipation, planning, and intelligence became the prerequisites of a campaign. The prolonged sitting of the Cavalier Parliament channeled pent up demand into unpredictable by-elections. Aspirants had to be ever-vigilant to seize their chances. If opportunity had knocked, it was probably already too late. "Mr. Allestry is yet living, but is on the point of expiring every hour," the predatory Anchitell Grey wrote in 1665 as he hovered about Derby. "While it pleases God to continue him I can make

---

[1] Historical Manuscripts Commission Reports, *13th Report*, Appendix VI (Manuscripts of Sir William Fitzherbert), p. 13.
[2] W. D. Cooper, *Letters to and from Henry Saville*, p. 45.

no further progress than give the corporation their fill of sack and tobacco."[3]

Once declared, a candidacy meant ceaseless effort. Sir Phineas Pett's campaign at Rochester was a model of expended energy and uninterrupted motion. He plotted a seven-pronged assault upon the Crown, the church, the treasury, and the admiralty to win an election that was never held.[4] Better understanding yielded better results. Through the use of Court informants, aspiring candidates anticipated elections; through the use of local agents, they fended off rivals. A precise understanding of the constituency, of its returning officer, patrons, and electorate, was now imperative. "Pray get from Mr Dickinson a copy in every parish of each man who pays the poor which will give you a true state of the electors," John Hatcher was advised in 1676.[5]

An air of expectancy enveloped parliamentary selections. Obsessive candidates shared their preoccupation with the politically astute as well as the socially curious. The frenzy of 1679 revived newsbooks and accounts of elections, both dormant since the Revolution. The *Domestick* and *Protestant Intelligencers* provided pithy accounts for those capable of reading between their closely printed lines. The private correspondence of the gentry, unrestrained by the prudent reticence of publishers, was also full of election news. Indeed, the range of information that could be acquired and communicated was impressive: "Lord Russell stands for Bedfordshire, Mr Montague for Northamptonshire, and Mr Sacheverell for the town, not for the shire. Sir Nicholas Carew at Gatton, Sir Robert Peyton for Middlesex... Powle will be chosen at Cirencester."[6] Yet published and private accounts also revealed a fascination with selections that transcended, or rather bypassed, political interest. Newsbook editors had an instinctive feel for the curiosity of their readers. Along with electoral results they also distilled the best local gossip. Most letters and notes tracked the fortunes of kith and kin. Members of the Verney family competed to be first to titillate old Sir Ralph with the strivings of their friends and relations. His London-based son John reported on events in Sussex, Kent, and Middlesex, as well as in the City; his sisters on Warwickshire, Hertfordshire, and Surrey; his cousin Wil-

---

[3] Historical Manuscripts Commission Reports, *15th Report*, Appendix VII (Manuscripts of the Marquis of Ailesbury), p. 174.

[4] John Smith, ed., *The Life, Journals and Correspondence of Samuel Pepys*, II, 55–57.

[5] Andrew Trollope, "Hatcher Correspondence Relating to Parliamentary Elections," *Associated Architectural and Archaeological Societies' Reports*, 23 (1895–96), pp. 136–37.

[6] Historical Manuscripts Commission Reports, *13th Report*, Appendix VI (Manuscripts of Sir William Fitzherbert), p. 12.

liam Denton on Cambridgeshire; while his eldest son Edmund garnered local news from Buckinghamshire and Bedfordshire constituencies.

This coalescence of social and political interest aroused by selections can also be seen in the nature of choice. In the localities, rank, prominence, and service remained critical, if not decisive, criteria. The social considerations that had dominated selections were revived with the monarchy. In many places the tempests of civil war and revolution served only to shake loose those whose holds had grown precarious and to revivify those whose grasps were firm. The ones who weathered the storms were better rooted than ever in local hierarchies, now being fortified by the invigoration of the lieutenancy and the distribution of new corporate charters. The Revolution also left its mark in more subtle ways. It perpetuated divisions over religious and political issues within local elites. "I have had the happiness to serve twice for your corporation through the favor of some of my friends among you," James Herbert reminded the mayor and jurats of Queenborough in 1681. "Yet by the opposition of others, it was upon terms so severe as a stranger might have expected it."[7] Though it remains premature to describe competing local hierarchies, there now coexisted within the structures of counties and boroughs men who could offer leadership in line with the wild swings of political opinion. Their suitability as members of Parliament became temporally determined. Those who were unacceptable during the backlash after 1661 were eagerly selected to preserve the Protestant succession in 1679. They were cast back into the wilderness in 1685 only to be rehabilitated three years later. In late Stuart England political affiliations qualified and disabled with cheerful evenhandedness.

Such shifts in opinion as can be gauged by the choice of members of Parliament were shifts in the opinions of the elite. Even in the crisis years surrounding 1679 one can detect little initiative from the electorate. The rise in competitive contests expanded their participation in the selection process, but it was participation orchestrated from above. The role of freemen and freeholders must still be explained in terms of consent rather than of choice. But consent is not the equivalent of passivity. Many contests were short-circuited by the refusal of the electorate to be drawn into personal and factional struggles; many candidacies were rendered short-lived by the realization that they were unacceptable to the electorate at large. Yet candidates continued to be nominated through channels dominated by county gentry and corporate officials; patronage continued to exert an almost gravitational force on borough selections;

---

[7] C. E. Woodruff, "Notes on the Municipal Records of Queenborough," *Archaeologia Cantiana*, 22 (1897), p. 185.

and the interest the Court developed in selections added another weighty layer. Nor is there much indication that communities and their leaders held fundamentally divergent views about liberties and loyalties. This is all the more remarkable given the penchant of the Crown to politicize office holding. It is a further indication of the independence of local leaders. The process of parliamentary selection depended upon that independence to adjudicate political and religious matters.

II

The effects of the Revolution were not as pronounced in counties as in boroughs. The restoration of the traditional geographic pattern of seats in 1659 and the reintegration of local elites shortly thereafter returned the knights of the shire to the pinnacle of the selection process. Competition for county places was again governed primarily by social considerations and competitors chosen from a narrow group of county families. But among the factors that helped differentiate county hierarchies, political and religious allegiances were now prominent. The consolidation of the governing elite after its century of expansion left more mouths to feed than the number of pieces into which the cake of office and reward could conveniently be sliced. The enlargement of the bench, of local commissions, and of the lieutenancy were symptomatic of the oversupply. In the absence of war, the later Stuart inflation of honors, which buoyed the aristocracy and pumped new life into the rank of baronet, was insufficient to satisfy the aspirations of the ambitious. Communities were well supplied with socially acceptable candidates suitable to a variety of political circumstances. The vicissitudes of politics between 1679 and 1689 presented more than one opportunity to rotate the stock.

An abundant social elite, stable yet variegated, controlled county selections. If anything, domination of knightships by the peerage and greater gentry was more complete than ever. The post-Restoration inflation of honors was one of rank. The titled sons of dukes and earls became social leaders among the county gentry and thus natural choices as parliamentary representatives. Between 1661 and 1689, Hampshire and Leicestershire were never without one knight of the shire who held a courtesy title; Yorkshire was without one only once.[8] In Lincolnshire, the Irish peer, Viscount Castleton, earned the unique distinction of being

---

[8]   In 1685 Hampshire chose Viscount Campden and the Earl of Wiltshire, and in 1689 Wiltshire and his brother Lord William Poulett; Leicestershire chose Lord Roos and Baron Sherard in the winter of 1679; Yorkshire returned Lords Fairfax and Clifford in the three Exclusion Crisis parliaments.

returned for his county without interruption from the Restoration to the Glorious Revolution.[9] Aristocratic heirs commonly held places in Bedfordshire, Buckinghamshire, Derbyshire, Lancashire, Monmouthshire, Rutland, and Shropshire. Repetitive selections – though an imperfect measure because of political factors that made them likely during the Exclusion Crisis and unlikely in 1685 – also reveal the continued power of the local gentry. Lowthers, Musgraves, and Fenwicks in the north; Onslows, Pelhams, and Derings in the south; Strangways, Robartes, and Rolles in the west; Barnardistons and Hobarts in East Anglia; Booths and Harleys on the marches – these were all traditional choices. Sherards in Rutland, Mildmays in Essex, Thynnes in Wiltshire; Staffordshire Bagots, Leicestershire Greys were the familiar names of knights of the shire.

The hold exercised over county seats by the elite – the aristocracy in its social sense – served to inhibit electoral contests. Though selection as knight of the shire was no longer seen as a test of social status, forestalling or embittering competition, there were other reasons to avoid contests. After the Restoration, the cost of candidacy and the number of free-spending candidates rose astronomically. Even unopposed selections were expensive. This became a significant factor in dissuading potential competitors. While many excuses were made in 1685, Sir George Fletcher's was repeated throughout the period: "That which weighs most with me is the charge and attendance."[10] The new attitudes toward candidacy also limited contests. Contestants were more willing to abandon lost causes and better able to anticipate them. As in the earlier period, the number of contests was not a measure of the level of either political conflict or political control. Their greater frequency reflected the changes initiated by the Revolution – changes including, but not limited to, increasing politicization.[11] Most county contests were still three-cornered rather than two-partied. They were as much the result of personal rivalries and county feuds as of political and religious divisions. Frequently, all of these factors were at work. There were, on average, contests in a third of the counties in each general election between 1661 and 1689.[12] Sixteen English shires conducted no more

---

[9]   Castleton attributed his acceptance by all shades of opinion to the double-barreled distinction that "I am no pensioner nor plotter." Historical Manuscripts Commission Reports, *11th Report*, Appendix V (Manuscripts of the Earl of Dartmouth), I, 82.

[10] Westmoreland Record Office, Rydall Hall Mss., D/RY 2855. For a fuller discussion of election expenses see Chapter 8 of this book.

[11] For contests, see Chapter 7 of this book.

[12] These figures are given as a rough guide only. Contest counting is a mug's game. The aggregates are too small not to be affected significantly by the chance survival

than a single contest during these six general elections, while eight others, with four or more, accounted for nearly half the total.[13]

This domination was achieved and maintained by the preservation of many of the traditional means of winnowing candidates. After the Restoration, the most effective device was the gentry meeting; but there is scattered evidence to suggest the survival, if not always the success, of other conventions. In the competition between Sir Wilfred Lawson and Sir George Fletcher in Cumberland, it was recommended that the rivals "cast lots for the county and that the loser should have the place for Cockermouth." Derings and Twysdens were again offered lots in 1679, though with no better results than their fathers had achieved in 1640.[14] The mediation of courtiers can no longer be seen primarily as a device to prevent contests, but of the many instances it is worth noting that Charles II echoed Elizabeth I when he personally requested that another Earl of Warwick absent himself from an Essex selection because of the contentions his presence aroused.[15] Less controversially, geographical rotations continued in operation in a number of counties. East and West Sussex; the Wiltshire chalk and cheese country; the forest and vale of Berkshire – all were natural divisions of county interests. Kent, which had a tradition of discouraging repeat selections – "few having the honor to be chosen twice knight of the shire" – abandoned it in the face of the rivalry between the Derings and Twysdens.[16] It continued, however, to allocate one seat to both eastern and western districts, and its contests

of evidence. The definition of a contest – more than two candidates on the day of election – still makes for hard cases. I have relied upon the information supplied in B. D. Henning, ed., *House of Commons 1660–90*, I, Appendix IX, with the addition of four contests: Rutland 1661; Yorkshire 1679 (October); Leicestershire 1685; Kent 1689. The first two are clerical errors in the compilations, the fourth an apparent error in the constituency history. For Leicestershire the evidence is Huntington Library, Hastings Manuscripts, 4816. "On Tuesday last they began to poll and Sir Edward Abney held out very briskly." Thus the count is 1661, 11 (28%); 1679 (March), 18 (45%); 1679 (October), 17 (43%); 1681, 9 (23%); 1685, 16 (40%); 1689, 10 (25%).

[13] Cornwall, Dorset, Herefordshire, Huntingdonshire, Monmouth, Shropshire, and Staffordshire have left no evidence of contests in general elections between 1661 and 1689. Berkshire, Hampshire, Northumberland, Rutland, Surrey, Sussex, Wiltshire, Worcestershire, and Yorkshire each had one contest. At the other end, Cambridgeshire, Essex, Kent, and Lancashire had four; Gloucestershire, Middlesex, Norfolk, and Oxfordshire had five.

[14] Historical Manuscripts Commission Reports, *12th Report*, Appendix VII (Manuscripts of S. H. Le Fleming), p. 24; B. D. Henning, ed., *House of Commons 1660–90*, I, 275.

[15] P. Braybrooke, ed., *The Autobiography of Sir John Bramston*, pp. 119–20.

[16] M. Bond, ed., *The Diaries and Papers of Sir Edward Dering*, p. 116.

in this period were all three-cornered. So, too, were those in Westmoreland, where the county was divided between the "barony" and the "bottom."

More commonly, counties relied upon preelectoral meetings of magistrates and leading gentlemen to select nominees. Lancashire leaders were summoned to quarter sessions in 1679 so that they "may then there with unanimity and due consideration impart their opinions what persons may most properly be pitched on to do his Majesty's and the country's service."[17] Solid evidence of preelection meetings exists for twenty-seven English counties, and suggestive evidence survives for others. "In the counties of Wiltshire and Warwickshire . . . the gentlemen agree beforehand and they only meet at the place of election for form sake," the Earl of Ailesbury recalled in disparaging the lack of such sensible arrangements in Bedfordshire.[18] Sir Justinian Isham proposed to his Northamptonshire neighbors "what upon the matter is practiced in many counties already: the chief gentlemen in every hundred or division to meet at some public place a little before the election."[19]

Gentry meetings usually occurred at quarter sessions or assizes where the magistracy of the county would be present. But if these proceedings were not conveniently scheduled, informal gatherings were arranged. "Several of the eastern and western gentlemen of this county met at Captain Coker's at Mappowder," Thomas Strangways reported from Dorset in the winter of 1679.[20] Derbyshire gentry assembled hastily in 1685 "in order to agreeing of Parliament men. . . . We had a very full appearance on so short a warning."[21] Lord Windsor, Lieutenant of Worcestershire, organized that county's conclave in 1681, as did Lord Lieutenant Sunderland four years later in Warwickshire.[22]

We are not well informed about the dynamics of successful preelectoral meetings. Form and content must have varied from place to place and have been governed by circumstance. Sir Justinian Isham recommended that the Northamptonshire candidates in 1661 be "such of them that

---

[17]   Historical Manuscripts Commission Reports, *14th Report*, Appendix IV (Manuscripts of the Lord Kenyon), pp. 110–11.

[18]   W. E. Buckley, ed., *The Memoires of the Earl of Ailesbury*, I, 183. The counties for which there is no compelling evidence of gentry meetings are Bedfordshire, Cornwall, Durham, Essex, Gloucestershire, Huntingdonshire, Middlesex, Northumberland, Oxfordshire (*pace* Ailesbury), Somerset, Suffolk, Surrey, and Sussex.

[19]   Northamptonshire Record Office, Isham Correspondence, IC 3377. I owe this reference to Victor Stater.

[20]   B. D. Henning, ed., *House of Commons 1660–90*, I, 212.

[21]   Historical Manuscripts Commission Reports, *12th Report*, Appendix V (Manuscripts of the Duke of Rutland), II, 86–87.

[22]   British Library, Additional Mss., 29,910, fol. 172; *Calendar of State Papers Domestic Series 1685*, p. 62.

have most of the gentlemen's voices, or rather votes in paper to avoid any observation of the choosers."[23] Meetings called to resolve anticipated difficulties, like the religious divisions in Northamptonshire, were different from those that affirmed recognized decisions. "This county [of Buckinghamshire] hath ever since the dissolution professed their willingness to adhere to their last choice. . . . At the assizes, which were lately, the gentlemen and grand jury declared themselves of the same opinion."[24] When meetings were simply extensions of sessions, it is likely that they maintained their legal organization. At assizes in Northamptonshire in 1661 and Warwickshire in 1685, the sheriff took the lead.[25] But when assemblies were called specifically to determine candidates, the initiative could rest with interested parties, mediators, or social superiors. Sir Walter Wrottesley called for a preelectoral meeting in Staffordshire after organizing support for his own nomination in 1679; for the Cavalier Parliament, Derbyshire gentlemen nominated William Cavendish and John Frescheville in their absence and then petitioned them to stand; while Lord Windsor chaired Worcestershire's meeting in 1681.[26]

Naturally, a large meeting of county gentry interrupted the flow of correspondence among them and made subsequent narratives superfluous. The most common reports were of results. "My Lord Morpeth and myself stand for Cumberland, Sir Richard Graham for Cockermouth, Sir P[hilip] H[oward] and [Sir] C[hristopher] M[usgrave] for Carlisle. All agreed."[27] Only unusual developments were likely to attract comment. "The fanatics would have set up Mr Willimot against Mr Allestry, but, when he understood it was not by a general consent, he declined it," the Earl of Rutland was appraised from the Derbyshire meeting of 1685.[28] Lord Windsor's demand that Thomas Foley agree to forbear a subsequent election in exchange for support in 1681 was obviously newsworthy and was reported out of the county. When Foley refused "then my Lord Windsor desired the gentlemen to subscribe what every

[23] Northamptonshire R.O., IC 3377.
[24] British Library, Add. Mss., 29,910, fol. 135. Richard Hampden to John Swynfen, July 31, 1679.
[25] Northamptonshire R.O., IC 499; *Calendar of State Papers Domestic Series 1685*, p. 62.
[26] P. M. U. Ward, "Members of Parliament and Elections in Derbyshire, Leicestershire, and Staffordshire between 1660 and 1714," unpublished M.A. thesis, Manchester University (1959), p. 149; British Library Add. Mss., 34,306, fol. 11 and Huntington Library, Hastings Manuscripts, HAP 20; British Library, Add. Mss., 29,910, fol. 172.
[27] Westmoreland R.O., D/RY 2126. I am grateful to Eveline Cruickshanks for a photocopy of this document.
[28] Historical Manuscripts Commission Reports, *12th Report*, Appendix V (Manuscripts of the Duke of Rutland), II, 87.

man would give to bear the charge of the poll against Mr Foley."[29] As always, the more difficult the situation the more we know about it. Whatever their results, the purpose of preelectoral meetings was to secure agreement and to achieve unified choices – "to prevent clashings and bandyings at the great popular meeting for the elections."[30] "The Lord Roos and Lord Sherrard were invited to stand," a Leicestershire electoral petition proclaimed. "This meeting was designed to unite in the election, that so trouble and charge might be prevented."[31] When the Yorkshire magistracy learned that three candidates were canvassing in the county in the winter of 1679 they summoned an assembly where one of the contenders "generously retired in order to save the confusion, charge, and trouble of a contest."[32] A meeting of Shropshire gentry in 1685 convinced Richard Newport to refrain from attempting the seat he had held in four successive Parliaments, while after Nottinghamshire assizes in the same year "the judges sent to Sir Scrope [Howe] to desire him to desist, which he did."[33] In Cambridgeshire, efforts were made to avoid a contest by postponing the county election until the day after that of the town.[34] To achieve accord, candidates contemplating county contests were sometimes promised safe seats in boroughs. The Marquess of Worcester was offered a place for one of his nominees at either the county or the town of Monmouth; Richard Norton and Andrew Henley made a pact to share seats at Hampshire and Portsmouth in 1660; Viscount Morpeth was shuffled off to Carlisle in 1681 to settle difficulties at Cumberland.[35]

[29] British Library, Add. Mss., 29,910, fol. 172. N. Baker to John Swynfen, February 14, 1681.
[30] Historical Manuscripts Commission Reports, *Report on the Frankland–Russell–Astley Manuscripts*, p. 39.
[31] Public Record Office, State Papers, 29/411 pt 2/120.
[32] Historical Manuscripts Commission Reports, *Report on the Manuscripts in Various Collections*, II, 393.
[33] *Calendar of State Papers Domestic Series 1685*, p. 103; Althrope House, Spencer Mss., John Millington to Lord Halifax, March 16, 1685. I am grateful to J. P. Ferris for a transcript of this letter.
[34] For the confusion surrounding this election see B. D. Henning, ed., *House of Commons 1660–90*, I, 146. The original election was postponed until February 20 and the borough election was held on February 19.
[35] *Calendar of State Papers Domestic Series 1679–80*, p. 74; British Library, Sloane Mss., 813, fol. 16; Westmoreland R.O., D/RY 2380. The evidence is clear that there was no contest at this election, despite Reinmuth's assertion to the contrary. The Carlisle return of Morpeth was made on February 28 and the county election was held on March 2. I concur with Eveline Cruickshanks's reconstruction of these events. B. D. Henning, ed., *House of Commons 1660–90*, pp. 182–85. Howard Reinmuth, "A Mysterious Dispute Demystified: Sir George Fletcher vs. the Howards," *Historical Journal*, 27 (1984), pp. 298–99.

As political behavior altered and political differences widened, pre-election compacts became the final prop against a possible landslide of contests. If they could not conciliate every contention at the eleventh hour, they could serve other purposes at earlier stages. The persuasive power of numbers, especially numbers of community leaders, helped discourage all but the most determined contestants. This was one reason why conclaves were hastily assembled when expectations of a parliament rose. Herefordshire gentry gathered on rumors of a session in 1675 and allotted both county and borough seats.[36] The pairing of Lords Fairfax and Clifford, who held the Yorkshire seats in the three Exclusion Crisis parliaments, was arranged three years before their selection.[37] Peer pressure could also exert itself during the meetings by dissuading dissatisfied countrymen from opposition. No less a person than the Earl of Shaftesbury was cowed into silence at a meeting of Dorset leaders in 1675.[38] Finally, if contests could not be avoided, they might at least be regulated. Sheriffs could use sessions or special meetings to announce plans for peripatetic polls, as was done in Buckinghamshire, or candidates might be brought together to agree upon procedures. In the only Rutland contest of this period, the candidates pledged at assizes that there would be "no laboring for voices." Before the 1675 by-election in Norfolk the sheriff, candidates, and leading gentlemen met in the grand jury room of Norwich Castle to negotiate articles for regulating the poll.[39]

It is hard to judge the effectiveness of preelection compacts in overcoming divisions within the counties. For one thing, they were more likely to be held in shires where rifts among the governing elite were either unimportant or did not manifest themselves at elections. Predictably, there is no direct evidence of gentry meetings for counties like Gloucester, Middlesex, or Oxford, which were contested in five of the six general elections. If special assemblies could lower tensions in some places, they could raise them in others. Secondly, a struggle between politically coherent county groups might also result in a struggle for county institutions. There was of course no formula for organizing meetings, no established list of individuals to be canvassed or invited. The rhythms of seventeenth-century life meant that important county figures would always be absent from such gatherings, even if they coincided

---

[36] *Calendar of State Papers Domestic Series 1675–76*, pp. 460–61.

[37] Arthur Gooder, *Parliamentary Representation of the County of York*, II, 172.

[38] Historical Manuscripts Commission Reports, *15th Report*, Appendix VII (Manuscripts of the Marquis of Ailesbury), pp. 177–78.

[39] For Buckinghamshire, Huntington Library, Temple–Stowe Mss., STT Elections Box 1 (7); for Rutland, B. D. Henning, ed., *House of Commons 1660–90*, I, 362; for Norfolk, Historical Manuscripts Commission Reports, *6th Report* (Paston Manuscripts), pp. 371–72.

with sessions. At hastily summoned assemblies they might be absent by design. "I invited such gentlemen as I knew to be of approved loyalty to meet yesterday at Warwick," Andrew Hackett reported to the county's lord lieutenant in 1685.[40] A Monmouthshire meeting in 1680 was held to prevent the Marquess of Worcester from controlling both of the county's seats.[41] The meeting that the Earl of Yarmouth organized in 1681 was equally partisan: "By my last post my son Paston wrote to our most considerable friends to make their interest strong that we may not have Sir John Hobart entailed on us as Parliament man. . . . Pray get a meeting of some of our friends that we may be unanimous."[42]

For all of their chances of success, however, gentry meetings frequently failed. Some of these disappointments were inevitable, especially when meetings were called to try to terminate campaigns that were well under way. For all of their hopes and fears "how fatal a tumultuous election might prove to the peace of our country," the Lancashire magistracy could not persuade any of three rivals to desist in 1679. But many others miscarried because of the hardening of attitudes, a crystallization of opinion that could not be softened. After the Derbyshire gentry agreed on candidates in 1685 "Mr Sacheverell . . . laughed at us and declared he would be at the election," though the sheriff, who refused his candidacy on grounds of nonresidency, laughed last.[43] In the same year, a year notable for rejecting members who had sat during Exclusion, Viscount Brandon disrupted the plans of the Lancashire gentry by declaring that he would "spend £1,000 in a poll."[44] Shaftesbury's dissatisfaction with Lord Digby's Court connections, after his own fall from favor, led to his rejection of a compact to which he had been a party in Dorset.[45] Richard Knightley opposed the collective will of the Northamptonshire gentlemen who had assembled for assizes in 1661. Though "openly declaring how heartily he wished the good agreement of the country," he was determined to represent the Presbyterian interests of the county.[46]

If unity was more difficult to achieve, it was still devoutly to be desired. *Nemine Contradicente* had not lost its appeal. "Nothing is more to be desired than a good understanding among countrymen," Sir John Lowther of Sockbridge declared in 1681 when a contested election

[40] *Calendar of State Papers Domestic Series 1685*, p. 62.
[41] *Calendar of State Papers Domestic Series 1679–80*, p. 483.
[42] British Library, Additional Mss., 27,448, fol. 5.
[43] Historical Manuscripts Commission Reports, *12th Report*, Appendix V (Manuscripts of the Duke of Rutland), II, 86–7; Huntington Library, HA 1250; HA 7744.
[44] Westmoreland R.O., D/RY 2883.
[45] Historical Manuscripts Commission Reports, *15th Report*, Appendix VII (Manuscripts of the Marquis of Ailesbury), pp. 177–78.
[46] Northamptonshire R.O., IC 499.

threatened Cumberland. "The first thing that contributes to a national settlement must be unanimity in elections."[47] Such sentiments were echoed throughout the country and were not simply wistful remembrances of times past. Lord Herbert of Raglan praised Sir Baynham Throckmorton's selection at Gloucestershire in 1664 as "the more pleasing to me because the first . . . that ever was in the memory of man without opposition."[48] Sir William Hickman wrote to Lord Halifax in dismay when a contest was threatened in Nottinghamshire. "I am sorry that you had not that promise of never standing of your brother Pierrepont. I heartily wish some way could be for accommodating. I know some have desired it."[49] Charles Gerard, second Earl of Macclesfield, boasted of his honor "to be chosen in three Parliaments without any opposition from the gentlemen or freeholders of Lancashire." He remained silent about his two contested triumphs.[50] More fitting still were the ideals of Sir Walter Bagot. His seven unanimous selections as knight of the shire in Staffordshire were remembered on his tombstone.[51]

During the Exclusion Crisis – and, quite differently, in 1685 – unanimity had political objectives as well. At different moments rallying cries like "No Popery" and "Church and King" could unify rather than divide. The terror induced by the Popish Plot and the abrupt dissolution of parliaments to prevent James's exclusion from the Crown strengthened the determination of communities to express their political will in the choice of members. This meant repetitive selections. "We are like to choose the same members that we chose last time," Sir Ralph Verney wrote from Buckinghamshire assizes in the summer of 1679.[52] The *Domestick Intelligencer* reveled in reporting the unanimous returns of sitting members "without cost or trouble" in the autumn of 1679 and again in 1681. The Northamptonshire knights were agreed "in a quarter of an hour."[53] Lord Cavendish and William Sacheverell were returned for Derbyshire in 1679 "without spending a penny" and in 1681 without appearing at the election.[54]

[47] Westmoreland R.O., D/RY 2370.
[48] Historical Manuscripts Commission Reports, *15th Report*, Appendix VII (Manuscripts of the Marquis of Ailesbury), p. 174. Lord Herbert's youthfulness may excuse his overstatement.
[49] Althrope House, Spencer Mss., Hickman to Halifax, February 8, 1679. I am grateful to J. P. Ferris for a transcript of this letter.
[50] B. D. Henning, ed., *House of Commons 1660–90*, II, 386.
[51] William, Baron Bagot, *Memorials of the Bagot Family* (1824), p. 79.
[52] British Library, M/636/33. Sir Ralph Verney to John Verney, July 23, 1679.
[53] *The Domestick Intelligencer*, no. 21, September 16, 1679.
[54] Historical Manuscripts Commission Reports, *13th Report*, Appendix VI (Manuscripts of Sir William Fitzherbert), p. 13; *Protestant Domestick Intelligencer*, March 15, 1681.

Yet caution must be exercised in evaluating this kind of evidence. The proximity of selections ensured some overlap, as successful campaigns were easily revived and unsuccessful ones abandoned. This must account for the oddity that no county chose six different men to the three parliaments. Moreover, counties that exhibited this kind of unanimity in 1679 and 1681 were equally unified in presenting loyal declarations after the Rye House Plot, sending congratulatory messages on the accession of James II, and displacing their previous members in 1685. "The whole county is opposed to Sir Scrope Howe," John Millington wrote of the Nottinghamshire member in the three Exclusion Crisis parliaments. They "declare to Sir William Clifton that if he join with Sir Scrope Howe he will hazard his election."[55] Howe withdrew after the meeting of the county gentry. In most places, committed partisans chose the beaches rather than the water when the tide was running against them. But if the explanation is complex, the pattern is simple. Thirteen counties returned the same men to all three sessions, while twenty-two others returned the same pair twice. Yet when James II summoned his first parliament four years later, the run of repetitive selections was halted. Only eight of the thirty-three surviving knights who had sat in all three parliaments were selected for their counties in 1685.[56] Interestingly, only five were rejected at the polls, two of them in Bedfordshire.[57] The twenty others did not have to get their feet wet to know that the political waters were icy.

III

Patronage continued as a dominant force in the process of borough selections. Deeply rooted, its many varieties flourished alike in the sunlight of popular acceptance and in the shady compacts of corporate leaders. Its principal function remained unaltered: Communities were provided with services, and patrons were provided with influence. "You may depend upon a return of gratitude from me suitable to the obligation you have laid upon me," the Earl of Danby forthrightly assured the corporation of York in 1673.[58] These bonds of reciprocity were strength-

[55]   Althrope House, Spencer Mss., Millington to Halifax, March 16, 1685. I am grateful to J. P. Ferris for a copy of this letter.
[56]   Sir Robert Carr (Lincolnshire) and Sir John Hobart (Norfolk) both died before 1685. In addition to the twenty-six men chosen in pairs, nine others were chosen by their counties in all three elections.
[57]   Those rejected were Lord Russell and Sir Humphrey Monoux in Bedfordshire; Sir John Guise in Gloucestershire; Viscount Brandon in Lancashire; and Thomas Foley in Worcestershire.
[58]   British Library, Add. Mss., 28,051, fols., 22–3.

ened by an increase in the value of both service and patronage. The nation's burgeoning commercial prosperity brought forth a flowering of ports, market towns, and administrative centers. The protection and expansion of their rights and privileges depended in large part upon powerful patrons. The cleansing of the waterways that nourished Thetford's economy, for example, was made possible by the town's election of Secretary Williamson in 1669.[59] Similarly, the explosive growth of government service presented opportunities for the enrichment and glorification of the individual. Not the least of the qualities necessary to rise at Court was local influence: "The King will then observe...that Sir Robert Carr hath a greater interest," Lord Roos was warned when his patronage at Grantham was challenged.[60] As the interdependence of center and periphery increased, the symbiotic nature of patronage came more sharply into focus.

No precise formula can be devised to predict the success or failure of individual patrons, just as no definition can be advanced of natural ties. Parliamentary patronage was based upon a perceived identity of interests, and perceptions are an elusive subject for study. The most common metaphors for the relationship remained those of patriarchy and the body politic. But with communities more often divided than in the past, organic images were not always appropriate. Frequently an offer from one patron could be rejected as a threat to the liberty of the subject, while that of another was accepted as a free gift of favor and fortune. Rival factions within a town, embittered by intermittent purges of leadership, might encourage a competition between patrons. With the Earls of Exeter, Lindsey, Stamford, and Viscount Campden all potential patrons at Stamford, it is little wonder that divisions in the town featured prominently at parliamentary elections. As the Earl of Lindsey reflected: "How powerful a conjunction of families are and how ridiculously insignificant they make themselves when upon all occasions they do not express a high concern of one another."[61]

The most stable relationships between parliamentary patrons and communities were those based on propinquity. The ownership or control of land by a prominent neighbor continued to exert the strongest claim. Russells at Tavistock, Herberts at Wilton, and Howards at Castle Rising are but a few of the more familiar examples of manorial lords who acted as patrons. "The borough of Christchurch is my own borough, the manor

---

[59] See their letter to Williamson after the election. *Calendar of State Papers Domestic Series 1668–69*, pp. 549–50.

[60] Historical Manuscripts Commission Reports, *12th Report*, Appendix V (Manuscripts of the Duke of Rutland), p. 48.

[61] British Library, Egerton Mss., 3330, fol. 28.

is my own and one or both of the burgesses have been always elected on the recommendation of the Lords of the place," the second Earl of Clarendon declared in 1681.[62] The tie between manor house and borough was not easily loosened. Yet the patronage nomination became progressively restricted to one of the two seats. At Great Bedwin "the borough submitted themselves in the choice of one of their members to the nomination of the Lord Bruce, who in the right of his Lady is the Lord of that town . . . and for the other burgess the borough desired to be left to their free choice."[63] This did not imply a dichotomy between nominated and elected places. Just as frequently, boroughs restricted the powers of one patron to leave room for the choice of another. In the protean politics of post-Restoration England, two patrons were better security than one.

An equally common basis for a patronage relationship was the possession of local or county office. High stewards and recorders continued to be parliamentary patrons to the boroughs they served, though their tenure in office was now regulated by the pleasure of the monarch. Hull, which had a need for patrons close to the throne to defend its county status, actually presented its steward, the Duke of Monmouth, with a purse of gold when his nominee was persuaded to withdraw from the 1678 by-election. Seven years later their steward, the Earl of Plymouth, boasted "that I shall recommend the persons whom they shall choose."[64] At Stafford, which also had Monmouth as steward, "it has been usual here on all elections of parliament men to accept for one such person as the high steward of the borough recommended."[65] No better statement of the expectations of a local officeholder can be found than that penned by the second Duke of Albemarle, Chancellor of Cambridge University. Upon hearing that university electors had been canvassed for candidates before his own nominations, Albemarle wrote to the Senate: "I have conceived the university had done me the honor (in choosing me Chancellor) to make me their head. . . . I hope it cannot be thought strange that I therefore assume a privilege which the members of every ordinary body yield to their head." Pointedly, Albemarle disparaged the notion "that you have done me the honor to make choice of me that I might

[62] *Calendar of State Papers Domestic Series 1680–81*, p. 165.
[63] *Smith's Protestant Intelligencer*, No. 9, February 24–28, 1681. Similarly, Henry, Lord Howard had "a free offer and assurance from the town of Aldeburgh to recommend one at least." C. Robbins, "The Election Correspondence of Sir John Holland of Quidenham, 1661," *Norfolk Archaeology*, 30 (1952), p. 133.
[64] B. D. Henning, ed., *House of Commons 1660–1690*, I, 477; *Calendar of State Papers Domestic Series 1685*, p. 23.
[65] *Calendar of State Papers Domestic Series 1682*, p. 456.

do you all the service that should lie in my power but never receive any from you."[66]

Alongside community-based officers were those whose functions bestrode center and locality. By the late seventeenth century lords lieutenant began to exercise parliamentary patronage based upon service and influence. This developed from the strong military presence that had existed in 1660 and 1661 and was fortified by the continuing importance of the militia. The lord lieutenant was a useful conduit between Court and country whose influence in parliamentary selections could be of aid to each. The Duke of Albemarle helped smooth many of the tangled selections in Essex boroughs, acting as a mediator among the gentry and as a power broker for the Crown.[67] The Marquess of Worcester was no less conspicuous as a parliamentary patron in Gloucester, Herefordshire, and Monmouthshire, where he held the lieutenancies, though his heavy-handed approach was often resented. In the Monmouth elections during the winter of 1679 it was reported "the Lord Marquess wants one of the knights to be his son and to have the nomination of the person for the borough, which the gentry think too much."[68] Yet he was influential in every Gloucestershire borough, and when Bristol rejected his nominee at a 1685 by-election he tersely reminded the corporation how he had been "put upon all your commands when any favor is to be obtained for you."[69]

The power of the lieutenant's sword was double-edged. Occasionally the service that he offered a community was freedom from the nuisance he could create. The Earl of Lindsey's lieutenancy in Lincolnshire was sharply felt in the county's parliamentary boroughs.[70] The threat of troops on election day was always a potential weapon of the lieutenancy,

[66] C. H. Cooper, *Annals of Cambridge*, III, 609. Albemarle's experience as a recorder, an office he held in five parliamentary corporations, is also worth quoting: "His Majesty has done me the honor, to appoint me Recorder of several towns in their new charters and others have upon their own choice requested I might be so; of all which there is not one corporation, that has suffered themselves to be engaged in this matter [selection of M.P.'s], though great interest has been made with some, till they have first had information of my intentions, whom I shall please to recommend to them."

[67] As well as being lord lieutenant, Albemarle was recorder of Colchester and Harwich and was influential in Maldon elections. In 1685 he persuaded Sir John Bramston to accept election in hope of staving off a contest "but it fell out quite otherwise." P. Braybrooke, ed., *The Autobiography of Sir John Bramston*, p. 164.

[68] *Calendar of State Papers Domestic Series 1679–80*, p. 74.

[69] Bristol Record Office Mss., 12,964, fol. 2. For Gloucestershire elections see Rudite Robinson, "The Parliamentary Representation of Gloucestershire, 1660–90," unpublished Ph.D. thesis, Yale University (1975).

[70] For Lindsey's use of troops at Grantham see Clive Holmes, *Seventeenth Century Lincolnshire* (1981), p. 240.

although in fairness it must be noted that parliamentary towns were commonly the likeliest places for quartering, provisions, and entertainment. In 1679 the Duke of Monmouth ordered the Grenadiers out of Guildford to deflect criticism of their presence, a course imitated by the Earl of Derby at Lancaster in 1685.[71] Yet it is easy to overlook the personal nature of the local militia and its role as another social connection in a community. When John Grey stood for Leicester in 1677 his nephew, Lord Roos, sent letters among the electors. He requested that "all and every of you who have any commission from my father in the militia or have any other dependence upon him and me... that you give your votes for Mr. Grey."[72]

In addition to the general military influence of the lords lieutenant, individual towns maintained their peculiar relationships with officials whose powers were more national than local. Although the Scottish border was putatively pacified, governors of Berwick Castle were still appointed.[73] On the Isle of Wight, Sir Robert Holmes acted as a most assiduous lieutenant, building up a personal interest in Yarmouth and on occasion seating himself or his brother at Newport and Newtown.[74] But the best known and most important of these quasi-military figures was the lord warden of the Cinque Ports. The relationship between the warden and the ports remained complex. Since the wardenship of Lord Cobham early in the century, there had not been a lord warden who could claim a local influence in either Sussex or Kent. This meant that nominees were less likely to be drawn from these counties and their all-too-abundant supply of aspiring gentlemen. This led to pressure on the ports for seats or patronage from neighboring magnates who knew of their economic problems at first hand, as well as from powerful absentee wardens who insisted upon traditional rights.

The difficulty after 1660 was that the lords warden were too powerful and too insistent. After Charles II's restoration he named his brother, James, Duke of York, to several important military posts. As lord warden, James successfully reasserted the traditional right of a single nomination in each of the ports. Only Seaford, enfranchised in 1640 and

---

[71] *Calendar of State Papers Domestic Series 1679–80*, p. 87. Westmoreland R.O., D/RY 2894.

[72] Historical Manuscripts Commission Reports, *12th Report*, Appendix V (Manuscripts of the Duke of Rutland), p. 35.

[73] The Widdringtons in the 1660s and the Duke of Newcastle thereafter were patrons at Berwick. See B. D. Henning, ed., *House of Commons 1660–90*, I, 344–45.

[74] Holmes sat twice for Newport and once for Yarmouth, while his brother sat four times for Newtown. In the survey of constituencies prior to 1688 all three corporations were considered to be controlled by Sir Robert Holmes. George Duckett, *Penal Laws and Test Act*, I, 432.

thus not obligated to honor Elizabethan traditions, refused his nominee in 1661, and only Winchelsea rejected his candidate in a by-election to replace the member that the warden had initially nominated. But many of the port by-elections were contested, and the days were long past when "a sheet of paper does the business."[75] After the Duke's exclusion from office by the Test Act, Charles II assumed the office himself. He scrupulously avoided direct nominations during the elections to the Exclusion parliaments, but the plans laid for the resumption of parliaments in the 1680s included the reassertion of patronage in the Cinque Ports.[76] Only New Romney resisted the claim, basing its objection on the technicality that the right of nomination did not belong to the warden by "ancient and uninterrupted instance and practice."[77] But it did not refuse the nominees of James II when he resumed the office after his brother's death.

The parliamentary patronage of these military officials was but one part of a fledgling effort at the national management of elections which had been unknown in the early seventeenth century. Royal interest in elections was no longer academic. Samuel Pepys secured his initial place in the Commons when the Duke of York recommended him to Lord Howard for a vacancy at Castle Rising in 1673. The diarist wrote a fawning letter thanking Howard for his favor upon "a humble creature of his royal highness."[78] Heneage Finch "has been heard to say that he would not concern himself about his election, but leave it to his Majesty."[79] In 1685 the Duke of Albemarle was "by the King's direction" ordered to build an interest at Clitheroe for Edmund Asheton.[80] The Duke of York, the Duke of Monmouth, and Charles II were all prom-

---

[75] By-elections presented complexities for both the warden and the ports, especially as the Cavalier Parliament lengthened. The Duke of York was continually approached, as he was by Sir William Temple in 1666, to make recommendations on vacancies whether or not the vacancy was created by one of his own nominees. Thomas Courtenay, *Memoirs of the Life, Works and Correspondence of Sir William Temple*, p. 241.

[76] Whether Charles II intended to call Parliament after 1681 is a moot question. In 1683 he was certainly exerting pressure on the ports to avow explicitly the lord warden's patronage rights. New Romney's legal advisor had an uncomfortable meeting with the lieutenant of Dover Castle on this point. He told the lieutenant that the corporation's "loyalty would prompt you to comply with his majesty's desires in electing whom his majesty would recommend. But he said that his majesty insisted upon the right of the Duke, intimating that the Duke thought himself concerned." Kent Archive Office, New Romney Records, Aep/fol. 47.

[77] Kent A.O. NR/Aep/fols. 51–54.

[78] J. R. Tanner, ed., *The Further Correspondence of Samuel Pepys*, p. 273.

[79] *Calendar of State Papers Domestic Series 1685*, p. 192.

[80] Historical Manuscripts Commission Reports, *14th Report*, Appendix IV (Manuscripts of the Lord Kenyon), pp. 179–80.

inent in Liverpool's 1670 by-election. Candidacies were advanced and withdrawn on instructions from the summits of power, making Court favor a factor in parliamentary selections. This direct intervention by the Crown, even when camouflaged by intermediaries, added an entirely new dimension to patronage relationships and set the course for what would eventually emerge as the "Court interest." Yet this destination was not to be reached for nearly half a century, and it is important that it not be anticipated. For all the Crown's power, there were real limitations on its influence in the selection process.

First, the constitutional role of parliaments remained sufficiently unstable to counterbalance any effort to organize government patronage on a wide scale. The forces that impelled individuals to gamble their fortunes on elections did not motivate the Crown. After the replacement of the Triennial Act, parliaments were again summoned and dismissed at royal pleasure. By keeping one parliament in session for eighteen years and dissolving another within weeks, Charles II demonstrated that he had a more potent weapon, if weapons were needed, than electoral management. Secondly, government, or the Court, was not a coherent entity in the late seventeenth century. The use of singular nouns here is more a matter of convenience than description. Charles II, the Duke of York, and the Duke of Monmouth constituted potentially divergent interests, especially in the latter part of the reign. To them was added the changing cast of ministers who vied among themselves for power and among the royal triumvirate for favor. Small wonder that parliamentary boroughs received nominations from "Court" supporting different candidates for the same seats. Finally, even when Court patrons were not in competition with each other there was no mechanism for coordinating nominees until the abortive campaign of 1688. Not even the opportunity provided by the limited number of by-elections to the Cavalier Parliament resulted in government planning, the demarcation of ministerial responsibility, or the development of a patronage office.

A Court divided by personality, by religion, and by faction could not speak with one voice. But even if it could, its wishes would be muted by the traditions involved in the selection process and by the dual nature of representation, which necessitated the coordination of center and locality. As it was in the reorganization of the boroughs, central government was dependent upon local power brokers for its information and ultimately for its influence. Credible nominees were those who had some natural tie to the community, a factor that exerted a powerful check upon officials who made their homes and careers in the capital. Similarly, local patrons like stewards and lieutenants would have some stock of their own dependents from which to fill the seats at their disposal. The Earl of Bath placed sons and nephews in the Cornish boroughs of which he was recorder; five sons and three grandsons of the second Earl of Lindsey absorbed the conscientious patronage of Sir Montague and Robert Bertie.[81] The conduct of courtiers was cut from the same cloth, with six Finches and six Hydes clinging tenaciously to coattails that had both local and national stitching.[82] Even Danby could manage a brother and two sons, though their various elections were spread across five counties.[83] These considerations curtailed discretionary patronage, while the tradition (during Charles's reign) that the Crown remained aloof from actual nominations necessitated the use of intermediaries who could wield local power. As Danby told Newcastle in 1679: "The King . . . desires you will promote as much as you can the choice of good members in those places which are influenced by your Grace."[84] This subinfeudation of parliamentary patronage diluted the spirit of loyalty between Crown and M.P., particularly in times of political crisis.

The absence of central coordination and the presence of local restraints on both patrons and candidates limited Court management to a potential rather than an actual force in the process of selection. Nevertheless, the potential was increasing. In the reign of Charles II the Dukes of York and Monmouth, and in the reign of James II, Lords Jeffreys and Sunderland became national patrons whose powers transcended the territorial influence of even the greatest magnates. Their support was sought by aspirants as a seal of approved loyalty, and they provided nominations and testimonials on a national scale. The Duke of York must be credited with creating the admiralty interest that would flourish until nineteenth-century reform. As parliamentary representation had such a coastal flavor, it was logical that languishing seaports would be transformed into bustling dockyards by the navy. Monmouth's influence was more personal, especially as he became the hope of a Protestant succession. His accumulation of military and local offices owed everything to his position at court. Jeffreys, who could never manage a seat for himself, became

---

[81] B. D. Henning, ed., *House of Commons 1660–90*, I, 640.

[82] B. D. Henning, ed., *House of Commons 1660–90*, under the entries "Hyde," "Finch."

[83] All three were first chosen at by-elections in 1677 for patronage seats at East Looe, Corfe Castle, and Berwick. Each was elected after difficulties: at East Looe the candidate of the speaker of the Commons was forced to withdraw; at Corfe Castle the electors chose a local man who resigned the seat to Viscount Latimer; at Berwick victory was secured for Lord Dunblane by the expedient of disenfranchising dissenters. British Library, Egerton Mss., 3330, fols. 73, 75; *Calendar of State Papers Domestic Series 1677–8*, p. 80; British Library, Egerton Mss., 3330, fol. 87.

[84] Historical Manuscripts Commission Reports, *13th Report*, Appendix II (Manuscripts of the Duke of Portland), II, 153.

a parliamentary patron overnight, undertaking to oversee elections from the bench in 1685. His Norfolk circuit that year dispensed justice and Court influence simultaneously. To Sunderland fell the task of organizing the most ambitious election scheme undertaken by the Stuarts, the management of the Parliament of 1688. This was to be accomplished after a sophisticated survey compiled information, for the first time, about electors, patrons, and candidates.

The expansion of the government's efforts at managing patronage does not imply that it enjoyed universal success. The Crown faced the same competition as any local patron and had its best results in places, like Windsor, where some natural tie existed. Without a local connection, Court patronage cast its fate upon the same winds that blew for all patrons. The assertion of the admiralty's claims, for example, was not accepted unequivocally. Dunwich rejected the admiral's nominee, Thomas Allin, in 1671, and then accepted his son at their next vacancy.[85] Aldeburgh refused Pepys in 1669, although this was more a reflection upon the candidate than upon the patron.[86] Portsmouth's reception of admiralty influence reveals the complexities of these relationships even more clearly. When the Duke of York nominated the navy's treasurer in 1661, he had to stifle opposition by assuring the town that he was not "indifferent to the success of it."[87] By 1679 the issue was less the right of patronage than who would exercise it. George Legge, the town's governor, had already promised the place to the naval official Sir John Kempthorne when he received a peremptory demand from the admiralty that he provide instead for the chancellor of the exchequer. This he refused to do, standing on his promise and on Kempthorne's credentials. His obstinacy provoked from the admiralty both a rebuke and a threat: "Were it fit for us . . . to contend about superiority of interest . . . that of the navy . . . [will] be found to stand upon higher ground . . . if that corporation go by the same measures of profit in disposing of their favors which other, no less wise, bodies do."[88]

Nor was the admiralty alone in failing to secure nominees. When Danby was elevated to the House of Lords he designated the seat he vacated at York for his eldest son. The corporation, already engaged to one of its own freemen, rejected the ministrations of its steward, the Duke of Buckingham, as well as Danby's own insistent entreaties: "Certainly it is the first time that any man's interest was ever thought equal

[85] Public Record Office, Admiralty, 2/1746/77.
[86] J. R. Tanner, ed., The Further Correspondence of Samuel Pepys, p. 258.
[87] Public Record Office, Admiralty, 2/1745/34.
[88] Tanner, ed., Further Correspondence of Pepys, p. 346.

to that of my Lord Treasurer's in promoting trade in England."[89] Similar examples could be cited in the experience of most parliamentary patrons. It is thus doubly unfortunate that rejection of a Crown nominee has come to imply rejection of the Crown. This could sometimes be the case – during the Exclusion Crisis, Thomas Thynne observed that "the prejudices against courtiers are pretty strong" – but it was not necessarily so.[90] Certainly no estimate of the gulf between "Court" and "country" should be calculated based upon the fate of candidates with ostensible Court backing. For one thing, more aspirants approached Court personalities for support after they had entered the running. This made them less nominated than approved – a subtle but important distinction. For the most part their successes were private and local; their failures should not be considered public. Nor should we forget that many patronage nominations, whatever their source, were rejected as superfluous or inappropriate by the communities involved. As patronage was not a power relationship, its rejection was not a sign of impotence.

This again points toward the interdependent relationship between patrons and communities that allowed for choice rather than domination. Castle Rising accepted Lord Howard's nomination of Pepys in 1673 only after the candidate had presented testimonials to his religious orthodoxy.[91] Litchfield consistently refused nominees of its successive stewards, and Coventry turned out its borough lord in 1661.[92] Even the Cornish boroughs, whose very existence has symbolized the corrupt nature of patronage, present complexities. Throughout the post-Restoration period they preferred a local gentleman in each constituency, and their two great patrons, the Earls of Radnor and Bath, were descended from ancient Cornish families. Though reorganized Cornish boroughs expressed a willingness to grant nominations to Bath in the 1688 survey, they also insisted that those named be Protestant Cornishmen.[93] There was no contradiction between accepting patronage relationships and rejecting individual patrons. Thus the poignant dilemma faced by Marlborough's freemen in 1661. Having committed

---

[89] Historical Manuscripts Commission Reports, *14th Report*, Appendix IV (Manuscripts of the Lord Kenyon), p. 97.

[90] Quoted in B. D. Henning, ed., *House of Commons 1660–90*, I, 385.

[91] J. Smith, ed., *The Life, Letters, and Journals of Samuel Pepys*, I, 142. Three King's Lynn clerics affirmed "that he hath constantly manifested himself to be a firm protestant according to the rites of the Church of England."

[92] B. D. Henning, ed., *House of Commons 1660–90*, I, 384, 429.

[93] G. Duckett, *Penal Laws and Test Act*, I, 379–80. Eleven Cornish constituencies responded: "The Mayor and corporation promise to elect two such members as their present recorder shall recommend, or approve of, provided they are of the protestant religion and their countrymen."

themselves to a nominee of the Herberts and to a man of their own choice, one of "discreet, moderate, and pious" views, they received a recommendation for a third candidate from Francis Lord Seymour. "We indeed find ourselves in a great perplexity being greatly desirous to preserve your honor's favor toward us and yet careful also to preserve the peace of our consciences."[94]

IV

Interdependency, natural ties, government influence, community choice: all were aspects of late seventeenth-century patronage. Though they can be analyzed separately, in context they merged, as can be seen in the 1670 by-election at Liverpool. To expand its flourishing trade and preserve its rising prosperity, Liverpool needed the succor of well-connected patrons and members of Parliament. In 1670 the death of its senior member, William Stanley, created an inconvenient vacancy. William Stanley had been an ideal M.P., combining local, county, and national prominence. Formerly Liverpool's mayor, Stanley served also as a Lancashire deputy-lieutenant and as a cornet in the Horse Guards under the Duke of Monmouth.[95] It would not be easy for the town to find another candidate "that will be faithful to us and such a one as we may increase our interest at Court," which Mayor Thomas Johnson forthrightly asserted "is that we want."[96]

There was no shortage of potential benefactors. Foremost was the lord lieutenant, the Earl of Derby, brother of the deceased member and head of the Stanleys of Knowsley. The family's far-flung patronage empire had suffered the fiscal depredations of the Revolution and the political challenges of parochial interest in the county.[97] At Liverpool, the competition came from Lord Molyneux and a number of prominent gentlemen including the town's remaining M.P., Sir Gilbert Ireland.[98]

---

[94] British Library, Add. Mss., 32,324, fol. 75.

[95] For Stanley see B. D. Henning, ed., *House of Commons 1660–90*, III, 475–76.

[96] E. B. Saxton, "Fresh Light on the Liverpool Election of 1670," *Transactions of the Historical Society of Lancashire and Cheshire*, 93 (1941), p. 59.

[97] B. Coward, "The Social and Political Position of the Earls of Derby in Later Seventeenth Century Lancashire," *Transactions of the Historical Society of Lancashire and Cheshire*, 132 (1982), pp. 127–54.

[98] The alliance, which included Sir Roger Bradshaigh and his brother-in-law Sir Geoffrey Shakerley, had a Catholic flavor but was also based on Molyneux's extensive landholdings, his dispute with the town over common rights and the construction of a bridge, and personal hostility to Derby. J. A. Picton, *Selections from the Municipal Records of Liverpool*, pp. 275–77; and M. Mullett, "The Politics of Liverpool, 1660–

Among local worthies there was Edward Moore, one of Liverpool's largest landowners and least popular personalities, and John Birch, a Lancashire native who had performed valuable service for the borough in Parliament.[99] All had claims to a share of the town's affections – each had his stock of past performance and his promise of future favor. Though it would be difficult to challenge a Stanley at Liverpool, an election constituted an important part of the process of validating the hierarchy of local power.[100] But that was not its only function.

Local patronage lay like the first soft layer of tissue over the vital organs of the corporation. On top of it was the substantial mass of muscle represented by the central government. The by-elections to the Cavalier Parliament were studied with eager attention by ministers of the Crown, indeed by the Crown itself, with an eye toward potential advantage. Within a week of William Stanley's death, Sir Gilbert Ireland had been petitioned with no less than six requests for his powerful support.[101] Two letters were written on behalf of the Duke of Monmouth, followed by a third from Monmouth himself, in favor of Thomas Ross. Four letters named Sir George Lane, Irish secretary of state, who was supported no less impressively by the Duke of Ormonde, the Earl of Ancram, and Viscount Molyneux. It is instructive that neither Molyneux nor Ormonde wrote directly to Ireland.[102] Rather they used his friend Sir Roger Bradshaigh as intermediary, as eventually did the Duke of York. Even Ireland's brother-in-law, Robert Worden, wrote "at the commands of a very great man."[103] The other local patrons were similarly beset. Monmouth's recommendations for Ross were sent to both the Earl of Derby and Edward Moore. John Birch, whose politically

---

[99]   88," *Transactions of the Historical Society of Lancashire and Cheshire*, 124 (1973), pp. 31–56.

[99]   For Moore, see Thomas Heywood, ed., *Moore Rental*, Chetham Society, 12 (1847).

[100]   I cannot accept Mullett's interpretation that the Earl of Derby had little to do with this election or that it represented a rejection of patronage relationships by the town. The suggestion that Sir Gilbert Ireland acted as Derby's "campaign manager" (p. 41) is fantastic, and Mullett neglects the vital preelection meeting organized by Derby to persuade Ireland to withdraw the candidacy of Sir George Lane. Mullett, "Politics of Liverpool," pp. 39–44; Historical Manuscripts Commission Reports, *10th Report*, Appendix IV (Moore Manuscripts), p. 118.

[101]   The correspondence received by Ireland is printed in A. Hume, "Some Account of the Liverpool Election of 1670," *Transactions of the Historical Society of Lancashire and Cheshire*, 6 (1853–4), pp. 1*–24*.

[102]   It is clear that Molyneux wished to remain in the background and that even Bradshaigh feared that his connection with Molyneux might undermine his nominee "that what comes from me may be the worse taken by the Leirpoltonians." Ibid., p. 10*.

[103]   Ibid., p. 4*.

sensitive ear was more firmly pressed to the ground, was the first to hear the name of Sir William Bucknall, revenue commissioner in Ireland.[104] Indeed, Bucknall's name was soon on everyone's lips. After Monmouth's persistent appeals to Ireland, Moore, and Derby, Ross was forced to withdraw: "This morning his Majesty sent to me...with a command to desist from pretending to be burgess of Liverpool, his Majesty resolving that one, Sir William Bucknall shall, if possible, be the man."[105] By the time of a preelection meeting called by the Earl of Derby, Bucknall's aspirations had been supported by letters from Prince Rupert, the Duke of Monmouth, the lord keeper, the chancellor of the duchy, and two leaders of the Cabal, Ashley and Buckingham.[106] Such a confluence of powerful backers overwhelmed Sir Gilbert Ireland and the supporters of Sir George Lane. At the meeting, which had been designed to gain a consensus for Bucknall, Ireland gave vent to his frustrations: "The mentioning the King was against the privilege of the Commons of England and that if these were suffered the King might as well call burgesses in the House of Commons by special writ."[107] His emotional oration, which concluded "then good night to the liberty of the subject," surprised the Earl of Derby and can hardly be viewed as a detached reflection on governmental patronage. A week later he had procured a letter from the Duke of York in support of Lane's sagging candidacy.[108]

It is worth observing that the pressure of governmental patronage was on local mediators rather than upon the constituency itself. They were expected to transform recommendation into nomination, and nomination into election. John Birch, who of all the patrons stood furthest from the direct interplay for power, penned the most honest advice: "If you have of your own number that you think fit, I, by all means, advise you to him as most natural." But if the town were to choose outside, Birch recommended Bucknall for his interests in Ireland, his "great interest with the King...and so able to serve you and give checkmate to your opposers."[109] Edward Moore, after half-heartedly advancing his own

[104] Ibid., pp. 4*–5*. For Bucknall see B. D. Henning, ed., *House of Commons 1660–90*, I, 741–42.

[105] Thomas Ross to Edward Moore, November 10, 1670. Historical Manuscripts Commission Reports, *10th Report*, Appendix IV (Moore Manuscripts), p. 117.

[106] Historical Manuscripts Commission Reports, *10th Report*, Appendix IV (Moore Manuscripts), p. 118.

[107] Ibid.

[108] Upon delivering a copy of the Duke's letter to Ireland, Sir Roger Bradshaigh wrote, "I wish one of them had been in your hand when you had the knattering humor in your mouth with the good Earl." A. Hume, "Some Account of the Liverpool Election of 1670," *Transactions of the Historical Society of Lancashire and Cheshire*, 6 (1853–4), p. 16*.

[109] Ibid., p. 4*.

claims, pressed Bucknall upon the corporation as well. His interests at Court and over trade in Ireland made him an ideal representative for the town "the advantage of which your ordinary freeman and their wife and child will duly find."[110] The Earl of Derby petitioned in the same vein. Having first recommended Ross, he wrote to give notice of Ross's withdrawal "and in his room by his Majesty's order [Sir William Bucknall]" whom Derby supported "by duty and inclination."[111] As Birch, Moore, and Derby argued the brief for Bucknall, Sir Gilbert Ireland pleaded the cause of Sir George Lane. Yet it was less Lane's success than his own on which Sir Gilbert based his case: "I pray gentlemen, make me not wholly an insignificant fellow with you . . . and also very ridiculous to all persons else that know me (who notwithstanding my former expense of so much time and money) shall now behold me stand affronted by your town."[112]

Parliamentary patronage remained a series of complex symbiotic relationships. Local influence was based upon natural affiliations, though these might vary from the ancient standing of the house of Stanley to the power of a sitting member of Parliament. Whatever its origins, local interest was recognized and became the granary from which national management could feed. We can see a two-way process at work in which "bottom–up" considerations were as potent as "top–down" pressures. Both Sir William Bucknall and Sir George Lane were suitable candidates for Liverpool M.P. because they could protect the town's critical Irish interests. The ultimate selection of Bucknall served to bolster trade, improve "Court interest," and pleasure local benefactors. This was the mix of ingredients that made a nominated candidate more attractive than a purely local one. By channeling Bucknall's nomination and guiding his selection, Birch, Moore, and the Earl of Derby had all served the community.

The usefulness of the local patron to the Court was proportionate to his ability to guide such choices. When the Duke of Ormonde heard that Ireland was advancing the candidacy of Sir George Lane he declared that "Sir Gilbert Ireland is a very honest gentleman and if ever it be in

[110] E. B. Saxton, "Fresh Light on the Liverpool Election of 1670," *Transactions of the Historical Society of Lancashire and Cheshire*, 93 (1941), p. 67.

[111] A. Hume, "Some Account of the Liverpool Election of 1670," *Transactions of the Historical Society of Lancashire and Cheshire*, 6 (1853–4), p. 13*. I see no reason to accept Mullett's suggestion that he was insincere. Derby appeared ready to advance whichever candidate emerged from court and took the leading role in organizing the meeting at which it was hoped Lane's candidacy would be withdrawn. Mullett, "The Politics of Liverpool."

[112] A. Hume, "Some Account of the Liverpool Election of 1670," *Transactions of the Historical Society of Lancashire and Cheshire*, 6 (1853–4), p. 16*.

my power I will serve him."[113] But as this selection makes clear, the "Court" came in a variety of sizes and shapes. There was certainly no coordination at the center. The Duke of Monmouth indiscriminately sprayed local brokers with letters nominating a candidate whom he had to withdraw; the Dukes of Ormonde and York supported a candidate who also withdrew.[114] With one Irish official backed by the Duke of York pitted against another Irish official backed by the King, there was more than enough room for maneuver by both the community and its would-be patrons. Success in guiding a parliamentary selection thus provided a local patron with national prestige. Rather than acting, as had his ancestors, as an independent power broker, the late seventeenth-century local patron was increasingly ground between community and Court. He needed favor from both, and for both he produced the valuable services of parliamentary patronage.

[113]   Ibid., p. 17*.
[114]   It is certain that Lane had decided to end his candidacy before the election and that those who had been pledged to him were set free. The remaining potential candidate, Henry Ashurst, also withdrew before the election. The only confusion that remains derives from Sir Gilbert Ireland's splenetic comment three days before the choice: "I am in no hopes but Bucknall will carry it, however he shall not have the plate with running alone for I am resolved to hobble up some blind courser or other which may probably at least bring it hereafter to the decision of the judges." At this date he was counting on Ashurst to play the "blind courser" and, after his withdrawal, it is unknown if anyone else did. Ibid., pp. 22*–23*, 20*.

7

Contesting and Winning

I

"NO FAGGOTS, No faggots, Mr Papillon is fairly chosen." The chaotic scene at the port of Dover in 1673 was not unlike many that took place during the by-elections to the Cavalier Parliament. The transformation in the nature of parliamentary selection meant that contests were better planned and more vigorously pursued than ever before. Whatever the attitudes of the participants, whether the old mixture of social aspiration and civic duty or the new unalloyed drive for political power and personal interest, candidates engaging in electoral contests now acted purposefully. Thomas Papillon was a man of honor and principle who conducted an incomparably scrupulous campaign. His concern for the town's welfare was paramount, his desire for its unity publicly attested. Yet never once did he consider giving way in the competition. "I will not desist or lay down on any account, but await the issue which God in his providence shall give."[1] Admiral Sir Edward Spragge knew little of the town of Dover and less of its traditions of selection. He pursued his seat just as he pursued the Dutch squadrons against which he had made his reputation. He spared neither men nor money to keep the wind in his sails. Spragge entered his electoral contest as he entered battle – to achieve victory.[2]

The port of Dover, one of the ancient Cinque Ports, was dominated by its castle and its pier, physical reminders of its role in military and naval affairs. After the Restoration these twin protuberances were nominally under the government of James, Duke of York, lord warden of the Cinque Ports and lord admiral. The lieutenant governor of the castle was the warden's direct representative in the ports; the burgeoning bu-

[1] Kent Archive Office, Papillon Papers, U1015/020/19; *Dictionary of National Biography*, under the entry "Papillon."
[2] B. D. Henning, ed., *House of Commons 1660–90*, III, 468–69.

reaucrats who administered the fleet were his minions at the admiralty. Trade and war, especially naval encounters with the Dutch, brought prosperity to Dover. Townsmen engaged in producing, packaging, or purveying stores and provisions flourished. Nor was there any shortage of merchants or craftsmen in a port which, throughout the seventeenth century, was a haven for Protestant refugees. Dover was the point of entry for Huguenots and Walloons, even if they passed on to London, and a settled community to which they could return in search of business and cultural connections.[3]

Dover's parliamentary representatives reflected the influence of their special government. The town traditionally granted a nomination to the lord warden, and the lord warden traditionally nominated the lieutenant governor of the castle. Their other seat was used, after the Restoration, to amalgamate naval dependence with religious independence in the choice of members of the Montague family. In 1661 the Duke of York nominated Sir Francis Vincent, lieutenant governor of the castle, and the town paired him with George Montague, cousin of the Earl of Sandwich, Dover's representative at the convention of 1660.[4] But when Vincent died in 1670, the lieutenant governor of the castle, Colonel John Strode, could not replace him, for he already occupied a seat in the Commons.

This presented difficulties all around. The vacant place was the one in the gift of the lord warden, who would be reluctant to surrender his claim to a nomination. Yet this particular seat was normally reserved for the lieutenant governor of the castle, who because he was resident at Dover could most easily make his interest there. He too was jealous of his privilege. To complicate matters further, Sandwich's heir, Lord Hinchingbrooke, had now come of age, and the Earl was anxious that he gain some parliamentary experience. The competing claims of warden, lieutenant governor, and admiral were ultimately compromised. The three agreed that Hinchingbrooke would have the warden's endorsement, but that the Duke of York would not propose another nominee should there be a subsequent by-election.[5]

Against Hinchingbrooke stood Sir Arnold Braemes, who had repre-

---

[3] The standard histories are S. P. H. Statham, *History of the Castle, Town, and Port of Dover* (1899) and J. Bavington Jones, *Annals of Dover* (1916). Neither is wholly reliable for the political events narrated here.

[4] B. D. Henning, ed., *House of Commons 1660–90*, I, 493–95.

[5] Kent A.O., U1015/020/29. It is not known whether this engagement was solicited by the town, uncertain about the precedents for nominations to vacated places, or by Strode, unhappy at not being able to name a candidate who might act as caretaker for his own interests. The compromise may well have been that only one Montague would stand at the next general election.

sented the town in 1660. Their competition created conflicts of loyalty as well as opposition. Braemes's base of support was the castle, the Anglican church, and the customs office. Yet he was not the "Crown's" candidate. Hinchingbrooke appealed to the admiralty interest, though despite his nomination by the Duke of York he found his greatest strength among the town's Protestant dissenters.[6] Divisions were sharpened by a raucous mayoral election that preceded the contest for the parliamentary seat. A snap election, in which nominations reverted back to a procedure abandoned in 1644, embittered town politics.[7] The Privy Council was forced to intervene, and the two parliamentary candidates were inevitably drawn into the fray. Braemes supported John Carlisle, clerk of the passage, an outspoken supporter of enforcing religious uniformity within the town. Hinchingbrooke threw his weight behind Richard Barley, a man whose religious dissent was coupled to a rigid and prickly personality. In the end, Hinchingbrooke triumphed. Barley became mayor and Braemes was defeated by 130 voices to 69.[8]

The 1670 elections, both mayoral and parliamentary, left a bitter legacy. "The new mayor winks at all conventicles and at the law and charters too," Carlisle reported to Secretary Williamson. "We are a sad divided people." "Let Sir Arnold's party (as we are forced to distinguish them) do their worst; we fear them not," one of the victualling clerks

---

[6] There was more than a little confusion about Hinchingbrooke's candidacy, and this can best be seen in the attitude of John Carlisle. When Hinchingbrooke was first proposed, Carlisle enthusiastically endorsed him in order to please the Earl of Sandwich. *Calendar of State Papers Domestic Series 1670*, p. 288. As the campaign progressed and Hinchingbrooke became entangled with Carlisle's mayoral opponent, he switched to Braemes. But first he checked with Secretary Williamson about the attitude of the Court: "Does the Court desire that Lord Hinchingbrooke should be burgess for Dover or is Sir Arnold Braemes looked on as a fit person?" *Calendar of State Papers Domestic Series 1670*, p. 494. As always, the "Court" was not a monolith.

[7] The procedural dispute was complex. Until 1644 the mayor and jurats had nominated candidates for the freemen to select. The system appears to have been rotational, in the sense that both of those nominated would eventually be selected. Sitting mayors were frequently reselected for a second term. In 1644 the freemen were given the right to participate in nomination, presumably naming the candidate who was not the sitting mayor. In 1664 the old system was reinstituted; in 1667 the new system was restored. In 1670 Mayor Matson secured Carlisle's nomination by unilaterally reviving the restricted policy. Barley protested, and two separate elections were held. The Privy Council ordered a return to the restrictive procedure but also opted for a new election with Barley as a candidate. Why Matson wanted to exclude Barley is unclear. Matson was a dissenter and subsequently one of Papillon's supporters. *Calendar of State Papers Domestic Series 1670*, pp. 411, 445.

[8] Hinchingbrooke's support of Barley is recorded by Carlisle. *Calendar of State Papers Domestic Series 1671*, p. 486. The Dover poll was "Hinchingbrooke 130, Braemes 69 with 31 absent, 16 neutral: total electorate 246." Kent A.O., U1015/021.

boasted to Thomas Papillon.[9] But the divisions in the town were not simply between conformists and dissenters. Dissent in a town like Dover took too many forms to be united by a common enemy. The fissures between Presbyterians and sectaries had never been bridged, while the existence of at least two licensed foreign congregations further complicated alliances. So did the mayoralty of Richard Barley, punctuated as it was by the selective enforcement of the Conventicle Act.[10] In the two years in which he held office Barley succeeded in alienating both his own supporters and his potential allies: "The ridiculous carriage of late of Mr Barley, the present mayor, hath made him more enemies that he had before."[11] By the summer of 1672, it was already clear than opposition to Barley would coalesce around another group of dissenters rather than around Carlisle and the churchmen.

The death of the Earl of Sandwich in May 1672 brought these conflicts to a head. Hinchingbrooke now took his place in the Lords and the seat he had briefly held was again vacant. Preparations were made immediately to find a successor. Within weeks, a group of Dover dissenters had pitched upon Thomas Papillon, victualler of the Navy. A Huguenot descendant with a reputation for godliness, Papillon had purchased the neighboring estate of Acrise with the profits of trade and office.[12] With his local, naval, and religious appeal, Papillon was more than a match for Arnold Braemes. Indeed, it was quickly apparent that Braemes would not enter the contest and that Papillon's rival would be the native-born Abraham Jacob, "a merchant of good esteem, a good estate near the town, intends to reside here, a commissioner of Dover Harbor."[13] Jacob's family, prominent Dover Huguenots, were in the vanguard of the opposition to Mayor Barley. At first, Jacob appeared a more powerful rival than the candidate produced by the lieutenant governor of the castle, Admiral Sir Edward Spragge. Spragge was an outsider backed by Strode to defend the castle interest. He was also a naval hero with considerable influence at Court, who claimed approval for his candidacy from both the King and the Duke of York. But the lord warden, true to his word, had not nominated Spragge and had also expressed his approval of Papillon's candidacy.[14]

Spragge's campaign, directed by Strode, mixed blackmail and blan-

[9] *Calendar of State Papers Domestic Series 1671*, p. 15. Kent A.O., U1015/020/3.
[10] To be fair, Barley was hauled before the council for his initial hesitancy in enforcing the act. Carlisle reported with glee the closure of Anabaptist and Presbyterian houses of worship. *Calendar of State Papers Domestic Series 1671*, pp. 65–6.
[11] Kent A.O., U1015/020/17.
[12] A. F. W. Papillon, *Memoirs of Thomas Papillon, London Merchant* (1887).
[13] Kent A.O., U1015/020/4.
[14] Kent A.O., U1015/020/8; U1015/020/29.

dishment. Those who owed their livelihoods to the fleet – pilots and seamen especially – were put on notice for their jobs, while beer and ale flowed from the town's numerous taverns.[15] Jacob was equally open-handed in treating freemen ("tis reported that £1,500 or £2,000 will be spent"), for the prize he sought included the mayoralty for his cousin Richard.[16] In the three-cornered contest for Parliament he was likely to show last, but in a two-horse race for the mayoralty, particularly against the despised Barley, the family could easily win. A new mayor might realign the loyalties of the town's dissenters and induce Papillon to withdraw. Nevertheless, rumors circulated that Jacob would "engage his party to join with Sir Edward (he inbursing Mr Jacob the money he is out)."[17]

These two elements of the campaign, the free flow of ale and the imminent mayoral contest, were both liabilities for Papillon. Like everything else he did, his candidacy was an undertaking of principle. "I have no other design than to do good to the town." He entered the competition on invitation, but full of "fears and perplexities of spirit...lest something of evil might be occasioned from my endeavors and intentions of good."[18] The sight of townsmen at alehouses, idle or incapacitated, sickened his closest friends in Dover. Though their complaints raised tactical issues – "if the common sort of your party be not kept...many of them may be drawn into the other parties" – these were no match for moral ones.[19] Affording such men entertainment in competition with Spragge and Jacob made him equally guilty of their debauchery. Papillon was uncompromising. "I am convinced unlawful ways are not to be used, though for the obtaining just and lawful ends. I cannot but think such things unlawful that occasion persons to neglect their families and callings to spend their time in tippling houses." Instead of threats, Papillon proposed to disburse £50 "to such of the poor who are freemen or the widows and children of freemen for buying coals and corn...or necessaries to set them on work." If there was to be a competition for spending, let it be for charity "to turn the tide of expense from evil to good."[20]

Papillon was equally high-minded about the mayoralty. Barley's two

---

[15] "The governor says he is sure all the pilots and seamen will be for him and that Sir Edward will not spare for cost therein." Kent A.O., U1015/O20/8.

[16] Kent A.O., U1015/O20/11.

[17] Kent A.O., U1015/O20/21.

[18] Kent A.O., U1015/O20/23A.

[19] Kent A.O., U1015/O20/13. Wivell informed Papillon bluntly enough: "As you have most of all the sober, religious interest in the town, yet their number is short (more the pity) of the common sort, the rest of your number."

[20] Kent A.O., U1015/O20/23A.

terms had deeply divided the "sober, religious interest in the town." His determination to seek a third year strained the coalition of Papillon supporters past the breaking point. "He is as fond of being mayor again as a child is of a rattle; and the town as weary of him."[21] Papillon's managers were faced with an impractical choice: to convince Barley to yield his nomination to Abraham Stocks, a plea that had already gone unheeded, or to convince their supporters to back Barley as the lesser of evils, an argument never very compelling among dissenters. Both failed. With support from churchmen, from his own coreligionists, and from those who deserted Papillon, Captain Richard Jacob was chosen mayor. The result in no way lessened Papillon's determination to contest the parliamentary seat. He believed that "it is too much for one family to engross all."[22] But to one of his cast of mind, Jacob's election posed a different problem, that of opposing constituted authority. Papillon would allow no doubt about his intention to cooperate with Jacob. Immediately after the result was known, he wrote to his followers pledging unqualified support for the new regime. "Since Providence hath called him to the place, I wish him joy therein . . . that he may be an instrument of good to the town and answer the ends of magistracy."[23]

Papillon might well have been concerned about magistracy, for he now had both the lieutentant governor and the mayor against him. Neither were likely to match his scruples. Strode's tactics were to pressure the supporters of both Papillon and Jacob into assisting Spragge. The petty officials who abounded on the docks were most vulnerable. Strode had no hesitation about approaching Edward Wivell, clerk of the victualling office and Papillon's campaign agent: "The governor fell upon me with so many high words about this business . . . some touching yourself as well as me." It is not known what combination of inducements and intimidation finally led to Wivell's defection, but he was not the only supporter drawn away.[24] Charles Valley was one of the pier dwellers and the town's chief brewer. With his neighbor Henry Teddeman he was thought to command "between thirty and forty votes in their clear account."[25] Valley was owed money on a contract that could be collected more easily in London than in Dover. Initially he asked Papillon to expedite payment, but after Jacob, another London merchant, entered the race, he demanded that the bills be bought outright. "Mr Jacob has

[21] Kent A.O., U1015/020/17.
[22] Kent A.O., U1015/020/18.
[23] Kent A.O., U1015/020/19.
[24] Kent A.O., U1015/020/14; U1015/020/20. Wivell's defection is a shadowy business. See U1015/020/29.
[25] Kent A.O., U1015/020/6.

offered to pay the money upon the bills if he would bring over what party he had to [Jacob's] side." Papillon contemptuously refused the same offer: "That were to buy men's votes, which I do think unlawful and not to be countenanced."[26]

This thinning of ranks became a more serious matter when Abraham Jacob joined forces with Sir Edward Spragge. The alliance was logical enough once the mayoralty had been settled. It is quite clear that the Jacobs saw themselves involved in a local power struggle in which they could hold the balance between the castle interest and the extreme dissenters. It was the latter that were most threatening in local affairs. Papillon's election as M.P., certain if Spragge and Jacob divided their common support, would only strengthen the opposition. Thus Abraham Jacob's resignation of his interest to Spragge may have been a quid pro quo for castle assistance in the mayoral election. Once the alliance was cemented, Captain Richard Jacob had as much at risk as did Spragge. He assumed responsibility for persuading the neutral and the vulnerable. His son Robert prowled the docks reminding laborers of the press and craftsmen of their contracts. His daughter Elizabeth raised the issue of licenses with innkeepers.[27] The close-fisted persuasions of the Jacobs were softened by Spragge's open-handed approach. Besides the money which he spent freely in town, it was noised about that Sir Edward would contribute £300 to the town and £500 toward the creation of a wet dock.[28]

These exertions buoyed Spragge's numbers considerably, but he had a great distance to go. Lord Hinchingbrooke had held a majority of over sixty when he defeated Arnold Braemes in 1670, and the intensity of this campaign, now entering its sixth month, ensured a larger turnout than before. In September Wivell had estimated that Papillon could count on thirty votes more than his competitors combined, and the movement on the margins since then had been insubstantial.[29] Papillon entered the new year with a comfortable lead and with the knowledge that Lord Chancellor Shaftesbury had issued the election writs in advance of the new parliamentary session. His only remaining fear concerned the hostility of Mayor Jacob toward his supporters. He tackled the subject

[26] Kent A.O., U1015/020/21; U1015/020/23A. See also the interrogatories prepared for the case before the Committee of Elections. U1015/023/28A.

[27] Kent A.O., U1015/023/28B. On the day before the election Papillon informed his wife that "the mayor sent for all the pilots and told them what a man Sir Edward Spragge was and that they should vote for him." A. F. W. Papillon, *Memoirs of Thomas Papillon* (1887), p. 125.

[28] Kent A.O., U1015/023/13.

[29] Kent A.O., U1015/020/21. "We are still the major party by about thirty votes, as we reckon."

forthrightly in a letter to the mayor. Papillon set out his qualifications, his support, and his intentions to do the town's service. He then implored that "you would see that the election when it shall be may be carried with all fairness and indifferency both in respect to time of notice, votes, and returns," concluding less than candidly, "which every man that knows Captain Jacob gives me assurance I shall not need in the least to doubt."[30]

In fact, by the middle of January 1673 it was widely held that Strode and Jacob would deprive Papillon of the seat by fair means or foul. All along Spragge had asserted that "if he got a return he would do well enough."[31] Until then their strategy had centered upon building a majority among the nearly 250 freemen. When this failed they began to pursue more circuitous routes. The least tortuous was to attempt to hold the election on a corporation franchise where the balance of votes was closer and the inducements to corporate welfare more potent. There had always been suspicions that this was what Strode intended: "Some are yet of the opinion that the governor's game yet aimed at is the getting the old decree established by King and Council for electing the burgesses by mayor, jurats, and common council."[32] But even with allies in the committee of privileges, it would be difficult to defend a newly constricted franchise, especially if sanctioned by "King and Council." If a way was to be found around the earnest Papillon, it would be better for it to avoid a constricted franchise. Jacob, Strode, and Spragge had somehow to turn a majority among the corporation into a majority among the freemen.

On January 31, 1673, a special meeting of the corporation was hastily called by Mayor Jacob. At such short notice not all members could attend, and some whose summonses had mysteriously failed to reach them were locked out after proceedings had begun. The meeting, too, was hurried, prayers being neglected and the reading of the traditional decrees dispensed with.[33] Only two items of business were to be transacted – the repeal of the by-law that required freemen by purchase to pay no less than £10 for their privileges, and the swearing in of over fifty new freemen gratis.[34] The meeting did not go smoothly, though Mayor Jacob was able to stifle debate on the repeal of the by-law and

---

[30] Kent A.O., U1015/020/28.
[31] Kent A.O., U1015/020/21.
[32] Kent A.O., U1015/020/11.
[33] Kent A.O., U1015/023/26; U1015/023/14. "The mayor at the said meeting refused to have prayers made or the Acts for behavior and regulating the proceedings in such assemblies read."
[34] Kent A.O., U1015/023/14.

turn away a number of townsmen who offered themselves as candidates for freemanship. The fifty-three new members had all been hand-picked, and they had all agreed to give their votes for Sir Edward Spragge.[35]

The scene on election day, February 1, would have been less dramatic but for Dover's method of selecting members to Parliament. "Not, as upon a heath that the most in show carry it, or the greater voice hath the day, but here the whole roll of freemen are called, one after another, present or absent."[36] The roll was called, the most ancient first, and thus the newly created freemen all waited together until the end. Before their turn came, 137 votes had been recorded for Thomas Papillon and 106 for Sir Edward Spragge. "No faggots, No faggots, Mr Papillon is fairly chosen," came the cry. But the mayor and lieutenant governor would brook no opposition. Strode demanded order, threatening to bring troops from the castle to ensure the completion of the roll call. Fifty-three names remained, "47 appeared and every one voted for Sir Edward Spragge."[37]

II

The most interesting analysis of the Dover election came from Lawson Carlisle, son of the clerk of the passage. While Papillon's supporters began the laborious process of preparing their case for the Committee of Elections, Carlisle wrote to Secretary Williamson: "Yesterday morning we had a very fair choice for a burgess and Sir Edward Spragge has carried the day by forty votes. But if my father and the rest of the jurats and common council men had not thought to have made about fifty freemen the day before the election, the fanatic party had been too much for us, but we hope to have done them down."[38] As communities became divided over local and national issues, over religion and politics, the traditional ideas about unity and unanimity were placed under severe strain. One of the principal forces making for contests and for the unscrupulous measures taken to win them was the sharpening of political divisions within the nation. These existed at many levels and often combined with local, familial, and personal disputes. Even after the Restoration it was rare for an electoral contest to be dominated by purely

[35] Kent A.O., U1015/023/15. "To admit freemen only such as would vote for Sir Edward Spragge." Some documents refer to 53 freemen, others to 52.
[36] Kent A.O., U1015/021.
[37] Kent A.O., U1015/023/26; U1015/023/13. "Faggots is a title there usually given to such as are hired to supply false musters."
[38] *Calendar of State Papers Domestic Series 1672–73*, p. 510.

ideological issues. But ideological issues were now in evidence and were openly espoused.

The impact of ideology upon the social life of local communities remains a subject shrouded in mystery. At the national level we can easily identify ideological issues, their proponents and opponents, and the structures through which they made themselves felt. Reading the issues of the *Protestant* or the *Domestick Intelligencer* allows us to draw distinct lines about the momentous political events of the day. Unlike any others in the seventeenth century, the parliaments of 1679 and 1681 can be said to have been elected when a single political issue dominated national affairs. This was to have a decisive impact upon both the electoral process and upon Parliament itself. But decisive is not the same as pervasive, and we must appreciate that even in an atmosphere as supercharged as the Exclusion Crisis, ideological issues were only one of a number of factors at work in parliamentary selections.

Indeed, the politicization of the process derived from a number of distinct developments. First, of course, was the perpetuation of religious divisions within communities. As at Dover, alignments could be confused, and it was usually only particular minorities whose behavior could be predicted. But known religious affiliations became a means of identifying candidates, either for support or opposition, and they must have been so obvious in small communities that they went unremarked. The bishop of Bristol, who in the early seventeenth century might have had the obligation of composing a contest, in the late seventeenth century worked to encourage one: "[Mr Moore] whose dissenting principles are as evident as the other's loyalty . . . so threaten[s] the interest of our King and Church (considering his interest [is] made by the Earl of Shaftesbury) that I cannot . . . suffer the design to pass without opposition."[39] Candidates were frequently labeled, accurately or not, as "fanatics" by their opponents or "honest" by their supporters. The second Duke of Albemarle condemned Sir William Wiseman, who "corresponded underhand with Mr. Mildmay and the rest of the fanatics" in Essex.[40] A group of Marlborough's dissenting burgesses defined their candidate as "discreet, moderate and pious."[41] Sir John Guise divided the freeholders of Gloucestershire along religious lines in analyzing the 1685 contest: "At this election the protestant interest was undoubtedly the strongest."[42]

A second feature in politicizing elections was the identification of candidates with national personalities. This was not only the case when

[39] W. D. Christie, *The Life of the Earl of Shaftesbury* (1871), II, 218.
[40] British Library, Egerton Mss., 3331, fol. 96.
[41] British Library, Additional Mss., 32,324, fol. 75.
[42] Sir John Guise, *Memoirs of the House of Guise*, pp. 134–35.

nominees were associated with unpopular patrons, but more generally when they were linked to a political figure who was out of favor in the community. Edward Verney believed that Lord Norris had lost his influence "for stickling so highly for my Lord Treasurer in so much that at Oxford the people hooted him out of town crying 'no Lord Treasurer, no Papist.'"[43] His brother John told a similar story of Sir John Werden: "He lost his election at Reigate; not that they had any dislike to him, but they said because he was secretary to the Duke and because he voted in the last parliament for his master's continuance in the Lord's House."[44] By the late 1670s this could, on occasion, simply be identification with the court itself. By 1685 it could be identification with the opposition, as Sir William Leveson Gower discovered: "There are reports spread at the Court that reflect on you in promoting elections of such as are not principled to contribute [to] the supporting [of] his Majesty and Crown."[45]

Finally, elections were now influenced by the ideological divisions that were coming to be identified by the labels Whig and Tory. Elections to the parliaments of 1679 and 1681 took place in the fervent political atmosphere of the Popish Plot and Exclusion Crisis. At Westminster, Sir William Waller "set up so late and treated so little that most thought it imprudent. But though at first [his] number seemed a cloud no bigger than a man's hand, before night it covered the whole heavens. So great is the merit of priest catching, and so little the credit of a courtier among the mobile."[46] In Cheshire, the 1681 election was the first in which party tactics were used, including canvassing by one candidate among the tenants of another.[47] It was not until 1685 that such tactics appeared in Northamptonshire, prompting Sir Roger Norwich to declaim against "the faithless and untoward generation of viperous Whigs."[48] The Nottinghamshire county election in 1685 ritualized ideological division: "There was one thing remarkable ... lengthways upon a long pole carried at the end of which was a black box and a great piece of parchment like a banner, upon which was writ in large character – 'No Black Box, no bill of exclusion, no association.' After the election was over the box

---

[43]   British Library, M 636/32. Edward Verney to John Verney, February 20, 1679.
[44]   British Library, M 636/32. John Verney to Sir Ralph Verney, February 17, 1679.
[45]   Historical Manuscripts Commission Reports, *5th Report* (Manuscripts of the Duke of Sutherland), p. 186.
[46]   Historical Manuscripts Commission Reports, *13th Report*, Appendix VI (Manuscripts of Sir William Fitzherbert), p. 13.
[47]   *Victoria County History of Cheshire*, II, 116. Lord Cholmondeley was so offended by this that he described it as "a thing so treacherous and base that he did not think [Cotton] had so little of a gentleman in him."
[48]   Northamptonshire Record Office, Isham Correspondence, IC 1383.

and the parchment were burnt in New Market place before all the people."[49] In 1689 it was the issue of the Association that dominated the Kent election. Although the county gentry were loath to have a contest – much to the chagrin of Sir Edward Dering – they insisted that Sir William Twysden take the Kentish oath. When he refused, the pairing he had made with Sir John Knatchbull was dissolved.[50]

As always with ideological issues, it is easy both to underestimate their presence and to overestimate their effect. The London publication of lists of the "worthy" and the "vile," of supporters of the Duke and exclusionists, makes it entirely possible that these were frames of reference at elections about which no comment was necessary. It is, in fact, surprising that there was so little overt labeling of candidates after 1679. But we must continue to guard against the temptation to connect what individuals did at Westminster with their election in the localities. There were too many communities that returned both supporters and opponents of Exclusion to "back-project" ideology into their choices. Not even the behavior of courtiers or those brought in by Court patronage was wholly predictable. Sir Thomas Littleton sat for Yarmouth in the Isle of Wight at the behest of Sir Robert Holmes in 1681. Yet "great Littleton" proposed a regency of William of Orange to follow Charles II's death.[51] Sir Charles Sedley, perhaps observing so many careers advanced without regard to ideological niceties, believed that Whigs and Tories were "much of the same stuff at bottom, since they are so easily converted one into another: I mean self-interest."[52] Certainly there were many late seventeenth-century illustrations of the principle that politics makes strange bedfellows.

Throughout the Revolution the town of Northampton displayed unflagging zeal for the parliamentary cause. It was a vital garrison during the civil wars and remained a stronghold of Puritan enthusiasm during the 1650s. It retained its right to return a member to Parliament under the Instrument of Government, and its choices in 1654 and 1656 were unexceptionable at a time when many others were not. Northampton traditionally returned its recorder and, with the corporation firmly in the hands of its parliamentarian leaders, it did so again in 1660. But the return of Francis Harvey, a leader of "the sober and discreet party of the town," was challenged by one of the town's disaffected Presbyterians. Though the Presbyterians and the "sober and discreet" citizens had

[49]   Althrope House, Spencer Mss., John Millington to Lord Halifax, March 23, 1685. I am grateful to J. P. Ferris for a copy of a transcript of this letter.
[50]   British Library, Additional Mss., 33,923, fols. 469–70.
[51]   B. D. Henning, ed., *The House of Commons 1660–1690*, II, 751.
[52]   Ibid., III, 410.

more in common with each other than with those who were likely to gain power after the Convention did its work, the contest led to a disputed election in which the corporation's exclusive franchise was overturned. Corporate leaders immediately set out to restore their privileges, but both the 1661 general election and a 1662 by-election were contested among the town's residents.[53] This last contest, between Sir William Dudley, county sheriff in 1661, and Sir James Langham, a Presbyterian benefactor who had represented the town in 1659, was fought when the lines between conformity and dissent were beginning to harden. Fragmentary evidence suggests a fierce but equal struggle that was ultimately declared void by the Committee of Elections. A new writ was ordered for 1663.[54]

In the interim the governors of Northampton were subjected to the rigors of the Corporation Act. A wholesale purge of town leaders took place under the careful scrutiny of Sir William Dudley, who had John Brayfield installed as mayor.[55] The wrenching choice between loyalty to Crown and loyalty to conscience divided Northampton's governors. While many were driven out of office, others conformed and pledged their voices to Sir William Dudley in the upcoming parliamentary selection.[56] Sir James Langham's decision not to pursue the seat seemed to ensure Dudley his place. With the governing body compliant, and without apparent opposition, there was every reason to revive the claims for the statutory corporation franchise, and Dudley and Mayor Brayfield made plans to conduct the selection on that basis.

While these preparations proceeded in town, Sir James Langham sought a candidate to oppose Dudley. His motives blended piety with pique and remain difficult to disentangle. He was undoubtedly concerned to protect his ousted supporters from further retribution, but he was equally chagrined at seeing his family's long-standing interests in the town set aside. He was also canny enough to realize that only a candidate untainted by political or religious extremism could capture a sufficient

---

[53] Ibid., I, 339.

[54] *Journals of the House of Commons*, VIII, 436.

[55] C. A. Markham and J. C. Cox, *The Records of the Borough of Northampton* (1897), I, 138. Sir James Langham was prepared to attest that after the election in 1662 Dudley had boasted "that there would be no new election until he had a mayor that would return whom he would have." Northamptonshire Record Office, Finch–Hatton Papers, FH 1755.

[56] It must be remembered that many "purges" of corporations resulted from individuals' refusing to take oaths rather than from the ejection of particular members on specific charges. There appears to have been a little of both at Northampton. Rainsford, the sitting M.P., who had strong contacts among the godly in town, had given his interest over to Dudley, and Lord Montague feared that most of Langham's party was already pledged. British Library, Add. Mss., 29,551, fols. 1, 5.

number of the town's conformists from Dudley. The first of the many ironies of this election was that in order to express his ideological opposition, Langham sought a candidate with views indistinguishable from those of Sir William Dudley. He found Christopher Hatton.[57]

Hatton entered the Northampton by-election with no other motive than to secure a seat in the House of Commons. Eldest son of Viscount Hatton, his family was well connected within the county, and both father and son had impeccable royalist credentials. Hatton may have had his own inclination for the seat, but he needed Langham's local interest one way or the other. To that he added the traditional means of canvassing, gaining nominations from the Duke of York, the Earl of Manchester, and his cousin Lord Montague, as well as the support of Richard Rainsford, the town's sitting M.P., should Dudley decide to withdraw. As Dudley and Hatton were cousins, this was not beyond possibility. Rainsford thought that "he being related to you . . . would not give your pretensions any opposition."[58] In this case, however, the ties of blood were well diluted by a decade-old dispute between Sir William and Hatton's mother over an inheritance.[59] When Dudley was approached to stand down, it was proposed as a way "to make reparation . . . and renew the ancient friendship between your families."[60] But Dudley had built his interest too carefully to be bought off so cheaply. He offered Hatton his support for the seat that the elderly Rainsford, recently dispatched to Ireland, might soon vacate. Whatever personal animus he held toward Langham's recalcitrant supporters, he did not identify Hatton with their views.

Dudley had the support of the corporation, of Rainsford, and of a segment of former Langham supporters. He had polled nearly equal with Langham in the previous election, and he might have been expected to carry the seat in either franchise except for the fact that the purge of the corporation bitterly divided the town. Along with Langham, a cadre of displaced religious enthusiasts sought a champion to oppose Dudley. They fixed upon Hatton like lampreys. "Your eminent worth and goodness having kindled in us an immortal fire and zeal for your honor, we,

---

[57] That Langham sought out Hatton is based on the evidence of Viscount Hatton as well as on Dudley's colored account. Northamptonshire R.O., FH 4084; British Library, Add. Mss., 29,551, fol. 8.

[58] British Library, Add. Mss., 29,551, fol. 1.

[59] The exact nature of the dispute remains obscure. It involved the inheritance of Dudley's sisters, Lady Hatton's nieces, and land purchases of Lord Montague. It began after the death of Dudley's father in 1652 and was still seething in 1660. See letters under those dates in British Library, Add. Mss., 29,550.

[60] British Library, Add. Mss., 29,551, fol. 8.

your vessels shall most religiously perpetuate it."[61] Led by Salathiel Lovell, they attempted to draw Hatton into town affairs, informing him of the machinations of Dudley and Mayor Brayfield and assuring him of a majority among the town residents. It is hard to fathom what Hatton made of such appeals. He knew that the seat would entail a contest and probably a dispute in the Committee of Elections and that until both were resolved he needed the support that had coalesced around the ousted corporate leaders. But there is little reason to suppose that he harbored sympathy for dissent or took any actions to protect his vulnerable supporters other than what was necessary to secure his own election. The correspondence from Lovell was unsolicited and largely unanswered.[62] Hatton conducted his campaign from London.

The campaign centered around forcing Dudley and the mayor to hold an election on the enlarged franchise. Hatton's canvass of local gentry revealed that sharp practices might be expected. When the mayor was pressed to announce the day of election at county assizes – "so that such as were concerned in it might not be kept there in suspense" – he demurred. When notice finally was given "instead of publishing it to the town...he sent only to those of the House."[63] Lord Montague believed that Brayfield "will do anything that Sir William will have him," and such fears stirred Hatton's father to action.[64] The Viscount penned a remarkable letter in nomination of his son, who "wants not the value of the highest nor the esteem of the best." This he sent to Brayfield with a reminder of his own past services to the town and a promise to "contribute some considerable interest in return for your kindness." Viscount Hatton professed himself unable to credit rumors that the election "should be according to favor and compact," for he was "confident of your integrity." He was equally confident of "the consequences [that] would follow such an action... since I suppose you would firmly believe that my son would not tamely sit down with such an affront, nor want friends to show themselves."[65]

But Hatton's threat of the censure of the Commons, by no means an idle one in a town that had its mayor imprisoned for election irregularities, had been anticipated. Dudley had offered to bear the costs that

---

[61] Ibid., fol. 9.

[62] Ibid., fol. 12. Hatton had undoubtedly replied to one of Lovell's letters stating that he was concerned by the open support some leading dissenters were giving to his candidacy. Lovell replied that "who ere it was that informed you that the presence of Mr Francis Harvey might prejudice your proceedings they are very much mistaken."

[63] Northamptonshire R.O., FH 3497.

[64] British Library, Add. Mss., 29,551, fol. 5.

[65] Northamptonshire R.O., FH 4084.

might be incurred – as much as £2,000, it was alleged.[66] Moreover, the question of the franchise could only be settled by limiting the election to the corporation and then defending the action in law. Though the town had experienced three electoral disputes in two years, only the Convention Parliament had ruled explicitly on the franchise. Legal sentiment had shifted with the Restoration. The corporation, before its recomposition, had declared its intention to challenge the 1660 decision, another of the ironies facing its ousted members who were now organizing the populace.[67] The election of Dudley by a united corporation was an excellent case on which to make a stand, especially if Dudley were to absorb the costs.

Accordingly, Brayfield prepared both for the corporate election and for the opposition it would arouse. He sent notice of the receipt of the precept only to corporate members and designated the cramped quarters of the town hall as venue.[68] Anticipating the crowds that were likely to demand voices, he rounded up a sturdy contingent to serve as guards ("near forty desperate and loose persons ... [armed] with clubs full of iron spikes") both to escort the members of the corporation to the hall and to man the doors against intruders.[69] However extraordinary it was, and by the time the precept had been read Hatton supporters had gained entry to the lower hall at the cost of some hard knocks, Brayfield was presiding over an official meeting of the corporation. He was intent upon maintaining its dignity. After the precept was read, two aldermen who supported Hatton demanded "which way he would proceed to election, if by the House they would have nothing to do with it," while another of this company leaned out of the window to orchestrate a cry of "Hatton" from those below. Affronted, Brayfield dragged the indecorous intruder from his perch "and threatened to lay several by the heels when they spake of Mr Hatton's interest."[70] All the while he refused the demands of the commonalty for voices. Dudley was declared chosen and the precept sealed with his name.

---

[66]   The imprisoned mayor was John Twigden, now one of Hatton's supporters. Markham and Cox, *Records of Northampton*, II, 498. In Hatton's election petition it was claimed that Dudley had indemnified the mayor. Northamptonshire R.O., FH 1755.

[67]   Markham and Cox, *Records of Northampton*, II, 498. As always, the legal questions were complex. In a paper that Geoffrey Palmer had prepared when arguing a Short Parliament franchise case, it was attested that only towns like Northampton, which had statutory exceptions, could have a corporate franchise. Northamptonshire R.O., FH 1750.

[68]   Northamptonshire R.O., FH 1755.

[69]   Ibid.

[70]   Markham and Cox, *Records of Northampton*, II, 498; Northamptonshire R.O., FH 1754.

Outside the hall the crowd had continued to swell. Anticipation of the dispute had brought Sir George Burwell, Northamptonshire's sheriff, to town. His presence, first in the hall and then at the Market Cross, may have prevented a riot.[71] Hatton's followers, who had kept up their cry throughout the election of Dudley, now organized a counterelection, appointing a poll at the cross. Clerks were named and books set out, though supporters of only one candidate appeared. Four hundred names were enrolled for Hatton.[72] But try as they might, they could not persuade Sheriff Burwell to issue a double return. Salathiel Lovell importuned him for four hours without success, and Hatton was forced to fight his case in the Committee of Elections after Dudley was seated. He triumphed easily.[73]

The mixture of principle and opportunism that underlay this electoral contest exemplifies the ways in which ideology affected the process of parliamentary selection. Dudley, whose first campaign was made possible by the enlarged franchise, now wanted it restricted. Lovell and the ousted corporate leaders, who had pledged to restrict the franchise, now wanted it enlarged. The loyal corporation reluctantly refused the nominee of the Duke of York; the religious dissidents reluctantly embraced him. Factionalism propagated bewildering misalliances. After three contests in two years, the purge of the corporation had been intended to restore both the corporate franchise and unified selections. It is clear that compromises were made to maintain the positions of some who might have been purged and that the withdrawal of Langham, and perhaps that of Francis Harvey, from competition for parliamentary seats was part of the agreement. The intensity of feelings aroused both by Dudley and by the purge was the principal cause of the invitation to Hatton and of the contest that followed.

Like Dudley, Hatton was an outsider; but unlike his cousin he was uninvolved in the town's divisions. His strength as a candidate lay in his ability to attract support among the local conformists, who might protest the loss of their voices or the sudden changes in town affairs but who would not be drawn to a candidate associated with dissent. Indeed, there was never a suggestion that one of the local zealots, perhaps one of those who had remained inside the corporation, should stand against Dudley. Hatton was not a rallying point for dissidents and was never

[71] Northamptonshire R.O., FH 1755.
[72] Ibid. The sophistication that resulted from so many recent contests was apparent in the statement of Hatton's petitioners that they had taken votes "whose number amounts to above four hundred there being not above six hundred persons in the town that have votes."
[73] British Library, Add. Mss., 29,551, fol. 19.

presented as such. He accepted Langham's interest as necessary to build a majority, but he appealed to the corporation through local and national patrons. He acted as an independent agent committed to protecting neither the new franchise nor the "sober and discreet" citizens. The support he gathered was amalgamated by local discontents and personal attraction as well as by religious principle. No evidence suggests that Hatton valued one element more than another. He brought to the event little more than a determination to be elected – first by getting Dudley to withdraw, then by insisting on an open contest, and finally by a dispute at Westminster. He certainly did not scruple, in his election petition, to recall Mayor Brayfield's parliamentarian background, sending a man "at his own charge against the King at Worcester with horse, pistols, [and] money."[74] Such memories of the past must have been as chilling to Hatton's supporters as to his opponents.

III

As elections became more regular so did their procedures. The acceptance of contests as a common occurrence necessitated the transformation of the cumbersome methods by which they were conducted. Before the revolution, procedure was used as an obstacle to contests. The shout, the view, and the primitive arrangements for polling, like the Yorkshire undersheriff's notched stick, aided the process by which returning officers and magistrates effected composition. Logistical difficulties, long delays, and the longer deliberations of candidates and officials all worked to prevent divisive elections. While supporters were gradually moved from market cross to common field or the paraphernalia for clerks and overseers listlessly collected, tempers might cool or reason prevail. The engrained prejudice against the poll demanded even greater obstruction than that achieved in the preliminary stages of the contest. Disputes over the form of the poll, the qualifications of electors, and the manner in which they should be counted wore down all but the most persistent contenders. Given its objectives, the prerevolutionary system was not ineffective.

But it was not designed to adjudicate contests. Even in the early seventeenth century it was clear that few procedural safeguards existed to ensure an equitable resolution. Candidates were impotent in the face of hostile returning officers, and returning officers grew hostile in the face of contests. Not even primitive rules existed to guide them, as the frequent resort to the memories of community elders attests. There was,

---

[74]   Northamptonshire R.O., FH 1755.

presumably, no member of the corporation at Higham Ferrers who remembered the Short Parliament election when a contest occurred in 1679: "The choice of members till this election has always been unanimous so no contest has ever arisen over who has the right to vote."[75] Nor were precedents established in selections always useful in elections. The contention of the sheriff of York in 1628 that the city's members were traditionally declared within minutes of the reading of the writ could not be denied. "But to that it was replied that never before above two were in election."[76] While committees of elections were capable of judging matters of fact, they proved less able to establish guidelines, let alone principles of conduct. Sir Edward Coke's assertion of the inalienability of the franchise was less momentous in the absence of regulations for polling. If it was held that the poll should not be refused, there was no attempt made to establish its primacy. Resolutions based on the shout and the view remained valid and difficult to overturn. The decision in 1628 that a freeholder could not be compelled to give his name when swearing to the value of his estate demonstrates the continued distaste for resolving elections by polls.[77] Procedures as critical as the manner of giving voices, which the shrewd Sir Edward Phelips had hoped to exploit in 1614, were still unresolved at the Restoration.

Nor were procedural matters to be settled at the national level. As before, reform was ground between the upper stone of overzealousness and the nether stone of cautious practicality.[78] Rules to limit gift-giving and overspending could never compete with the expectations of the electorate: "We found it impossible to hope for a voice in this town if we stuck to the new order of the House of Commons and not to the old custom of England," Henry Saville informed his brother. "Nay, we were fain to double our reckonings."[79] Attempts to reintroduce residency or property requirements and to ban placemen never passed the House at all.[80] It was improbable, in any event, that the full House could have achieved significant procedural reform. Having mastered the patchwork of custom and regulation that governed their own choices, sitting members had little incentive to alter them. What zeal did exist was aimed at discouraging abuses rather than at discovering their causes. Fundamental

---

[75] A. N. Groom, "The Higham Ferrers Election in 1640," *Northamptonshire Past and Present*, 2 (1958); *Calendar of State Papers Domestic Series 1679*, p. 104.

[76] M. Keeler, M. Cole, and W. Bidwell, eds., *Proceedings in Parliament 1628*, III, 147.

[77] *C.J.*, I, 884; Ibid., II, 507.

[78] See the conservative bill proposed in 1628, with its saving clause that no new rule would overturn established custom. *Proceedings in Parliament 1628*, VI, 12–14.

[79] W. D. Cooper, ed., *Saville Correspondence*, p. 45.

[80] *Calendar of State Papers Domestic Series 1673–75*, p. 113; E. and A. Porritt, *The Unreformed House of Commons* (1903), I, 204–6.

reform involved a reconceptualization of the process of selection. To ensure equity among determined competitors, reform would have to perpetuate – indeed to sanction – the religious and political divisions that poisoned many contests. The single legislative achievement of the Cavalier Parliament in this regard, the 1667 act barring Catholics from membership in the House, showed how unpopular was the protection of minority rights.

Thus procedure was left to adapt to shifts in local attitudes and circumstances without interference from above. This makes the similarity of change all the more remarkable. By the end of the 1660s the electoral contest had taken shape throughout the nation as an integral part of the selection process. If the rules of contests continued to be refined, with local variations inevitably present, there was no longer any attempt to forestall competitive choices by procedural obstacles. The election became a more structured event, with nominations, speeches, and demonstrations of support. Candidates commonly appeared at their elections to address the electors, nominate tellers in polls, and agree on local customs or their variations. Both candidates and magistrates prepared to resolve contests by counting the electorate, and this gave rise to a variety of new methods. Efficiency increased with experience.

Above all, the poll triumphed. Once communities accepted contests, it was imperative that they ensure their equitable resolution. The shout and the view, so effective in minimizing the divisiveness of past elections, were rapidly becoming obsolete. After the Restoration it was almost a maxim that a poll could not be refused. In the summer of 1679 there was an obvious disparity of support among the Hampshire county contestants. "The court was adjourned to the field where the parties might divide and the sheriff judge upon the view...[but] a gentleman's son of the county demanded the poll." The winning candidate "carried it (as it appeared on the view) five to one."[81] The eclipse of the view was only natural once precise results were desired. An attempted view at Middlesex in 1681 was abandoned, "the numbers being equal so that it could not be decided." In fact, the leaders of the two sets of paired candidates were separated by over four hundred votes.[82]

No longer functional, the view and the shout became part of election ritual. "They had the best shouters that ever came to a field," the *Domestick Intelligencer* reported of the candidates at Yorkshire in 1679. "They were heard three long Yorkshire miles."[83] Particularly in the counties, elections took on distinctly military trappings, as the armed

[81] *The Domestick Intelligencer*, no. 18, September 5, 1679.
[82] B. D. Henning, ed., *House of Commons 1660–1690*, I, 308–9.
[83] *The Domestick Intelligencer*, no. 24, September 26, 1679.

forces that appeared in 1660 and 1661 were succeeded by militia companies and the uniformed officers of the Crown. Countless county contests began with the massing of mounted supporters outside town in preparation for a great troop through. Led by powerful noblemen, with the candidates in their midst, the relative sizes of rival companies were readily apparent. But the troop through was not utilized to determine majorities: It was a competition of style, much as the shout was one of enthusiasm. In Essex the contending sides at the 1679 contest entered Chelmsford separately. Colonel Henry Mildmay's supporters arrayed within sight of the town and swelled with the confluence of other groups of freeholders on horseback. "Lord Grey met the Colonel in a most sumptuous habit, with his lead horse in rich trappings."[84] Supporters of Hampden and Wharton paraded with flags and trumpets behind the Duke of Buckingham during their enforced perambulation of Buckinghamshire in 1679.[85] Once gathered together in courtyard or before town hall, the respective companies raised the cry of their candidates into a clamorous din. All of this occurred before the reading of the writ.

The organization of the election remained very much a local affair. The nomination of candidates was its most mysterious aspect; the few glimpses that survive reveal an informality bordering on serendipity. In boroughs, prospective candidates increasingly sent letters of intention, though there is no evidence that magistrates were compelled to accept them or to present the names to the electors. Indeed, far more letters of intent than letters of resignation survive in corporate archives, suggesting that common fame guided the conduct of officials in making nominations. This was certainly the case in county elections where candidates simply presented themselves on the day of choice. That such slackness did not result in free-for-alls rather than in the familiar three-cornered and two-sided contests suggests a self-regulating mechanism too basic to attract comment. In the general elections between 1661 and 1689 only two out of two hundred and forty county selections were made from among more than four candidates – the Middlesex contest in 1685, which had six, including the redoubtable Sir William Smith, who had polled three in 1679; and the Hampshire election in 1679, where the fifth candidate may have been named only because he demanded the poll.[86]

Once the candidates were declared, it only remained for the returning officer to number their supporters. Such a seemingly simple task was

[84] "Essex's Excellency or the Gallantry of the Freeholders of that County," 1679.
[85] "A Copy of a Letter from a Freeholder of Buckinghamshire," 1679.
[86] B. D. Henning, ed., *House of Commons 1660–90*, I, 308; *The Domestick Intelligencer*, no. 18, September 5, 1679.

fraught with difficulties. There is nothing inherently equitable about procedure. Like law, it struggles with the precedents of the past and the preferences of the present to achieve socially acceptable rules and regulations. To be fair, procedure must be seen to be fair. This was made all the more difficult when both returning officers and candidates were novices without experience of electoral contests. Indeed, there was rarely a fount of experience from which to draw. Each election posed its own problems. Contests with two pairs of contenders had a different procedural logic from those with three individuals. Three-cornered contests could be either open competitions, competitions between a pair of candidates and an outsider, or competitions for the second seat only. Each demanded distinct treatment. Meanwhile, problems of franchise and venue remained as complex as ever. The politicization of the Committee of Elections provided little comfort. Their decisions were made with one eye on the manner of choice and the other on the member chosen.[87]

Out of this thicket many paths could be followed. Occasionally, the smoothest was for the candidates and returning officers to agree among themselves on the procedures to be followed. A decade after the Committee of Elections closed Tamworth's franchise, the candidates in the 1679 contest agreed to open it by campaigning and polling among the inhabitants.[88] The agreement at Richmond, also about the franchise, was more complex, as the town used burgages to define participants. "That no widow should vote ... neither minor nor guardians could vote. That divided burgages could not be admitted to vote.... And it was also agreed that demolished burgages could not vote."[89] Prior to the convention of 1689 the two candidates at Wallingford concurred that "those only should be admitted who are charged to the church and poor."[90] At the Dorset by-election in 1677 the contest was so bitter that it was decided "by consent the sheriff is to make a double return and the end is left to the Committee of Elections."[91]

It was not only franchises that were settled in procedural agreements. The Richmond articles included the stipulation "that a poll ought to be demanded by the persons to be elected before 12 o'clock." At the Norfolk by-election in 1675 the contenders entered into a signed compact covering every detail of the poll, though there were later accusations that

[87] J. R. Jones, "Restoration Election Petitions," *Durham University Journal*, 53 (1961), pp. 49–57.
[88] D. G. Stuart, "Parliamentary History of the Borough of Tamworth, Staffordshire 1661–1837," unpublished M.A. thesis, London University (1958).
[89] C. Clarkson, *The History of Richmond* (1814), p. 117.
[90] B. D. Henning, ed., *House of Commons 1660–90*, I, 135.
[91] *Calendar of State Papers Domestic Series 1677–78*, p. 112.

a vital clause to prevent double voting was deliberately deleted in the final draft.[92] At Yorkshire, the failure of the sheriff and one of the candidates to agree on procedures actually prevented the continuation of a poll which was to be adjourned to eight sites within the county.[93]

The emergence of the peripatetic poll cut another swath through procedural complexities. Especially in large counties, the site of an election could provide an estimable advantage to a candidate resident nearby. The venue of the sheriff's court, though not fixed, was customary, and service industries had developed in its wake. These provided a vested interest in a stationary poll; but even in the largest urban areas resources were too sparse to meet the crush of thousands of freeholders who might be forced to endure several days of polling. As the idea that each freeholder should be allowed his individual voice gained ground, the venue of a single county town, however centrally located, became an inhibition rather than a convenience. Itinerant polls, adjourned from place to place within the county, first received the attention of the Committee of Elections in the Parliament of 1659. As usual, issues of equity and advantage commingled. At the contest in Cheshire, it was alleged that a majority in one venue was overturned by moving the poll to another: "After three days polling in the castle where Brooks carried it, the court was removed to Congleton where Bradshaw did outnumber him."[94] Initially, the Committee of Elections was inclined to rule such a procedure illegal on the grounds that the sheriff could then extend or terminate the poll at will. But it was quickly realized that if the sheriff could not move the venue of his court, he could not perform most of his legitimate functions.[95]

In fact, the peripatetic poll broadened participation by allowing more individuals to give voices. This was a further indication that consent was replacing assent in the selection process. After two days of polling at Leicester "the town being straitened of provisions, it was unanimously agreed by all the competitors that the High Sheriff should proceed to adjourn the court from hundred to hundred and poll the freeholders... within the respective hundred wherein they lived."[96] Buckingham elections were adjourned from town to town in 1679 and 1685, though this was as much a result of the administrative feud between Aylesbury and Buckingham as anything else.[97] Large northern counties like Yorkshire

[92] C. Clarkson, *The History of Richmond* (1814), p. 117; Historical Manuscripts Commission Reports, *6th Report*, (Paston Manuscripts), pp. 371–72.

[93] Leeds Central Library, Mexborough Manuscripts, R14/172c.

[94] British Library, Harleian Mss., 1829, fol. 20.

[95] J. T. Rutt, ed., *Thomas Burton's Diary*, IV, 430.

[96] Public Record Office, State Papers, 29/411 pt. 2/120. "The Case of the Gentry, Clergy, and Major part of other the Freeholders of the County of Leicester," 1679.

[97] The adjournment of the August 1679 election from Aylesbury to Buckingham so

and Lancashire adopted peripatetic polls, Yorkshire planning eight separate sites before the poll was abandoned.[98] In Derbyshire the 1685
election "began at Derby Thursday last and brake off... till Monday
night at Ashbourne and afterwards to Bakewell and Chesterfield." The
poll in Northamptonshire at the same election moved from the county
town to Dodford, Oundle, Rothwell and Brackley.[99]

If the peripatetic poll enlarged participation, it also delayed decisions.
The Northamptonshire election looked very much like the abuse that
the Committee of Elections had feared in 1659. On April 25 "they made
another effort at Dodford by polling about a score or two... but the
books were soon shut up and the court adjourned to the first of May."
After further delays, a count on May 4 was also adjourned. The writ
was not dated until May 12.[100] The great cost of prosecuting a dispute
as against defending one meant that contenders challenged every possible
development. "The poll began and continued not above a quarter of an
hour before a dispute arose about a freeholder... Afterwards many exceptions of that kind were taken... as enforced the mayor to stop the
poll until it was appeased." This raucous contest at Weymouth in 1667
took several days to conclude among an electorate of barely two
hundred.[101]

County polls could generally be expected to last for days. In 1685 the
Leicestershire election took three days and the Cheshire contest six.[102]
At Dorset, in 1677, the by-election also lasted several days: "They have
each lost it by voices two or three times, and send into the country for
fresh ones."[103] It is difficult to distinguish between deliberate and legitimate delays. By the 1660s poll books were commonplace. Durham,
first enfranchised in 1675 and thus an excellent guide to conventional
procedure after the Restoration, kept a poll book at every election until
no rival candidates appeared in 1685.[104] Enrolling the electorate could

infuriated the supporters of Hampden and Wharton that they camped in a field
outside town and endured a rainstorm rather than spend money in Buckingham,
"there being no reason that Buckingham should get anything by this intrigue."
British Library, M 636/33. William Grosvenor to John Verney, August 20, August
21, 1679.

[98] For Lancashire, B. D. Henning, ed., *House of Commons 1660–90*, I, 283–84; for
Yorkshire, Leeds Central Library, Mexborough Manuscripts, Mx/R14/172c.
[99] Huntington Library, Hastings Mss., HA 7744; Northamptonsire R.O., IC 1384,
1386.
[100] Northamptonshire R.O., IC 1384, 1386.
[101] J. Hutchins, *History and Antiquities of the County of Dorset*, II, 435. I owe this
reference to J. P. Ferris.
[102] *V. C. H. Cheshire*, II, 117–18; Huntington Library, HA 3976.
[103] *Calendar of State Papers Domestic Series 1677–78*, p. 106.
[104] Durham R.O., "Poll Books."

be a lengthy process. The August heat caused several suspensions of the Essex poll in 1679 "for the ease of the court."[105] The number of clerks and the methods they adopted could have a decisive effect. At Cambridgeshire the limitation to two polling stations prolonged the 1679 contest. At Abingdon a contest was shortened when the clerks accepted all names presented to them and compared them to the ratepayer books afterwards.[106] Amersham had both a "short poll" of scot and lot payers and a "long poll" of inhabitants.[107] The parameters of efficiency were wide: Newcastle's magistrates counted six hundred voters "from 8 in the morning to 7 at night" in 1659; Norfolk's clerks tallied six thousand in a slightly longer day twenty years later.[108]

The formalization of polling procedures, whether through prepoll agreements, a peripatetic court, or by the simple expedient of providing clerks, poll books, and "indifferent gentlemen . . . to methodize and order the proceedings" did not inhibit the creative talents of candidates and returning officers.[109] There was hardly a ploy that was not tried at least once. Tactics at elections were sharper than ever, and sometimes even benefitted from the regularization of the process. If itinerant polls could be spun out until the desired result was achieved, they could also be ordered so as to give one of the candidates an early lead, as happened at Buckinghamshire in 1685.[110] Scheduling offered other advantages, especially among borough magistrates whose choice of dates was not limited by the schedule of the county court. One Peterborough by-election was arranged to coincide with an important horse race, an event more attractive to a number of county peers.[111] Even the order in which votes were taken could be manipulated. A dispute in 1661 over whether to poll electors for one or two voices allowed the mayor of Hereford to adjourn a bitter contest and return the candidates he favored.[112] Blatant tampering with the roll of freemen, burgage splitting, and dubious disqualifications are but a sample of the underhanded devices engendered by the intensity of late seventeenth-century elections.

[105]   "Essex's Excellency or the Gallantry of the Freeholders of that County," 1679.
[106]   B. D. Henning, ed., *House of Commons 1660–90*, I, 129, 146.
[107]   *C. J.*, XV, 48.
[108]   C. H. Firth, ed., *The Clarke Papers*, III, 174; *Domestick Intelligencer*, no. 19, September 9, 1679. "The poll continued from 11 in the morning to between 12 and 1 at night."
[109]   "The Case of Mr William Cooke," 1679.
[110]   British Library, M 636/39. Sir Ralph Verney to John Verney, April 9, 1685.
[111]   "The election will certainly be on Thursday next, and the reason of the design is that that is the day the horse race is to be which will take away several interested persons, as my Lord Exeter, my Lord Westmoreland, and divers others." Northamptonshire R.O., F (M) C 409.
[112]   Richard Johnson, *The Ancient Customs of the City of Hereford* (1882), pp. 208–9.

One expects no less than the shrewdest electoral practices from the Earl of Danby. His efforts to keep his sons and his brother in the lower House, as well as his constant attention to government interest at by-elections in the 1670s, are well attested.[113] His heir, Viscount Latimer, entered Parliament without even standing for a seat that was resigned in his favor and continued his career by feeding the venal appetites of the Buckingham magistrates.[114] His younger son, Lord Dunblane, achieved his first success at the age of eighteen through the agency of his father and the Duke of Newcastle. The seat designed for him was at Berwick, where the military governors of the town normally nominated a candidate. But by-elections always confused patronage arrangements, and at Berwick it had been decided before 1677 that the next vacancy should go to the historian and local landowner John Rushworth.[115] Danby's intervention for his son ensured a contest. The town's recorder, Richard Stote, was given the task of managing what appeared to be a losing cause. "I find the opposite party still exceed us in votes," he reported a week before the election.[116] Though it was clear that Stote could count on the town's mayor – "there shall be nothing refused him that is legal" – it was also plain that a victory would have to be achieved at the poll.[117] After much deliberation and consultation, Stote conceived a winning plan, "though perhaps such things have been rarely if ever practiced." He would except against the participation of Dissenters, first taking the precaution of having them excommunicated, "to disallow many, yea most of their votes."[118] After eliminating over fifty of Rushworth's supporters in this manner, Stote reported to Danby that his son had been elected. "After a troublesome contest with an unreasonable party opposite to us, we found many of them stood excommunicate."[119]

At Aldeburgh, Sir John Holland managed his own election in 1661. A client of the Howards, he expected to occupy the Norfolk seat at Castle Rising that he had held twice before, but confused communications left him with a nomination in Suffolk instead. Holland was intent on being selected "considering the importunity of my friends, the con-

[113] J. R. Jones, "Restoration Election Petitions," *Durham University Journal*, 53 (1961), pp. 49–57.

[114] Latimer's election at Corfe Castle in 1677 came about when Anthony Ettrick resigned the seat in his favor. *Calendar of State Papers Domestic Series 1677–78*, p. 80. For Buckingham see Chapter 8 of this book.

[115] British Library, Egerton Mss., 3330, fol. 63.

[116] Ibid., fol. 81.

[117] Ibid., fol. 85.

[118] Ibid., fols. 81, 85.

[119] Ibid., fol. 87.

sequences of the issue of this parliament, and the noise that has been of my serving."[120] A fastidious candidate who left little to chance, Holland was vexed at having to travel out of his county and depend upon messengers to conduct his campaign. Shortly after his nomination, he rode down to Aldeburgh to fete the magistrates and declare his candidacy. A few hours in town were sufficient to devise the tactics necessary to defeat a local rival. "We have agreed ... to conceal the precept for the election until there comes a south wind to carry away the seamen upon whose votes we hear [our competitor] depends."[121] But the outgoing tide which swept away opposition also stranded Holland in Norfolk "very much troubled that I cannot attend in person at the time of your election as I resolved."[122] He was forced to deliver his directions curtly and in writing. "Find the temper of the freemen and if you discover the least danger I am confident you will judge it advisable to make new freemen in the morning."[123]

At Peterborough in 1666 the town bailiff combined the advantages of scheduling the election and of admitting and excluding electors in manipulating the result. His own position of authority in the unincorporated town was precariously poised between the competing claims of the dean and chapter and the local landowners. A parliamentary by-election was an opportunity for the dean and chapter, which temporarily held the upper hand, to gain an ally. Three candidates contested the vacancy created by the elevation of Charles Fane to the House of Lords. Each was well connected and powerfully supported. Sir Vere Fane was the previous member's brother; Lord Fitzwilliam was the successor to a traditionally influential family; and Edward Palmer was the son of the attorney general, a potentially useful friend in a jurisdictional dispute. Bailiff Palmer maintained secrecy about the date of the election, provided only three days' notice, and then fixed it upon the day of the county horse race.[124]

Nevertheless, over five hundred townsmen appeared to give voices. "The election was agreed to be made by the poll and three clerks for each pretender."[125] After the books were shut, it was reckoned that Lord

---

[120] Caroline Robbins, "Election Correspondence of Sir John Holland of Quidenham, 1661," *Norfolk Archaeology*, 30 (1952), p. 132.
[121] Ibid., p. 136.
[122] Ibid., p. 137.
[123] C. Robbins, "Election Correspondence of Sir John Holland," p. 137. It is worth noting that Holland had been a member of the Committee of Elections in 1660 and was to be a member in the sessions of the Parliament of 1661.
[124] Northamptonshire R.O., F (M) C 409.
[125] Northamptonshire R.O., F (M) M 1261.

Fitzwilliam, at the top of the poll, had two hundred and forty voices; Edward Palmer, at the bottom, had one hundred and thirty-eight.[126] The books were then compared to those of the town's ratepayers, and for this purpose two overseers of the poor were drafted into service. It was soon apparent that the books of rates had more than a few recent emendations. Palmer's supporters had been elevated to solvency, while Fitzwilliam's supporters had been lowered to indigence. By the end of the day, the bailiff declared Palmer elected.[127]

Edward Palmer never took his seat in the House of Commons. Lord Fitzwilliam collected the signatures of his supporters and the names of potential witnesses in preparation for a dispute at the Committee of Elections. His case was similar to that of Thomas Papillon at Dover – indeed, eerily alike, as Palmer, like Spragge, died before it could be heard. Winning elections in post-Restoration England was as much a matter of preparing a case for the Committee of Elections as of mustering support for the poll. Beginning in the 1670s, printed petitions appeared in election disputes, setting out the plaintiff's case in the most vivid terms.[128] This was testimony, if any more was needed, to the fact that gaining a hearing at the Committee of Elections was as much a problem of public relations as of equity.[129] Papillon's election petition occupied pages of charges, evidence, and names of individual witnesses who could testify to his version of events.[130] Lord Fitzwilliam received the most expert and up-to-date advice regarding lawyers and procedures: "If you have any interest, or can make any, early apply yourself to Mr. John Vaughan...no man [is] more able nor knowing in parliament's procedures...Avoid all sharpness and especially all personal reflections, for that will but be your disadvantage."[131]

The emergence of elections as a dominant feature of the process of parliamentary selection can be seen in all these developments. Competition among the gentry for social distinction, for patronage, and for influence at court mixed with the emerging ideological divisions over politics and religion. The combination was potent. A seat in the House of Commons was now to be won against aggressive competitors in a struggle of personality, beliefs, resources, and will. More than any other factor – though many were at work – it was competing candidates that

---

[126]   Ibid.
[127]   Ibid.
[128]   See for example Public Record Office, State Papers, 29/411/pt. 2, 120.
[129]   J. R. Jones, "Restoration Election Petitions," *Durham University Journal*, 53 (1961), pp. 49–57.
[130]   Kent A.O., U1015/023/13, 14, 15, 26, 28a, 28b.
[131]   Northamptonshire R.O., F (M) C 412.

created the electorate. The fifty freemen brought in at Dover were to be the servants of Colonel John Strode and Sir Edward Spragge. It would not be very long before the relationship was reversed. Never again could county leaders or corporate officials assume that their selections would be peaceable. Never again could patrons assume that their influence would go unchallenged. The identity of interests that had once characterized parliamentary selections was fast becoming a memory of a vanished golden age. In its place came competition and strife. In its aftermath would come a new understanding of political participation.

8

Hard-Fought Elections

I

BY THE LATE seventeenth century, parliamentary selections were dominated by competition. Patrons competed for nominations in boroughs, gentlemen competed for precedence in shires, and the Court competed for both. Competition intensified every element of the selection process, from planning to polling. Aspirants launched their campaigns at the first hint of a vacancy or a session. Only days after Charles II unexpectedly dissolved the first parliament of 1679, a mad scramble had already begun. "At Buckingham, those that stand began on Friday, for Sir Peter Tyrell having notice of the dissolution . . . came immediately to the town and stayed most part of that night . . . spending money." The early birds were seldom alone: "Mr. Chaplyn uses his best endeavors for Sir Richard Temple; Lord Latimer has likewise sent; and so hath the Duke of Buckingham. So there is like to be a great contest."[1] The candidates competed for victory. They nurtured their interests in boroughs or their influence in shires in preparation for the battle for seats.

As we have seen, the most obvious manifestation of the competitive element in parliamentary selection was the rise of contests. They pervaded the process as much by threat as by actuality. If an election was not the result of every selection, it was the expected result. Candidates had to anticipate contests when announcing their intentions and when planning their strategy. They had to identify their supporters and their opponents in order to woo the one and defy the other. Candidates had to be inured to competition: "I have not yet heard of any slighting word spoke against me," Sir Ralph Verney wrote to his partner, Sir Richard Temple, in 1681, "but at such a time as this we must expect to hear all of our faults."[2] Contenders could not be expected to be deterred from

[1] British Library, M 636/33. Sir Ralph Verney to John Verney, July 14, 1679.
[2] British Library, M 636/35. Sir Ralph Verney to Sir Richard Temple, February 4, 1681.

the struggle by the mere presence of rivals. This meant that stronger measures had to be taken to run them off.

Thus competitive contests spawned disagreeable offspring – inducements, increasing costs, intimidation, and violence. Yet, paradoxically, the diminution of the social side of selection in favor of the political one depersonalized selections. Party politics, in the loosest sense, only emerged at the end of this period, but even in the 1660s candidates could be seen to represent certain groups or opinions. This meant that they had both more and less at stake – more in the pursuit of their cause, less in the risk to their personal worth. Once winning was the sole objective of candidacy, strategic withdrawals could be made on calculations of defeat rather than on fear of dishonor. Devaluing the personal aspect of the process allowed discretion to become the better part of valor.

The most common inducements to parliamentary electors were beef and ale.

> That Beef and Ale should yet prevail
> You need no longer wonder.
> For men of wit must still submit
> To fools of greater number.[3]

Treats of all kinds were provided to stiffen the resolve of wavering electors, and this was true without regard to the size of a constituency or its franchise. "The ale that the populace get at Buckingham will make them choose anybody that will bestow it," Sir Ralph Verney observed in disgust during the 1681 disputes.[4] But it was not the populace only that consumed the resources of candidates: "The people say the burgesses' pockets are full of money," Verney had reported two years earlier.[5] The tradition of treats had grown out of the social, celebratory aspects of parliamentary selection. Before the Revolution, men selected as members of Parliament had occasionally acknowledged the honor bestowed upon them by feasting the electors in county and borough. There was no element of bribery in the custom. It probably derived as much from ideas about hospitality as from feelings of gratitude, and the attendance of candidates at their elections was sporadic. Even at contests, where traditional behavior was certain to be misrepresented by opponents, the decision to provide provisions or shelter was aimed not at persuading electors but at acknowledging supporters.

Such values were transmuted with breathtaking rapidity after the Res-

---

[3]   *The Sale of Esau's Birthright or the New Buckingham Ballad* (1679).
[4]   British Library, M 636/35. Sir Ralph Verney to Alexander Denton, February 9, 1681.
[5]   British Library, M 636/33. Sir Ralph Verney to John Verney, February 10, 1679.

toration. The feast flourished, but no longer as a mere postelection celebration. "At Buckingham there is great feasting; Sir Richard Temple feasted the bailiffs and burgesses yesterday with venison and some think he will be one."[6] One of the chief purposes of election agents was to distribute money during the campaign. At Corfe Castle "Mr William Culliford, agent of my Lord Dunblane, gave some eighteen pence and some a shilling for the hindrance of work half a day."[7] The line between persuasion and bribery was all but rubbed out as candidates competed in lavishing gifts where they might do the most good. In 1669 Sir William Drake wore his opponent down in Amhersham by spending "forty pounds a day treatments" and built a market hall for the town after his election in 1681.[8] Sir William Ellis made an interest-free loan of one thousand pounds to the corporation of Grantham, though it did not ensure his election.[9] Neither did the initial generosity of Edward Backwell. His Christmas gifts to the poor of Wendover were questioned in the committee of elections, and he was unseated on charges of bribery.[10] Along with beef and ale, gifts to the poor were almost mandatory at borough elections. They too had their origins in a less politicized era when such charity was its own reward. Now they had become but another electoral inducement, although many candidates might share the view of Sir Ralph Verney, who agreed "to give ten pounds to the poor of Buckingham . . . and think that it is the best money that is spent on this occasion."[11] There can be no better evidence of transformation than the elegant arrangement reached at Dover in 1690. There the four candidates decided to distribute half a crown to each voter in lieu of a feast, with the charges borne by the winners.[12]

Inducements were but one of several factors that led to the spectacular increase in the cost of elections. It was only to be expected that rising demand would inexorably inflate the price of candidacy, but realization of this came slowly. Candidates, especially novices, were staggered by

[6]   Ibid. Sir Ralph Verney to John Verney, July 17, 1679.
[7]   *Journals of the House of Commons*, IX, 594.
[8]   Historical Manuscripts Commission Reports, *7th Report* (Manuscripts of Sir Harry Verney), p. 488. *Victoria County History of Buckinghamshire*, III, 141.
[9]   G. Davies, "The By-election at Grantham, 1678," *Huntington Library Quarterly*, 7 (1943–44), pp.179–82.
[10] B. D. Henning, ed., *The House of Commons 1660–90*, I, 145.
[11] British Library, M 636/35. Sir Ralph Verney to Sir Richard Temple, February 12, 1681.
[12] "We agreed and signed a writing... that after each man had given his vote he should deliver him half a crown in lieu of an entertainment." Kent Archive Office, Papillon Papers, U1015/024/6.

their outlays and, like Pepys, assumed they were unique. "I look upon the extravagant expense of my last election to have risen wholly from the accident of Mr. Offley's interposing himself." His victory at Castle Rising in 1673 was "the first election . . . that ever cost so many pounds as mine cost scores."[13] Sir John Lowther was equally surprised by the cost of selection in Westmoreland. "So much is time altered," he reflected on the outlay for the postelection feast in 1660, which he shared with Sir Thomas Wharton. "The bills of charges of that night . . . was ninety pounds a piece, which at former times cost not five pounds."[14] Lady Roos could afford to be philosophical as she observed John Grey's supporters "give in their accounts." "Upon examination of them [we] find that the election day cost near eight hundred pounds which, though a great sum, yet being we carried it, is not so much as the least repined at." It is not known if Grey was as cheerful.[15]

Those who would wear the garland were now in danger of bringing financial chaos down around their ears. Perhaps the most unnerving aspect of the inflation of costs was that ruinously expensive elections could never be predicted.[16] The crucial factor was neither the size of the constituency nor the nature of its franchise – it was simply the presence of a free-spending opponent. Pepys's misadventure at Castle Rising probably cost him seven hundred pounds, while a place at Okehampton cost Henry Northleigh four hundred and sixty pounds.[17] County seats, as befit the status of aspirants to them, were more expensive still. Twelve hundred pounds were expended during a Hertfordshire by-election in 1668.[18] A decade later at Buckinghamshire "we hear the charges at the election comes to fifteen hundred pounds, nay others say more, yet there was no opposition nor contest. . . . You may guess what it would have come to had there been any competitors."[19] John Evelyn, observing his

[13] J. R. Tanner, ed., *The Further Correspondnece of Samuel Pepys*, pp. 331–32.

[14] B. D. Henning, ed., *The House of Commons 1660–90*, I, 434. Lowther's surprise also derived from the fact that he had not anticipated standing. Cumberland Record Office, Lowther Mss., D/Lons/1A fol. 251.

[15] Historical Manuscripts Commission Reports, *12th Report*, Appendix V (Manuscripts of the Duke of Rutland), II, 40.

[16] Even routine selections were relatively expensive after the Restoration. It cost Sir Walter Bagot seventy-eight pounds at his first election for Staffordshire and an average of thirty pounds thereafter to entertain freeholders after uncontested selections. William Salt Library, Bagot Papers, D 1721 (Elections Bills).

[17] J. R. Tanner, ed., *The Further Correspondence of Samuel Pepys*, pp. 331–32; W. B. Bridges, *Some Account of the Barony and Town of Okehampton* (1889), p. 103.

[18] L. Stone, "The Electoral Influence of the Earls of Salisbury," *English Historical Review*, 71 (1956), p. 388.

[19] British Library, M 636/32. Sir Ralph Verney to John Verney, February 13, 1679.

brother's election, recorded that the electors "ate and drank him out near two thousand pounds by a most abominable custom."[20] Sir Ralph Verney feared that no one would stand for Berkshire in the first Exclusion Crisis parliament because of the cost: "I cannot prevail with Sir Humphrey Foster to stand there: He swears it cost him fifteen hundred pounds though he had no powerful adversary; my Lord Stirling protests he will not stand for it cost him two thousand pounds to sit a few months."[21] Such fears were justified, for in neighboring Bedfordshire the four contenders spent six thousand pounds.[22] But all this pales before the incredible fifteen thousand pounds that Sir John Banks and Cresheld Draper are said to have lost in contesting a Winchelsea by-election just prior to the dissolution of the Cavalier Parliament.[23]

It is difficult to imagine how such great sums of money could be expended in such short periods of time. In counties, of course, the principal outlays were for shelter and sustenance. In selections without competition, this meant the feast. Edmund Verney reported from Buckinghamshire in 1679 that "at the Red Lion they gave in an account of eight hundred and sixty dinners . . . they reckoned eight hundred bottles of sack spent."[24] Nearly all of Sir Walter Bagot's expenses in his five selections as knight in Staffordshire were for food and drink. Yet in keeping with the celebratory aspects of selection in a county where contests were still unknown, Bagot provided musicians, bell ringers, and in 1681 "seven gross of pipes" with eleven pounds of tobacco. Even in Staffordshire, however, the threat of a contest could raise the financial stakes. When there was some question as to who would partner Bagot in the winter of 1679, larger numbers of freeholders appeared to consume food and drink. The first 1679 selection cost Bagot three times the second, though at seventy-eight pounds a Staffordshire seat was an excellent value.[25] In general, the cost of county contests correlated with the length of the poll. Overnight adjournments were probably more expensive than peripatetic polls, but there was not much to choose between them.

In boroughs, the flow of ale could last for weeks, and the temptation to offer more costly inducements was ever-present. With the electorate confined within a relatively small area, the presence of a candidate or his agent during the campaign could make a decisive impact. The towns

[20] E. S. de Beer, ed., *The Diary of John Evelyn*, IV, 164–65.
[21] British Library, M 636/32. Sir Ralph Verney to Edmund Verney, January 30, 1679.
[22] British Library, M 636/32. Edmund Verney to Sir Ralph Verney, February 24, 1679.
[23] B. D. Henning, ed., *The House of Commons 1660–90*, I, 504.
[24] British Library, M 636/32. Edmund Verney to John Verney, February 20, 1679.
[25] William Salt Library, Bagot Papers, D 1721 (Elections Bills).

themselves had every incentive to encourage the process of persuasion. "I'm glad there is such feasting at Buckingham," John Verney wrote to his father during the second 1679 campaign. "These sudden dissolutions will possibly fill their pockets as well as their heads."[26] The cost of the campaign more than compensated for the fact that polls added little extra expense to borough contests. Sir Ralph Verney niggled at paying the poll clerks a pound each in 1681 – "when we took the poll for the knights of the shire we did not give the clerks a guinea a piece" – but Sir Richard Temple persuaded him of the wisdom of the outlay. The two were soon expending far more on hiring legal talent to protect themselves from the election dispute begun by their opponents.[27] Indeed, fighting an election in both constituency and Parliament was the costliest of all ventures.

As the stakes rose in selections, candidates and their agents became more interested in ends than in means. Larger investments led to larger expectations of return. If inducement was the shiny side of the new electoral coin, intimidation was the dull one. And the coin was liberally expended. Intimidation was not unknown in the early seventeenth century, but it was less frequent and less effective. Individual electors might be threatened with jury service or upgrading on the subsidy roll. Few were placed in as much terror as those Hertfordshire gentlemen who were threatened with being made sheriffs.[28] In the later seventeenth century, corporate officeholders were the likeliest targets of direct pressure, especially from the Court. The expansion of offices in the localities and their linkage to politics increased the Crown's persuasive powers. A *quo warranto* proceeding was the fist in the glove. Many were directed at purging recalcitrant burgesses, and all the new Caroline charters contained clauses allowing for removal at pleasure.[29]

Elections brought economic peril as well as prosperity. Though individuals remained the likeliest targets, late seventeenth century intimidation could involve entire communities. In 1660 a crowd of Leicestershire gentlemen threatened to boycott the town of Leicester if Sir Arthur Hasilrig was returned to the Convention. As the town's prosperity was dependent upon the local gentry, a concerted withdrawal of

---

[26] British Library, M 636/33. John Verney to Sir Ralph Verney, August 7, 1679.

[27] British Library, M 636/35. Sir Ralph Verney to Sir Richard Temple, February 12, 1681; Sir Richard Temple to Sir Ralph Verney, February 17, 1681.

[28] B. D. Henning, ed., *The House of Commons 1660–90*, I, 269.

[29] R. G. Pickavance, "The English Boroughs and the King's Government: A Study of the Tory Reaction of 1681–85," unpublished Ph.D. dissertation, Oxford University, (1976); John Miller, "The Crown and the Borough Charters in the Reign of Charles II," *English Historical Review*, 100 (1985), p. 53–84.

business would have had grave consequences. Hasilrig was not selected.[30] Colonel John Birch issued a similar warning to Weobly at a by-election in 1678. Owner of the town's principal manor, Birch demanded not so much a right of nomination as one of refusal, informing the town leaders that he would neither buy from them nor sell to them if he did not approve of their choice. This placed the town in a particularly vulnerable position, for its surviving M.P. had declared his intention to sue for fourteen years' back wages if the candidate he supported was not chosen.[31] At Eye, Lord Cornwallis was more selective in the punishment he meted out. He took up the town's taverns and simply refused to sell drink to his opponent's supporters.[32] Legal and administrative centers were open to the same forceful persuasions of the court as were individual burgesses. The threat to move assizes or quarter sessions was galvanic. New Romney's counsel assured the port's leaders that confiscation of their charter was the certain result of refusing the lord warden's right of nomination.[33]

The forms of intimidation ranged from a word in the ear to a box on one. "Brave doings at Marlow, breaking arms and legs and heads with stones."[34] "At Windsor . . . they cuff and cudgel one another every day."[35] In the popular election that followed the corporate choice at Buckingham in 1681 "the report goes that one poor man had his eye beat out and another had his ear bit off."[36] It is difficult to distinguish tumultuous violence during the heat of the moment from cold-blooded attempts to cow opponents. Both were increasing. The political hysteria surrounding the Popish Plot is one obvious explanation for increasing violence at elections; the intensity of competition is another.

Neither candidates nor returning officers were entirely safe during contests. Sir John Stonehouse, whose family had dominated Abingdon selections for generations, was attacked by a mob carrying the colors of his opponent and declined an appearance on election day.[37] Sir Humphrey Winch was ducked at Great Marlow and almost drowned before

---

[30] Mary Coate, "William Morice and the Restoration of Charles II," *English Historical Review*, 33 (1918), p. 376.
[31] B. D. Henning, ed., *The House of Commons 1660–90*, I, 267.
[32] British Library, M 636/33. Sir Framlingham Gaudy to Sir Ralph Verney, August 28, 1679.
[33] Kent A.O., NR/Aep/fol. 47.
[34] British Library, M 636/33. Dr. William Denton to Sir Ralph Verney, August 14, 1679.
[35] Historical Manuscripts Commission Reports, *13th Report*, Appendix VI (Manuscripts of Sir William Fitzherbert), p. 20.
[36] British Library, M 636/35. Sir Ralph Verney to William Coleman, February 10, 1681.
[37] C. J., X, 123–24.

his election in 1679.[38] Mayors and sheriffs were no better served. At Exeter an extraordinary scene followed the adjournment of the poll in March 1679. One of the contenders, William Glyd, "gets on the table ...seizes some of the poll books, kicks the Mayor in the shins and assaults the sheriff, and much doubt there was lest murder might be committed."[39] At Wallingford a decade later the mayor was "induced to make a double return" by threats "to cut off his ears and burn down his house."[40] In this atmosphere it is not surprising to learn that lives were now to be reckoned among the costs of elections. Deaths were reported at Leicestershire in 1679 and at Northamptonshire in 1685.[41] At the 1673 Chester by-election, nine men were fatally crushed in a stampede to the polling place.[42]

Curiously, inducements and intimidation shifted the attention of the candidates from each other to the electors. As a consequence of the competition for seats, aspirants began to court the electors. "At this election the poor men were courted as well as the rich," petitioners from Corfe Castle complained to the committee of elections in 1679.[43] Unquestionably, social and political forces were at work that expanded political participation at all levels of society. But in parliamentary selections the significant initiatives came from above. It was the willingness of community leaders to compete with each other and their determination to achieve victory that dramatically enhanced opportunities for members of other social strata. "There is great canvassing for voices on behalf of Mr Montague who hath spent forty hogsheads of ale at Northampton," a correspondent of Sir Thomas Isham wrote in the winter of 1679. "I am glad you are not one who would put himself to horrid inconveniencies for a little popular applause."[44]

It was the elite who created the contests that allowed larger numbers of individuals to participate at selections. Sir Ralph Verney's electoral agent at Great Bedwin stated the obvious when he reported on the pressures placed on electors: "What will be the issue none can foretell being in the hands of people not fixed and have great men of quality

---

[38] British Library, M 636/33. Dr. William Denton to Sir Ralph Verney, August 14, 1679.

[39] Historical Manuscripts Commission Reports, *Report on the Manuscripts of Lord Montague of Beaulieu*, pp. 174–75.

[40] B. D. Henning, ed., *The House of Commons 1660–90*, I, 135.

[41] B. D. Henning, ed., *The House of Commons 1660-90*, I, 295; Northamptonshire Record Office, Isham Correspondence, IC 1383.

[42] British Library, Harleian Manuscripts, 2125, fol. 166; *Calendar of State Papers Domestic Series 1672–73*, p. 587.

[43] *C.J.*, IX, 594.

[44] Northamptonshire R.O., IC 1161.

and interest on all sides of them using all their arts and power to shake them."[45] Yet it must always be remembered that participation and representation are not conceptual equivalents. When communities made harmonious choices, they could believe that if few participated at least all were represented. Contested elections increased participation at the expense of representation. The more sharply the ideological lines were drawn, the greater was the sense of political disenfranchisement on the part of the losers. The exhilaration of victory naturally increased the ignominy of defeat.

Similarly, it was divisions within corporate elites that encouraged franchise disputes. Potential disputants needed preliminary legal advice to establish proper grounds for their actions, and they needed considerable financial assets to pursue them at the Committee of Elections. Both were usually beyond the means of groups with putative claims to voices. Buckingham provides a model into which the differing circumstances of other places can be fitted. Once Sir Richard Temple had secured an entrenched electoral interest within the corporation, his opponents began to search for an alternative mode of opposition. In 1680 one of the aldermen of the faction opposed to Temple broke open the town chest in an abortive effort to make public the terms of the charter.[46] This led to a dispute at the 1681 election. The gentry leaders who opposed Temple and his partner Verney claimed that they had seen the charter "and that the right was in all of the freemen and the burgesses had concealed it from them very dishonestly."[47] They organized a popular election, after the corporation had made its choice, in which Temple not only participated but which he won.[48] It is hard to locate even the faintest stirrings of popular pressure for the recovery of lost rights, which in any case were not determined during the attenuated Oxford Parliament.

The courting of electors would eventually have great importance in transforming the selection process into an electoral process. By 1689, however, its most apparent contribution was to help depersonalize candidacy. With attention turned toward questions of electors, franchises, and establishing majorities, the interest of candidates in their opponents was reduced. There remained those occasions on which opposition was regarded as a dishonorable social snub, but this was an old-fashioned attitude usually held by only one of the contenders. When the Earl of

[45]   British Library, M/636/17. Thomas Gape to Sir Ralph Verney, March 29, 1660.
[46]   Huntington Library, Temple–Stowe Manuscripts, STT 246.
[47]   British Library, M/636/35. Sir Richard Temple to Sir Ralph Verney, February 2, 1681.
[48]   Ibid. Sir Richard Temple to Sir Ralph Verney, February 10, 1681.

Shaftesbury refused to assent to the candidacy of Lord Digby after a meeting of Dorset gentry in 1673, he maintained that it was a political decision. Digby saw it differently, and at a meeting between the two Digby poured such personal invective on the Earl that he was successfully sued for *scandalum magnatum*.[49] This was a remnant of a vanishing past. By the end of the century, candidates were interested only in the tactics of their opponents and their chances for success. They hardly acknowledged each other's existence in the contest, and there were none of the apologies and postelection recriminations so common in the early seventeenth century. Although what happened at Shaftesbury in 1681 was not typical, it was not simply symbolic. After the victory of Andrews and Bennett over Whitaker, "we presently went all to dinner together: Mr. Whitaker, Mr. Mayor, his brethren ... and many more. We were very merry and friendly altogether."[50]

II

"I have been at Buckingham and find I have but six voices and without seven I can do no good."[51] The quest for the seventh voice dominated the Buckingham parliamentary election of 1685. There was no pretense of achieving unanimity, no effort to avoid a contest, either by the candidates or by the mayor and twelve aldermen who composed the electorate. Despite a purge of dissident burgesses in a recent reincorporation, Buckingham's governors were pulled apart by ties of personal loyalty, political persuasion, and corporate and individual interests. There was little reason to attempt to unite them. Seven voices would carry the seat, and it was to the bare majority that the candidates addressed themselves. "I hope that we shall get seven on our side and then it is not much for the rest."[52] This single-minded purpose set the tone for the contest: Calculations were cold, and blandishments basic. No missed communication or misunderstanding set these events in motion, no personal animosity or offended honor colored the strife. Nor did the magistracy resist the divisiveness that the candidates encouraged. Rather they acted like innkeepers in a storm – reneging on promises, striking hard bargains, driving up costs – and rekindled the conflict whenever it dampened.

The electoral campaign was worthy of a military analogy. Sir Richard

---

[49] K. D. Haley, *Shaftesbury*, p. 254; Historical Manuscripts Commission Reports, *15th Report*, Appendix VII (Manuscripts of the Marquis of Ailesbury), pp. 177–78.

[50] W. A. Day, *The Pythouse Papers* (1879), p. 95.

[51] British Library, M/636/39. Sir Ralph Verney to John Verney, March 15, 1685. I would like to thank Major Ralph B. Verney for making these materials available.

[52] British Library, M/636/39. Edmund Verney to John Verney, March 16, 1685.

Temple, Sir Ralph Verney, and Edward Osborne, Viscount Latimer, each laid siege to the town of Buckingham. Temple, high steward in the 1684 reincorporation that he had obtained for the town, occupied the high ground from his bordering estate at Stowe. His partner Verney, whose properties in Claydon lay six miles to the southwest, was more vulnerable. In his seventy-second year, he had withdrawn from national affairs and, though scrupulous regarding his county duties as justice of the peace, was removed from the political maneuverings of the neighboring town. There his support was of a personal nature, relations fortified over decades, in good times and bad. Latimer's interest was less of propinquity than of potential for performance. Son of the Earl of Danby and a Buckinghamshire landowner by marriage, Latimer's political fortunes and prospective power rose and fell in tandem with his father's mercurial career.[53]

Each of the three proved superb generals. Their stratagems and artifices, assaults and retreats, left the outcome in doubt for the full three months of battle. Lines of communication were established between operational headquarters in London and the town, where trusted personal servants were sent on frequent forays. Lines of supply were maintained by the constant feasting of the thirteen and their families: "It is highly necessary that you make some little treat for the women," Temple advised the grudging Verney. "Send in Westphalia ham and neats' tongue from your own house."[54] They battered the borough with a barrage of appeals for support. From the beginning of March to the middle of May hardly a day passed without incident. Heavy artillery and heavier reinforcements were all brought to bear to secure the strategic objective of an electoral victory: "The more opposition, the greater is the glory [to] carry it."[55] Indeed, they relished the struggle.

But they relished it hardly more than did the town. Never were the forces of occupation made more welcome. At the first hint of siege the earthworks were plowed over, the cannons spiked, and the battlements slighted. The electoral contests to the three parliaments during the Exclusion Crisis, in which Verney had been chosen once and Latimer and Temple twice, had proven lucrative for a town in economic decline. Not only had the candidates spent freely at the inns and taverns, driving up the prices of local commodities and services, but as the struggle for favor was among local men, they were also motivated to patronize Buck-

---

53   Details of the parliamentary careers of each can be found in B. D. Henning, ed., *The House of Commons 1660–1690*, III.
54   British Library, M/636/39. Sir Richard Temple to Sir Ralph Verney, April 1, 1685.
55   Ibid. John Verney to Edmund Verney, March 19, 1685.

ingham traders and craftsmen.[56] Most importantly, the parliamentary contest had preserved what was left of the town's role as a county administrative center. Despite the growth and prosperity of Aylesbury, Buckingham remained the venue of summer assizes and a contender as site for county elections. All of this enriched the venal magistracy and the free burgesses who formed the town's trading companies. Their new charter – promoted, procured, and paid for by Sir Richard Temple in the furtherance of his parliamentary interest – increased their privileges and enhanced their power.[57]

Only one great prize had eluded the magistrates of Buckingham. This was the erection of a town hall in place of the one that had burned down in the early seventeenth century. "It being the county town of the shire, assizes are usually kept there, but having no town hall . . . they erect sheds for the purpose against the ruinous castle walls."[58] Nothing so threatened the town's hold over assizes as the absence of a permanent hall and the presence of one in Aylesbury. The circuit judges were perennially complaining of the uncomfortable temporary sheds that housed their proceedings each July.[59] Twice the corporation had returned members to Parliament on the understanding that a "contribution" would be made to this dimension of the town's welfare. In 1661 Sir Richard Temple, whose participation in local support of the Restoration had earned him royal favor, had convinced the magistrates that he could secure the permit for cutting down timber of sufficient length from the royal forests to construct the hall. His none-too-secret negotiations on this point had earned him the sobriquet, Sir Timber Temple.[60] When the story was repeated in 1679 it was no longer clear whether his opponents were more chagrined that the "Monster of Stowe Woods" had unlawfully offered to build the hall or that he had immorally failed to fulfill the pledge. In either case, Lord Latimer was then elected on the same platform. Again the town was disappointed, though Latimer did secure both permit and timber before financial stringencies forced him to abandon the project. In November 1684 the corporation reminded

[56] See the brief account in the constituency history "Buckingham" in B. D. Henning, ed., *The House of Commons 1660–90*, I.

[57] For the terms of the new charter see Public Record Office, State Papers, 44/66/320–22.

[58] Historical Manuscripts Commission Reports, *13th Report*, Appendix II (Manuscripts of the Duke of Portland), II, 289. Thomas Baskerville's Journeys in England.

[59] British Library, Additional Mss., 28,087, fol. 18.

[60] For this part of Temple's relations with the borough see Godfrey Davies, "The Political Career of Sir Richard Temple (1634-1697) and Buckingham Politics," *Huntington Library Quarterly*, 4 (1940), pp.51-54.

Latimer of his unfulfilled promise, but the year passed without the summoning of the parliament expected by the burgesses.[61]

The death of Charles II, in February 1685, activated the town and its parliamentary aspirants. Before the old King had been interred, Temple and Verney met in London to lay their plans for the now inevitable general election. Verney, an ever-reluctant candidate, had been persuaded by his sons Edmund and John to stand again for the seat that he had held in 1681.[62] Though after that contest he had few remaining illusions about the process of candidacy (and even those would soon be shattered), Sir Ralph still viewed selection as a mixture of suit and bequest appropriate to one who had first entered Parliament in the spring of 1640. "I would not have the town think I decline their kindness," he confided to his estate agent, William Coleman, who was sent to Buckingham to make Verney's intentions known.[63] His meeting with Temple was designed to iron out the complicated financial arrangement of a partnership between the frugal old man and his lavish neighbor. A seat in Parliament held an altogether different meaning for Sir Richard Temple. He had first been elected in 1654 – illegally, it was contended – to avoid paying his father's debts, and his election in 1661 actually released him from debtor's prison.[64] His extraordinary parliamentary career had led to office and enrichment; he regarded the cost of a parliamentary campaign as venture capital to be offset by subsequent profits. To ensure his place at Buckingham he had financed the acquisition of the new town charter, and he was prepared to spend liberally in the event of opposition.[65]

Opposition was certain, though it was not yet clear that it would come from Lord Latimer. Over the previous decade the principal challenge to Temple's hegemony in Buckingham had come from a group headed by Sir Peter Tyrell and Henry Robinson, a burgess of the town. With the backing of the Duke of Buckingham, they had amassed enough support in the winter of 1678 to unseat Temple.[66] Although Temple had regained

[61]   British Library, Add. Mss., 28,087, fols. 18, 20.
[62]   British Library, M/636/39. Sir Ralph Verney to William Coleman, February 25, 1685.
[63]   British Library, M/636/39. Sir Ralph Verney to William Coleman, February 19, 1685.
[64]   Calendar of State Papers Domestic Series 1654, p. 306; Huntington Library, STT Parl. Box 2, "Petition of Viscount Baltinglass"; B. D. Henning, ed., House of Commons 1660–90, III, 537.
[65]   No adequate account of the Buckingham reincorporation exists. The best is contained in an unpublished paper by George Abernathy, "The Borough of Buckingham, 1660–1697: A Struggle for Control." I am grateful to J. P. Ferris for providing me with a copy of this paper. See also Davies, "The Political Career of Sir Richard Temple," pp. 70–72.
[66]   In February 1679 Latimer had all thirteen voices, Tyrell had seven, and Temple had six. See the accounts of the election by Latimer, British Library, Add. Mss., 28,087,

his place in the summer, the group had continued to harass him with personal invective, lawsuits, and efforts to subvert his support among the town magistrates.[67] In 1683 they had attempted to have Robinson elected town bailiff. "The plot was craftily laid and Sir Peter Tyrell and Sir John Busby were at the bottom of it," but timely intervention by Verney and Temple foiled them.[68] It was to meet this menace that Temple had secured the new charter that excluded four of Tyrell's supporters from the corporate government.[69] Temple was named steward and the corporation's governors, formerly the bailiff and burgesses, were retitled "the Mayor and Aldermen of the loyal borough of Buckingham."[70]

This small emendation was of great consequence. For nearly half a century the free burgesses of Buckingham (inappropriately labeled the "populace" in these disputes) had challenged the exclusive franchise claimed by the corporation. In all but one post-Restoration election they had made double returns of their own candidates to initiate a dispute in the committee of elections.[71] The strength of their legal case lay in the ambiguity of the term burgess. Both freemen of the corporation and the elite thirteen were called burgesses, and the old charter could thus

fol. 1, and Edmund Verney, M/636/33. Edmund Verney to John Verney, February 13, 1679.

[67] It was this group which was responsible for the pamphlet attacks upon Temple and the accusation that he was a Catholic. The Duke of Buckingham prosecuted and secured a judgment against Henry Heyward, one of Temple's supporters. British Library, M/636/34. Sir Ralph Verney to John Verney, July 22, 1680; Edmund Verney to John Verney, July 20, 1680.

[68] Nominations for bailiff followed a rota system among the burgesses with two nominations being presented to the free burgesses (freemen of the companies) for election. Despite the partisan divisions in the town it is instructive that the bailiff in 1682 believed "this division in the town could not be answered to God nor man; the other party must come in and take their turn." Huntington Library, STT 288; M/636/37. Sir Ralph Verney to John Verney, May 3, 1683; Edmund Verney to John Verney, May 7, 1683.

[69] The four were Robinson, Mason, Browne, and Thomas Ethersay. See the correspondence between William Chaplyn and Sir Richard Temple, Huntington Library, STT 308-318. Tyrell's support was so undermined that when Temple held a celebration for the receipt of the new charter, Tyrell held a counter-demonstration, "which was looked upon as a slur put upon the new charter, but he need not care for that." British Library, M/636/39. Sir Ralph Verney to John Verney, August 21, 1684.

[70] The new charter also brought benefits to the corporation, and it should not be seen only in the context of Temple's electoral interests. New markets were obtained, the aldermen were made more secure in their places, and the requirements for free burgesses were tightened. Public Record Office, State Papers, 44/66/320-22.

[71] B. D. Henning, ed., *House of Commons 1660–1690*, I, 139. After the election in February 1679, it was Temple who considered championing the popular cause. Abernathy, "The Borough of Buckingham."

be read as providing for a broad franchise.[72] Restyling the corporate leaders as aldermen and placing the parliamentary franchise exclusively with them vitiated the case of the free burgesses. They were certain to test its legality: "Tis believed that they will choose such as the Mayor and Aldermen do not choose and they will do it without charge," Verney reported to Coleman at the beginning of March.[73] A popular candidacy worried Verney both because of its cost and because of the trouble it brought with it. Unlike Temple, Verney had refused to campaign under both franchises in 1681, and he was repelled by the debauchery associated with the free flow of ale in the town.[74]

At his meeting with Temple, Verney again voiced his principled opposition to campaigning among the free burgesses while agreeing to share equally in the costs of wooing aldermen. On February 20, Coleman was sent to Buckingham to announce Verney's candidacy and to discover if "any person or persons are like to stand against Sir Richard Temple, either by the interest of the aldermen or that of the common people." Coleman met with the mayor and those aldermen who, judging from past performance, were likely to constitute Verney's interest. From them he discovered that at the same time that Verney and Temple were making their plans, Lord Latimer was making his. He had already written to the corporation, seeking their election and reasserting his promise to build the town hall: "They had a letter from the Lord Latimer to be for him on account of their town hall, so as yet they have not come to any resolution." Yet Latimer's offer was not without effect. Among those upon whom Verney was counting, three others held fast on the supposition "that Lord Latimer could do nothing" in the building of the hall.[75]

It was this impression that Latimer set out to correct in announcing his candidacy. The imminence of a parliament had induced him to respond to the corporation's earlier request that he fulfill his pledge for the hall. Both parties now had even greater incentive to bring the matter

---

[72] Huntington Library, STT Parl. Box 2, "Report of the Committee of Privileges in 1660." In 1661 the certificate of return stated, "There is no double election made for the said corporation." Huntington Library, STT Elections Box 1 (4).

[73] British Library, M/636/38 (misfiled). Sir Ralph Verney to William Coleman, March 4, 1685.

[74] British Library, M/636/39. Sir Ralph Verney to William Coleman, February 19, 1685. "I would rather sit still than gain a place by such debauchery." Verney's refusal to treat the populace was well remembered in 1685, especially among those burgesses who profited from the sale of provisions.

[75] Ibid. William Coleman to Sir Ralph Verney, February 22, 1685. The waverers were Walter Arnet, George Carter, and Thomas Sheen; those who remained with Verney were Nathaniel Kent, Jonathon Seaton, and George Dancer.

to a rapid conclusion. Although his father, the Earl of Danby, had been freed on bail by Charles II, it was not yet clear that he would be returned to favor. In January, Latimer had been denied the reversion of the mastership of the rolls which Danby had purchased but, more favorably, the Earl's bail had not been rescinded at James's accession.[76] A seat in the Commons could thus prove a useful bargaining chip for both father and son; and no seat was more likely than Buckingham. The problem was how to convince the twice-shy aldermen that he would carry out his promise without giving them the opportunity to collect the hall as an outstanding debt. This was complicated, because any quid pro quo would be open to the charge of bribery. Latimer faced the twin dangers that if he did not build the town hall, or built it too soon, he might not be elected; but that if he did build the town hall, he might be unseated.[77] It was to extricate himself from this dilemma that he entered into negotiations with the mayor and aldermen.

His first step was to hire an architect, William Carpenter, to make a preliminary assessment. Carpenter surveyed both the site and the timber that Latimer had previously purchased and drew an estimate for a building fifty by thirty feet at an approximate cost of three hundred pounds.[78] With this blueprint in hand, Latimer approached the corporation. In a letter to the mayor he offered to defray all of the expenses outlined in Carpenter's plan and to allow the corporation to exercise supervision of the construction. The offer was conditional upon his return to parliament in the upcoming election. His proposal reached the mayor at the beginning of March and was the subject of a series of meetings that lasted long into the night of March 4.[79]

Although they agreed on little else, the aldermen all desired the erection of the town hall. When they had pressed Latimer in November, they had made it plain that they intended to proceed with the construction even if it were necessary to raise a public subscription.[80] The election presented them with another opportunity to have the hall financed, and this they all agreed was worth seizing. On everything else, however,

[76] Andrew Browning, *Thomas Osborne, Earl of Danby* (1951), I, 362–66.
[77] Nor was the reef around which the plan had to be navigated less jagged for his father. If Latimer was humiliated by the town it would strike at Danby's own political pretensions. If he was challenged for bribery, Danby's character would inevitably be drawn into the proceedings. See his letter, British Library, Add. Mss., 28,053, fol. 314.
[78] British Library, M/636/39. "Copy of the Bond," March 23, 1685.
[79] The content of these meetings was to become a subject of controversy. Coleman reported the receipt of Latimer's letter and meetings about it to Verney on March 5. British Library, M/636/39.
[80] British Library, Add. Mss., 28,087, fol. 18.

there was division; and because this opportunity had knocked before, previous failures still echoed. The aldermen had to find some way to ensure the building of the hall before they made their return. Moreover, the mayor, Hugh Ethersay, had to exhibit the same caution about bribery as did Latimer. At the initial meeting on March 4 he informed his brethren only that he had an offer of public benefaction from a "loyal" subject. It was his opinion that as the borough was now incorporated as the "loyal borough" they could all agree it was their duty to elect "loyal" subjects. During the afternoon Latimer's letter was read out, and a fuller, less harmonious discussion took place. The mayor's circumlocution now took on substance, and that night tempers frayed at one of the local inns. George Dancer grumbled that he was not for a "loyal bribe" and that Ethersay was a "shatterbrain" for suggesting that Latimer's election was the obligation of a loyal borough.[81] But beyond these incivilities the central problem remained: How could the arrangements be guaranteed to produce the hall? With Latimer as a principal there was no question of accepting anything on trust.

Negotiations began immediately. William Carpenter went to Buckingham to present his designs to the magistrates and to settle details with their building consultant. In a series of meetings they agreed on matters of costs, scheduling, and supervision and reported their results to the town leaders. At the same time, William Carter, Latimer's personal agent, arrived to carry out the more sensitive bargaining. He too engaged in a series of consultations, mostly with the mayor, to seek an agreement in principle that Carpenter's plan was satisfactory and that the corporation would elect Latimer.[82] As Carpenter recalled, "we met all thirteen and they seemed unanimously resolved and willing to acquiesce to our proposals."[83] By the middle of March, only the vexed issue of safeguards remained unresolved.

Latimer proposed that he enter a bond of performance for six hundred pounds as security for building the hall. The bond, two hundred pounds in cash, and the wood already provided would be held by Carpenter. The bond would carry the proviso that the mayor and aldermen would elect a burgess of Carpenter's choosing.[84] This stipulation would protect both sides against noncompliance. The corporation's legal advisor, William Busby, was troubled by the openness of the arrangement — "all ways were dangerous and I disliked the selling of voices" — and feared

---

[81]   British Library, M/636/39. "Information of Thomas Atterbury," April 20, 1685; British Library, M/636/40. "Testimony of George Carter," May 7, 1685.
[82]   British Library, Add. Mss., 28,087, fol. 25.
[83]   Ibid., fol. 45.
[84]   British Library, M/636/39. "Copy of the Bond," March 23, 1685.

that the proviso created a defeasance.[85] He urged that the "indifferent hand" that held the down payment and the bond be an independent agent unconnected to either candidate or corporation but trusted by both. This condition was ultimately accepted by Latimer. He drafted a letter to the still unspecified "country gentleman" setting out the circumstances of the negotiations over the town hall and Latimer's intention "that I may give them security for that and not hurt myself."[86]

Latimer's campaign was aimed against Verney. Both his experience and Carter's intelligence suggested that Temple's hold over a majority of the aldermen was unshakable. Their energies were directed toward prying loose second voices: "[Verney's] own interest is so small that I should certainly have two for one had not Sir Richard Temple joined with him"[87] By the middle of March his persuasive proposals were having their effect. Carter was able to report optimistically both on the negotiations for the hall and the prospects for success. On March 24 he wrote that a visit by Latimer to the town would settle the business conclusively – "I am now of opinion that your Lordship's presence will surmount all difficulties" – and sardonically added that "Sir Richard would be glad to have an opportunity to fawn upon you."[88]

Latimer's initial onslaught caught Sir Ralph Verney unaware, and he reeled from its impact. His first worry had been to avoid the cost of a popular election. It was not until the mayor and aldermen came to London to present the town's congratulatory address to James II that Verney discovered the attack upon his support within the corporation. Nine of the magistrates dined with Temple and Verney on successive evenings and all pledged themselves to Temple. Only four would give promises to Sir Ralph, the others "did resolve to be free from any engagement."[89] By the end of February, Verney had lost Mayor Ethersay and aldermen Hartley and Purcell from his thinning ranks.[90] He also learned from Alderman Pelham Sandwell that "about five years before they had promised Lord Latimer to be for him if he would make good his former promises."[91] Verney set out to recoup these losses by means of Coleman. "They must all be kept up and courted on this occasion," he instructed his subaltern; "use all means to improve my interest."[92]

[85] Ibid. William Busby to Sir Ralph Verney, March 24, 1685.
[86] British Library, Add. Mss., 28,087, fol. 20.
[87] Ibid., fol. 5.
[88] Ibid., fol. 27.
[89] British Library, M/636/39. Sir Ralph Verney to William Coleman, February 27, 1685.
[90] Ibid. Sir Ralph Verney to William Coleman, February 28, 1685.
[91] Ibid. William Coleman to Sir Ralph Verney, March 8, 1685.
[92] British Library, M/636/38 (misfiled). Sir Ralph Verney to William Coleman, March 4, 1685.

Hartley and Purcell were to be sought particularly. "You may say to them that I shall advance any public work that is for the good and honor of the town, but I must not say much of it now lest my adversaries call it a bribe."[93] But Coleman fought a rearguard action. By the end of the first week of March Verney could already count five votes against him.

Moreover, a new adversary had entered the lists – Lord Chief Justice George Jeffreys. As he was riding the Norfolk circuit that winter, Jeffreys decided to take a personal interest in the electoral affairs of the county where he held real estate. His principal purpose was to prevent the reelection of the exclusionist Thomas Wharton as one of the knights of the shire. First he convinced Thomas Hackett to contest Wharton's candidacy, and then he set about to menace the county gentry into rejecting their popular protégé.[94] Jeffreys employed Thomas Atterbury, a Buckingham burgess added in the reincorporation to protect Crown interests, to make known his displeasure with Verney for supporting Wharton. At Aylesbury assizes, Jeffreys publicly assailed Verney for being "a trimmer, that is one that is on both sides." Next he prevailed upon the sheriff to conduct a peripatetic poll during the shire contest, with the earliest sites nearest to Hackett's geographical strongholds.[95] By these means he hoped to bring Hackett in on Viscount Brackley's interest; Brackley was the other county candidate whose electoral strength encompassed both Court connection and local position. Should Hackett fail at the county, it was thought that Jeffreys had already promised him a seat at Buckingham as consolation.

Jeffreys's plans added another element of uncertainty to the election. With his Court influence he could exert additional pressures upon the mayor and aldermen, but whether these would be strong enough to succeed was unknown. As Verney observed, "If they humor him in their choice he will let the assizes be there and he will use his influence with the sheriff to have the elections at Buckingham."[96] Verney was sufficiently concerned to obtain a release from his personal pledge to Wharton so that he could counter resistance from Atterbury in town.[97] But the introduction of a fourth candidate was as much a problem for Latimer

[93]   British Library, M/636/39. Sir Ralph Verney to William Coleman, March 2, 1685.
[94]   B. D. Henning, ed., *House of Commons 1660–1690*, I, 136.
[95]   British Library, M/636/39. Sir Ralph Verney to William Coleman, February 28, 1685. There can be no question of a surprise adjournment of the poll. Correspondence among the Buckinghamshire gentry mentions the planned assemblies in different parts of the shire for a month before the election.
[96]   Ibid. Sir Ralph Verney to William Coleman, February 27, 1685.
[97]   Ibid. Sir Ralph Verney to William Coleman, March 5, 1685. Although Verney requested a release from his own pledge, he had already used his influence in support of Wharton with his neighbors and tenants.

as for Verney. Indeed, intervention by Jeffreys threatened everyone. His assertion that Hackett could stand against Temple "to have two good men," was no comfort to Latimer.[98] He knew that Temple's majority was secure and that unless Sir Richard withdrew he, Hackett, and Verney would compete for the same seat. Latimer would either have to oppose the Court candidate, hazarding his father's precarious position, or withdraw himself. If he did withdraw, the town could assert "that they would have chosen me if I had been upon the place and therefore expect my going on with the town hall."[99]

To Latimer's agonies were added those of Temple. As mayor, Ethersay was providing Latimer with every opportunity to consolidate his support – countenancing delays, organizing special meetings, goading his hesitant colleagues. Through him Jeffreys was now exercising his muscle: "His office being *durante bene placito*, he is afraid of being turned out."[100] At the end of March Ethersay let it be known that he was willing to wait until after the contest for the knights of the shire before bringing the town to its election.[101] In vain had Temple intercepted the writ and held onto it while Verney was building his majority.[102] They were faced only with the prospect of more waiting and scheming and the possibility of another powerfully backed contender in the fray. Such maneuvers and delays were disquieting for Temple; they seemed to threaten his own carefully constructed interest. Over the years he had invested heavily in the town and had much more at risk than a bond of performance. If the lord chief justice was going to bring his weight to bear against him, Temple's position in both court and country could collapse spectacularly.

Whatever collision with Jeffreys might lie ahead, it was Latimer who remained Sir Ralph Verney's primary rival. He and his sons continued their quest for the seventh voice, a quest that now took another strange turn. In 1680, at the height of the feud between Temple and Tyrell, the factional leaders had struck at each other's underlings in a series of lawsuits. Temple had prosecuted one Barton for slander and subornation of perjury after allegations that Sir Richard frequented Catholic services. Simultaneously, the Duke of Buckingham brought a charge of slander against Henry Heyward, a Buckingham barber and corporate burgess. At the midsummer assizes both the Duke and Sir Richard won massive

---

[98] British Library, Add. Mss., 28,087, fols. 33–34.
[99] Ibid.
[100] British Library, M/636/39. William Busby to Sir Ralph Verney, March 24, 1685.
[101] Edmund Verney first heard rumors to this effect on March 16. British Library, M/636/39. Edmund Verney to John Verney. Sir Richard Temple to Sir Ralph Verney, April 1, 1685.
[102] British Library, M/636/39. Edmund Verney to Sir Ralph Verney, March 10, 1685. Temple gave the writ to Edmund Verney, who finally delivered it on March 27.

damages. Neither Barton nor Heyward could pay the punitive fines levied against them, and they were subsequently sentenced to prison in the Fleet.[103] It was Sir Ralph Verney's misfortune to have been involved in the Heyward case: "The words were fully proved and I was foreman of the jury, but much against my will."[104] After the initial judgment in 1680, Verney was entreated to intervene with the Duke of Buckingham by both Temple and Heyward. It was then thought that the Duke would forgo the fine, having been vindicated from the *scandalum magnatum.* But Temple's judgment against Barton led the Duke to insist upon reciprocal mercy.[105] As a result the two languished in prison, making common cause in doleful Christmas Day appeals to prospective benefactors like Verney.[106] Heyward's case intermittently intruded into Buckingham town politics. Tyrell's allies sought to remove him from the governing elite, while Temple's allies defended him and preserved his place at the reincorporation. In 1685 Heyward's pathetic plight became further entangled when he was named in a bill for "ravishing an old simple woman."[107]

Heyward's fate assumed new importance as Verney's interest amongst the aldermen eroded. Heyward had supported Verney in previous elections and was Edmund Verney's barber at East Claydon. Although Sir Ralph did not effect his discharge, he had attempted to appease the Duke on several occasions. If Heyward could be brought to town for the election, even on bail, he might represent the elusive seventh voice. The prospect brightened considerably in the second week of March, when the allegations of rape were unexpectedly dismissed at assizes. Bail could now be obtained against the debt owed to the Duke through a writ of habeas corpus. As soon as assizes were concluded, John Verney was delegated to enter into negotiations with Heyward, negotiations as delicate as those that Latimer was conducting over the town hall. In return for a pledge of support, Verney would secure the writ and discharge Heyward's prison fees.[108] But while John Verney was seeking legal advice to bind Heyward without risking accusations of bribery, the Duke of Buckingham, for his own purposes, decided to settle the debt: "My

[103] British Library, M/636/34. Edmund Verney to John Verney, July 20, 1680; British Library, M/636/36. Sir Ralph Verney to John Verney, July 27, 1682.
[104] British Library, M/636/34. Sir Ralph Verney to John Verney, July 22, 1680.
[105] Ibid. Edmund Verney to John Verney, July 20, 1680; British Library, M/636/35. Sir Richard Temple to Sir Ralph Verney, July 29, 1681; Sir Ralph Verney to Sir Richard Temple, August 1, 1681.
[106] British Library, M/636/39. Heyward and Barton to Sir Ralph Verney, December 25, 1684.
[107] Ibid. Sir Ralph Verney to John Verney, March 10, 1685.
[108] Ibid. Sir Ralph Verney to John Verney, March 15, 1685.

barber, Henry Heyward is out of prison . . . upon condition that he pay one hundred and ten pounds," Edmund hastily informed his father. "He promised me faithfully to be for you."[109]

Heyward's release and return to Buckingham helped consolidate Verney's position. Though Sir Ralph frequently bemoaned the inconstancy of the aldermen and their determination to strike the best bargain – even if with the devil – by the end of March the contest stood delicately poised. Latimer's proposals – still without accord as to the gentleman to hold the bond – had persuaded six electors to his side. Verney, with support from Temple, had persuaded six electors to his side. The uncommitted Thomas Hillesden became the seventh voice. All efforts were now directed at his conversion, for the creation of even a temporary majority would firm waverers and encourage defectors. In truth, neither interest was well entrenched. Latimer could easily lose Arnet and Sheen if Verney made a solid offer on the hall. If Jeffreys intervened he would be deserted by Ethersay and Atterbury. Sandwell and Carter were uncertain Verney allies, waiting for the final settlement of Latimer's promises. Heyward was conspicuous by his frequent absences from town, raising fears among the Verneys that he had struck a secret bargain with the Duke for his release.

Hillesden was the key. His neutrality not only kept the outcome in doubt, it also prevented the conclusion of negotiations with Latimer. The commitment to build the hall was contingent upon a guarantee of Latimer's election, which in turn depended upon a majority in his favor. Thus much of the pressure on Hillesden came from the mayor who, with Latimer's other supporters, closeted him for long hours. "They said there were six for the Lord Latimer and that the town hall and all the business depended on him."[110] Hillesden did not budge. Some days later Carter wrote less than candidly that there was "a sort of uncertainty as to Mr. Hillesden, our seventh man," concluding, "I cannot believe [he] will start from us." It was Carter's opinion that Hillesden's concern was over the security of the arrangements for the hall: "His pretended doubt is that your Lordship may recall the money."[111] Indeed the hall was much on Hillesden's mind. He had told the mayor "that he should not give his vote until he was satisfied that there would be a town hall," but he had confided to William Chaplyn, Sir Richard Temple's agent, that he was confident that Verney and Temple would finance the project as well. It was now critical, Sir Richard implored Edmund Verney, that Sir Ralph

[109] Ibid. Edmund Verney to Sir Ralph Verney, March 10, 1685.
[110] Ibid. Sir Richard Temple to Edmund Verney, March 24, 1685.
[111] British Library, Add. Mss., 28,087, fol. 29.

come to town and make an offer, "according to which he would give his vote one way or another."[112]

Temple's intuition was better than Carter's, for he knew Hillesden well. He correctly assessed that Hillesden would rebel against the intimidation of the mayor if only he could be sure that his vote would not cause the loss of the hall. He had already lashed out, proclaiming more publicly than was politic "that he had not heard Mr. Mayor or any of the rest of them declare they had promised their votes upon this condition to my Lord," a representation so bald that "Mr. Mayor and the rest boggled and would not own they had promised their votes."[113] Hillesden could hardly feel scrupulous about the hall or about using votes as leverage in furtherance of town interests. He had been bailiff during the reincorporation and had driven a hard bargain with Temple over the benefits to be received by the town. More than any other he had saved Ethersay's place in the corporation, and he sharply resented his successor's behavior. The unremitting lobbying was bad enough, but it was worse in the cause of Latimer, who "when he was last chosen they all followed him calling him son of a traitor, courtier, pensioner, and papist."[114] If only Verney would stroke him now that his back was up.

Temple had experienced Verney's vacillation before, and he moved quickly to avoid its repetition. Sir Ralph's continued absence from Buckingham – "the great injury you have done your own concerns" – dictated a circuitous approach.[115] Temple decided to influence him through his family. His strongest chance was Edmund, Sir Ralph's feckless heir. It was Edmund who had advocated Sir Ralph's candidacy and who had served as his proxy on several occasions in town. Temple may have hoped that he could conclude the arrangements for the offer of the hall with Edmund. At the end of March he remonstrated with him to come to town and filled him with news of Hillesden's dilemma and the opportunity it presented.[116] Temple also attempted an approach from the feminine side – his wife invited Cary Gardiner, Verney's sister, for a visit during which she cast the rosiest hue upon the dark business of the hall. The mayor and aldermen "by their oaths they are bound to make all advantage they can to serve the town," she confided to her less worldly guest. Providing the hall now might result in future economies, for it would cost "but one hundred and fifty pounds a piece and she says the continuance of feasting of them will amount to a good part of it." Finally,

[112] British Library, M/636/39. Sir Richard Temple to Edmund Verney, March 25, 1685.
[113] Ibid. Sir Richard Temple to Edmund Verney, March 24, 1685.
[114] Ibid. Sir Richard Temple to Edmund Verney, March 24, 1685.
[115] Ibid. Sir Richard Temple to Sir Ralph Verney, March 22, 1685.
[116] Ibid. Sir Ralph Verney to Edmund Verney, March 24, March 25, 1685.

Lady Temple asserted that similar deals were struck at most elections and that only timidity could explain any hesitation.[117]

Sir Ralph's correspondence was filled with questions and advice about the hall. Throughout the initial month of campaigning he had resisted making a definite commitment. His reluctance was both high-minded and miserly; and in his ounce of parsimony there were some grains of common sense. If Latimer could not obtain a majority with his offer, then Verney would save the cost and the danger of a disputed election. But basically he balked at the idea of the transaction, of further lining the pockets of the avaricious aldermen. In the heat of the moment he could be drawn to rash acts – bailing the disreputable Heyward, for instance – but in the cold light of day, with his age and ill health to provoke his conscience, things looked different. "The truth is I have no desire to be a parliament man," he confided to his son John as the pressure built up to satisfy Hillesden. "It is not only chargeable and wonderful troublesome, [it] forces me to omit those things that are necessary in respect of my health."[118] Besieged on all sides, Sir Ralph's resistance collapsed. By the first of April, Edmund had delivered the precept to the mayor and had urged him to bring the contest to a speedy conclusion.[119]

For the first time in the contest the balance of power had shifted away from Latimer. William Carter continued to press Hillesden – "I had Mr. Hillesden with me till twelve last night but cannot get an assurance" – but by the end of the first week in April he had reduced his goal to converting him back to neutrality.[120] Latimer's plans now had to take a radical turn. He had accepted the prognostications of the mayor that the offer of the hall alone would gain the support of a majority of aldermen. The failure of this tactic left less promising alternatives. One course was for Latimer to reinforce his offer by a personal appearance in town. This might ease the doubts of those like Hillesden and George Carter by demonstrating the genuineness of his intentions. To allow time for him to meet with potential waverers, Latimer asked Ethersay to delay the town election even further.[121] This would enhance the risk that he would have to head off Jeffreys and Hackett, but as things now stood this was preferable to certain defeat by Verney. Another possibility lay in persuading one of the aldermen, by means other than the hall, to change sides. Carter thought Jonathan Seaton was the most susceptible

[117] Ibid. Cary Gardiner to Sir Ralph Verney, March 28, 1685.
[118] Ibid. Sir Ralph Verney to John Verney, March 29 and April 5, 1685.
[119] Ibid. Edmund Verney to John Verney, March 30, 1685.
[120] British Library, Add. Mss., 28,087, fol. 35.
[121] British Library, M/636/39. Sir Richard Temple to Sir Ralph Verney, April 1, 1685.

to the influence that might be exerted from Westminster. He held the office of understeward by royal pleasure and would fear the loss of its income.[122]

Abandoning the aldermen altogether presented another set of options. If Latimer could not obtain a majority he would have to hazard a disputed return. This could be achieved in two ways. The first was to accept election by the free burgesses and bring their case to the House. This would leave his fate in the hands of the Committee of Elections, where his influence might prove greater than it would in the town. Carter was confident that the burgesses would choose him, especially in light of Verney's public refusal to contest the corporation's exclusive franchise.[123] Election by the burgesses, of course, would alienate the magistracy, for they would have to oppose his return in order to protect their own privileges. If he failed in the dispute his interest in town would be permanently damaged. Additionally, a franchise dispute was likely to be opposed at court. Latimer's case might begin a landslide of challenges to the recent borough reincorporations. As he confessed in perplexity to his father, "I doubt the King would not approve of that way of election, besides the mayor would not return me on such a choice."[124]

The second alternative was to have the mayor make a false return. This would also necessitate a fight in the Committee of Elections, and until the dispute was resolved only Temple would be seated. As a seemingly uninterested party, he would be able to prod the committee and give evidence in Verney's favor. Again Latimer was confident that the mayor would do his bidding, but a false return would entail building the town hall and most likely paying any fine that was levied if Verney won the dispute. Both courses were dangerous, as Danby made clear to his son. The critical thing was that Latimer continue as a candidate whether or not he gained a majority. Withdrawal would cost him both the place in Parliament and the town hall. If Latimer were to accept a false return it should be on the understanding that he was only committed to building the hall if the election proved valid.[125] Either of these alternatives presented more difficulties than advantages, and both would initially leave him outside the House petitioning to get in.

One other option presented itself, one as bold as it was unscrupulous. It was more certain of success than reliance on the aldermen, and more beneficial than waiting for the result of a franchise or electoral dispute.

---

[122]   British Library, Add. Mss., 28,087, fol. 35.
[123]   Ibid., fol. 24. "I am offered by the heads of the populace for you. I give them fair words without meeting with them."
[124]   Ibid., fols. 3–4.
[125]   British Library, Add. Mss., 28,053, fol. 314.

Though it was likely to be the most costly, it was also likely to yield the highest return. Latimer could deal secretly with the mayor for a false return and secretly with the free burgesses for a double return. As the corporation would have to make the first choice, and deny the free burgesses their purported rights, Latimer would be named on the writ before the mayor discovered his perfidy. He would then only have to assure the free burgesses that he would finance their dispute through a partner and agree to guide it through the Committee of Elections. On these conditions they should have little objection to selecting him.[126] The advantage of being named on both returns was decisive. The rules of seating in disputes were designed only to ensure representation for each community, not to judge equity. Until the committee could untangle the disputes, only Latimer would be seated. To lose his place he would have to be defeated in two cases, both of which he could fight with delays. Best of all, Temple would not be in the House to act as a counterweight on the committee's proceedings.[127] It was this course that Latimer appeared ready to pursue when news arrived that Thomas Wharton had been selected knight of the shire.

Wharton's victory incensed Justice Jeffreys. Despite his efforts and his personal involvement, Hackett had been soundly defeated. Indeed, county sentiment was such that Wharton might have set Brackley aside had he wished to name his own junior partner.[128] The defeat was as much a blow to Jeffreys's pride as it was to his influence. To redeem the first he was ready to lash out at the nearest target, but to protect the second he needed to limit his own exposure. Whatever promises had been made to Hackett, there was now no question of an open electoral campaign that might result in another humiliation. If Hackett was to be brought in, it would have to be arranged before his candidacy was announced at Buckingham. Such an effort necessitated more allies than just the mayor and Atterbury. Jeffreys now needed Latimer.

The circumstances that drew Jeffreys to Latimer were mutually beneficial. During the previous weeks Latimer had met Jeffreys and used his father's influence in an attempt to dissuade him from entering Hackett into the contest. Their most compelling argument was that he and Hackett would only compete for the same voices. Alone, Latimer would have the best chance to defeat Verney.[129] After Verney's conduct at the shire

---

[126] In 1681 Temple had been selected on both franchises though of course there was no opportunity for the dispute to be heard before the sudden dissolution.

[127] British Library, Add. Mss., 28,087, fol. 35. "Your Lordship will be safe both ways and Sir Richard Temple himself forced to petition and wait without doors."

[128] B. D. Henning, ed., *House of Commons 1660–1690*, I, 136.

[129] British Library, Add. Mss., 28,087, fols. 33–34.

election – throwing all his support behind Wharton despite professions to the contrary – Verney's defeat would be almost as satisfactory to Jeffreys as Hackett's election.[130] But if Jeffreys were to team with Latimer without sacrificing Hackett, a strategy would have to be devised that might turn Temple out as well. This would have to be even more complex than the one contemplated by Latimer. While Mayor Ethersay might be persuaded to make a false return against Verney, too many aldermen were bound to Temple to expect that he could be set aside in the same fashion. Something more fundamental was required.

Temple watched the gathering storm with increasing discomfort. He had mistakenly assumed that Verney would easily acquire a majority of magistrates once their pairing was announced. If he had had any misgivings at the beginning, they had concerned defending the new charter from a dispute with the free burgesses. Latimer's near-success was not only surprising, it also demonstrated that Temple's hold over the corporate elite was less firm than he had supposed. The mayor had proven wholly unreliable. Temple had already approached the undersheriff in hope of altering the wording on the writ so that a majority of aldermen could initiate the election. This had failed, as had all efforts to apply pressure upon Ethersay.[131] Sir Richard was also vexed by Verney's ineffectual campaign. The prolongation of the contest had brought it to attention at Court. Rumors circulated, fanned by Danby, that Temple was juggling with the writ and interfering with Latimer's election. After the county contest, Jeffreys added his voice to the others, and along with stories of misconduct came allegations of disloyalty. Temple was forced to lie low at Westminster, hardly a posture for a would-be placeman, bemoaning to Sir Ralph that his support of Wharton might "prove not only fatal to you, but to your friends at Buckingham and me also."[132]

Almost incredibly, the battle for the Buckingham seats now intensified. Mayor Ethersay announced that he would delay the event until after the King's coronation, which added several more weeks to the campaign.[133] Abandoning hope of a false return, Latimer again reversed his field, sensing an opportunity to gain a majority among the magistrates. By the middle of April he had made his first appearance in town, personally appealing to members of Verney's interest to change their votes. "All imaginable endeavors have been used to get off one of my seven votes," Sir Ralph reported to his son John on April 16.[134]

[130]   British Library, M/636/39. Sir Richard Temple to Sir Ralph Verney, April 22, 1685.
[131]   Ibid. Thomas Barnwell to Sir Richard Temple, March 21, 1685; Sir Ralph Verney to John Verney, April 5, 1685.
[132]   Ibid. Sir Richard Temple to Sir Ralph Verney, April 11, 1685.
[133]   Ibid. Sir Richard Temple to Sir Ralph Verney, April 17, 1685.
[134]   Ibid. Sir Ralph Verney to John Verney, April 16, 1685.

When Verney's support proved unexpectedly solid, however, Latimer shifted his attention from Buckingham to Westminster. With Jeffreys's aid, it might be possible to persuade Temple to break off his pairing with Verney. If Temple would declare himself neutral for the second seat it would release a number of aldermen whose pledges had been made in Temple's interest.[135] If Sir Richard refused, some more drastic means would have to be sought to diminish his influence over the corporation.

Temple had to assess his tactics as much for the effect they would have after the election as for their efficacy during the contest. A loss of power over the aldermen could initiate another free-for-all and revive Sir Peter Tyrell's ambitions.[136] Even among his own followers the mercenary streak had shown thick. If he did not maintain his grip he would face additional years of fighting mayoral elections and plotting aldermanic accessions with no greater certainty that some ambitious newcomer would not overthrow his efforts with a single, well-timed push. Thus Latimer's demand that he renounce his partnership with Verney struck to the heart of Temple's interests in the town. If only it were as easy as that.

The depths of these difficulties were brought home to Temple when Latimer and Jeffreys unleashed their final assault. Unable to secure a majority of the Thirteen, they decided to shorten the odds. After Latimer's fruitless appearance in town, Thomas Atterbury went up to London to initiate a case of judicial misconduct against Alderman George Dancer.[137] The charges related to the boisterous meetings on March 4 when, in his cups, Dancer had called Mayor Ethersay a shatterbrain and uttered some equivocal remarks about loyalty. Atterbury, Ethersay, and William Hartley separately deposed that Dancer's conduct during the corporate meeting violated his oath and was grounds for dismissal from the governing body.[138] Dancer had been chosen as the sacrificial lamb because the case against him appeared the most damaging on the surface. His shouting match with Ethersay had taken place in the presence of a majority of the aldermen and could be dated, with disingenuous imprecision, on the day of an official meeting about the election. But discussions between Atterbury and Ethersay, the contents of which were carefully leaked, hinted that Nathaniel Kent and perhaps Jonathon Seaton could become future targets.[139] Success against Dancer might prove a persuasive object lesson.

---

[135] Ibid. Sir Richard Temple to Sir Ralph Verney, April 22, 1685.
[136] Throughout the contest, Temple had one eye on Tyrell and his activities. Ibid. Sir Richard Temple to Sir Ralph Verney, April 5, 1685.
[137] Ibid. Sir Ralph Verney to John Verney, April 16, 1685.
[138] Ibid. "Information of Thomas Atterbury," April 20, 1685. British Library, Add. Mss., 28,087, fol. 82.
[139] Ibid. Sir Richard Temple to Sir Ralph Verney, April 17, 1685.

The attack on Dancer energized Temple and Verney. As veteran legal gladiators they quickly grasped the multiple dangers of a prosecution. First, Temple organized a counterpetition defending Dancer against the charges of disloyalty. Eight aldermen, among others, protested that Dancer had always given his voice for loyal members of Parliament who supported the rightful succession of the Crown.[140] As steward, Temple took the deposition of Alderman George Carter, which set out the extenuating circumstances of Dancer's affray with the mayor and specified that it had taken place at night in an inn.[141] Verney alerted his son John to the complications that were likely to arise, writing twice in the same day and sending by different carriers. Depositions would be presented to the lord chief justice, who would have power to imprison Dancer or bind him over. John would have to be ready to appeal for a delay of the case or to arrange for bail on short notice.[142] Sir Ralph wrote directly to Jeffreys to plead that the hearing be postponed until after the election. He had little expectation of favor, but calculated that the appeal might be useful in a subsequent electoral dispute.[143]

Exoneration, imprisonment, defeat by an attenuated corporation – they had to prepare for all eventualities. Removing Dancer from the governing body, even temporarily, would recreate the deadlock that had existed before Hillesden's decision to support Verney. What would happen then? Latimer's attack had outrun his planning. Gaining the depositions and bringing the aldermen along had occupied all of William Carter's energies. He kept late hours with Latimer's supporters, coordinating their testimony and seeking technical advice from Jeffreys, who cautiously directed him to a legal agent.[144] Their hope was that the King, on receipt of the petition and affidavits, would remove Dancer from the corporation immediately. This might by itself tip the balance of the election by causing a defection or an abstention. It might also convert Temple to the course of least resistance: "Sir Richard thinks that if he left your interest to join with my Lord Latimer then no further proceeding would be against the charter by *quo warranto*."[145] But time was very short, and Carter wondered whether the corporation could remove Dan-

[140]   British Library, M/636/38 (misfiled). "Certificate in Defense of George Dancer."
[141]   British Library, M/636/40. "Testimony of George Carter," May 7, 1685 (this was when Verney received a copy).
[142]   British Library, M/636/39. Sir Ralph Verney to John Verney, April 20, 1685. Sir Ralph cautioned John not to take any action at this time but to be prepared to approach Jeffreys if necessary.
[143]   Ibid. Sir Richard Temple to Sir Ralph Verney, April 18, 1685.
[144]   British Library, Add. Mss., 28,087, fol. 44.
[145]   British Library, M/636/40. John Verney to Sir Ralph Verney, April 24, 1685.

cer if the King delayed: "Whether the six, with the mayor's casting voice may not do it themselves."[146]

This was a question that could only be resolved by reference to the charter. Each corporation had its own rules for the removal of incapacitated or maleficent governors. It only now dawned upon Latimer that his final ploy depended upon a clause in a charter that Sir Richard Temple had drafted. It was innocuous enough: "The aldermen to be chosen for life... unless put out for reasonable cause by the majority of the mayor and aldermen."[147] "Reasonable cause" was language flexible enough to cover the circumstances that Atterbury had woven together against Dancer. But where was the stipulation, so common in the new charters, that reserved for the King his right to dismiss at pleasure? In vain was the charter scrutinized. Its final proviso stated that mayor and sergeant, steward and deputy-steward, and all justices of the peace could be removed "by order of his [Majesty's] Privy Council."[148] Nowhere did it state that such power could be exercised over aldermen. Only by a majority of their own number could they be removed, without direction for the presence or absence of the accused, without provision for a casting voice at all. They needed a majority, a full, clear majority – a seventh voice.

If Latimer was crestfallen by the discovery, Jeffreys was dumbfounded. The new charters were carefully vetted to ensure the crown's prerogative over the boroughs and the borough's loyalty to the crown. The Buckingham charter had been scrutinized by Secretary Godolphin and had been granted less than a year before.[149] How could it have failed to protect the King's right to dismiss at pleasure? Jeffreys brought the matter directly to James II and urged him to take the most forceful action possible as a sign to the aldermen of the royal will. Without a hearing or an opportunity for the presentation of the counterpetition and George Carter's affidavit, Dancer was removed from the town's commission of the peace and replaced by William Carter.[150] Simultaneously, Jeffreys began to search for legal precedents that might regain the initiative against Dancer and, if necessary, the charter itself.

Temple and Verney had not yet repelled the counterattack, but at least they were fighting on terrain of their own choice. Had their opponents been aware of local history, they would have known why the

[146] British Library, Add. Mss., 28,087, fol. 44.
[147] PRO SP 44/66/321.
[148] PRO SP 44/66/322.
[149] PRO SP 44/70/30.
[150] British Library, Add. Mss., 28,087, fol. 39.

charter specified the most stringent standard for removing aldermen. During the years that Heyward had languished in prison, his opponents had attempted, with near success, to have him dismissed from the governing body. Nor did rotating mayors make the best tiebreakers in troubled times. Sir Richard Temple had put his trust in majorities, and he was now to discover whether or not it was well founded.

The same problem that vexed Jeffreys absorbed Temple and Verney. John Verney was sent to find the most powerful legal experts to discover the most likely interpretations of the charter. Neither Sir Henry Pollexfen nor Sir John Holt would offer opinions or accept John's prominently displayed purse of gold. The question was one of politics, not one of law.[151] John did learn, from less influential legalists, that the clauses were ironclad and that the mayor had no casting voice either in removing aldermen or in electing parliamentary burgesses. But there was little doubt that any number of aldermen could be set aside by due process, no matter how spurious the charges or perjured the evidence: "Twas nothing now to turn out men, many in a day, to disenfranchise them because of elections."[152]

Justice Jeffreys needed little corroboration from legal experts to realize that he was outflanked. If the King could not remove Dancer it would be impossible to resolve the issue of the mayor's casting vote before the election. Were they to continue to storm this hill they would have to employ all their reserves to remove two members of the corporation and thus create a clear majority. Nathaniel Kent had already been considered as a potential candidate for proceedings when it was decided to remove Dancer. Charges against him would have to be prepared and pressed forward by Carter and Latimer. Already the disarray was evident. Mayor Ethersay had announced a hall for the removal of Dancer on the supposition that he held the deciding vote. This had to be headed off after the aldermen had been primed to perform their distasteful task.[153] They had to regroup for an even more difficult confrontation, and time was shorter than ever.

In fact, the game was up. The aldermen of Buckingham knew more about purges in their ranks than either Jeffreys or Latimer. For months during the winter of 1683–84 they had argued and bickered, pleaded and begged both each other and Temple for inclusions and exclusions of the sitting burgesses. Four members of the governing body had then been removed. It was a catharsis few wished repeated. Ethersay's brother had been a victim, and the grievances the mayor had stored up he was

[151]   British Library, M/636/40. John Verney to Sir Ralph Verney, May 5, 1685.
[152]   Ibid. John Verney to Sir Ralph Verney, May 11, 1685.
[153]   Ibid. Jonathon Seaton to Sir Ralph Verney, May 16, 1685.

now expending with satisfaction. But for others the wounds had healed, and they had no desire to have them reopened. Each individual target exposed a different complex of personal loyalties and aroused deeper self-interested concern for the future. If the purgers were to be purged in turn, where would it end? The cracks were already apparent. Temple had obtained eight signatures to the testimonial for Dancer and he might even find another in defense of Kent. The opposition was vulnerable and isolated. On May 11 it broke: "Mr Atterbury would have turned them out from being aldermen but his own party would not join in so foul a practice against two of their brethren," Sir Ralph reported to John with considerable relief.[154]

"I send this only to tell that this morning Sir Richard Temple and myself were elected at Buckingham without any noise or trouble. Mr. Atterbury was not there nor did my Lord Latimer come down. So the whole twelve electors signed the book for Sir Richard Temple and seven signed it for me."[155] Such, on May 15, was the whimpering finale to the three-month struggle for Buckingham. It left Latimer humbled, Verney dyspeptic, and Temple an insomniac. The decisive result "without noise or trouble" was as unexpected as every other element of this remarkable contest. So many ends remained loose when Latimer's support collapsed that it was hard for any of them to imagine a suitable conclusion.

The sequel is a story in itself, but curiosity about it should be sated. Edward Osborne, Viscount Latimer accepted the election of the free burgesses but made no effort to follow the dispute. The syphilis he had contracted was already sapping his strength. He would not live to fight another day. Sir Ralph Verney, once his return was secure, carried out his reluctant pledge to share the costs of building the town hall. It still stands today, disfigured on one side by a road-widening scheme, with little reminder of its fantastic origins. George Jeffreys accepted defeat in the town with no better grace than he had in the county. He gained revenge of a sort, securing a *quo warranto* against the charter and purging the corporation to his own taste. His success was short-lived, washed away like the King he served in 1689. Sir Richard Temple continued his successful career of playing both ends against the middle, becoming a pensioner to both James II and William III. For Buckingham, the seeds planted by "Sir Timber" bore their fruit over the next century. If anything, the town enhanced its reputation for hard-fought elections.

[154]   Ibid. Sir Ralph Verney to John Verney, May 11, 1685.
[155]   Ibid. Sir Ralph Verney to John Verney, May 15, 1685.

Conclusion

SEVENTY YEARS separated the election of Sir Maurice Berkeley and John Poulett from that of Sir Richard Temple and Sir Ralph Verney. More than the seasons had passed away. The Somerset election of 1614 was part of a system that stretched back into the past, a system based on status, in which honor and obligation were paramount. The Buckingham election of 1685 was part of a system that stretched forward into the future, a system based on competition for rewards, in which patronage and principle were paramount. Though there were similarities in outward form, at its core parliamentary selection had been transformed. A process of social distinction and community assent had given way to one of political power and electoral consent.

These changes did not take place suddenly, but neither did they evolve gradually. For many county families parliamentary candidacy maintained its hereditary character. In the years between the Armada and the Glorious Revolution three generations of Berkeleys and Pouletts, of Temples and Verneys engaged in parliamentary selections. Activities that pass from fathers to sons acquire their own traditions. But over a longer span, the politicization of county life that the Revolution effected was easily recognizable and can be readily observed one generation removed. Between grandfathers and grandsons ideas about political participation, about the role of Parliament, and about the importance of selection had been transmuted.

It was John Temple, Sir Richard's grandfather, who had leapt too soon into the muddled Buckinghamshire selection of 1588, and who had to weigh the obligations of honor against those of friendship. On that occasion, the timely intervention of a privy councilor prevented a contest that candidates and freeholders abhorred.[1] A century later, in Buckingham town, the intervention of Lord Jeffreys complicated a con-

---

[1] See Chapter 3 of this book.

test that candidates and electors relished. Neither honor nor friendship weighed heavily with Sir Richard Temple. Sir Maurice Berkeley, Lord Fitzharding, also would have found the attitudes of his grandfather mystifying. Old Sir Maurice had spent most of the 1614 campaign apologizing to Sir Edward Phelips for standing in competition against his son and defending his candidacy to county magistrates and court officials. His grandson made a career in parliamentary elections, contesting two unsuccessfully in 1679 and winning four others, two of them in contests.[2]

It was the contest that symbolized the transformation of parliamentary selection. Though contests had always been part of the process, they had rarely been a purposeful part. Before the Revolution contests were indicative of failure. They occurred unexpectedly and haphazardly and involved issues of honor and reputation rather than issues of politics or belief. The structure of the selection process worked to inhibit them, as did the actions of potential candidates. Rotas among prominent families, the predesignation of borough officers, and the grant of nominations to patrons were more common features of selection than were contests. The code of conduct that assessed greater shame to defeat than it accorded honor to victory ensured that few would risk the one for the other. Moreover, when contests threatened it was the obligation of county magistrates, borough officials, and officers of the state to attempt to compose them. If communities were divided into factions or disturbed by religious dispute, then their leaders worked even harder to prevent eruptions at parliamentary selections.

The idea that harmonious choice best served the interests of local elites – magistrates, freemen, or freeholders – operated on several levels. First, it honored those chosen, individuals or patrons whose good will was tied to the welfare of the community. Divisive selections left bitter legacies. Second, it knit the local society together, whether a small corporate body or a mass of county freeholders. It was a ritual of affirmation that bound the participants to each other and recreated their collective identity. In corporations, selections were performed in the full regalia of office with a gravity that is hard to recapture. In counties, they were orchestrated by the sheriff and justices of the peace with the solemn legal trappings of quarter sessions or assizes. All of this was of more than symbolic importance in a society where individuals identified themselves with their community and gave primary allegiance to their shire. Finally, harmonious choice served the interests of the nation. Whichever

[2] B. D. Henning, ed., *The House of Commons 1660–90*, I, 632–33; 369–72. In February 1679 a Berkeley and Phelips finally paired together for the Somerset county seats. They were defeated.

of the many notions of Parliament prevailed – that it existed to do the King's business; that it was the grand jury of the realm; that it was the council of the monarch; or that it was the representative of the people – all were best served by members who bespoke the will of their localities.

These were potent inducements for communities to make unified choices. They outweighed the increasing ideological polarization of the late 1620s and in some places even outlasted the Revolution. But from the 1640s onward the survival of older forms and values came despite social and political circumstances rather than because of them. Parliament had proved itself too powerful for its membership to depend upon whim, or chance, or rota. Men's estates, indeed their very lives were defended or taken by those who held seats in the House of Commons. The competition between those who wanted to arrest it was the beginning of the quest for places in Parliament. Candidates were now motivated by impulses other than their own honor and merit, impulses that could be held superior to those of the individual. To promote King Charles, or King Jesus, or Noll Cromwell, candidates had already risked more than defeat in contested elections.

As values changed, so did methods. Conduct reprehensible to one generation became mere practicality to another. If there was merit in competing for a seat, then there was even greater merit in winning one. Careers at Court depended upon presence in the House of Commons, careers in the country upon patronage to it. After the Restoration, attention came to be fixed upon parliamentary constituencies – their composition, their patrons, and their electorate. Natural connections between individuals and boroughs were shored up. New connections were put in place. Making an interest became the preoccupation of the elite in court and country, and their competition drove up costs. Even safe seats soon required lavish expenditures. There were agents to fee, magistrates to coddle, electors to mollify. Most of all, there were opponents to stymie. Charters were scrutinized and challenged by one set of parliamentary candidates, redrafted and defended by another. Ironclad clauses were reinforced by the Crown and undermined by the Committee of Elections, or girdered by the committee and recast by the Crown. There was little of principle in the process.

Competition for places in Parliament led to new sophistication in the process of selection. As so much was calculated on victory, so much depended upon those who determined it. These could be returning officers, patrons, government officials, or the electorate. Circumstance varied in time and place and was largely dictated by the strengths and weaknesses of opponents. Secure patronage was the safest route, reliance upon a large electorate the riskiest. But each depended upon the ferocity of competition, the political savvy of the candidates, and the expectations of the electors. As these increased with the rapid succession of general elections during the Exclusion Crisis, more settled modes of resolving contests emerged. Frequent legal battles helped determine franchises. Rules for polling and counting voters were gradually standardized. The discretion of returning officers and powerful patrons was limited. All of these elements worked to develop an equity based upon majority decisions to replace the old equity based upon social standing or magisterial solidarity.

Yet there was nothing altruistic about this emerging majoritarianism. It arose from the competition within the elite for control of boroughs or the voices of county freeholders. It was seen as a falling off from a natural, organic unity – which had never existed in actuality so strongly as it did in memory – a falling off made necessary by the depredations of mankind. Despite the sententious rhetoric of losing candidates or far-seeing common lawyers, majoritarianism was not based upon notions of universal suffrage or the rights of man. It was as yet but a tactical development deployed to cope with the irreconcilable divisions within local society. A society which until recently had defined disagreement as dissidence was now awash in dissident groups. Religious congregations competed with each other and with the national church for the keys to the Kingdom of Heaven. Political associations that outlasted the Revolution hardened in the 1670s and 1680s. No county was without its former royalists and its former parliamentarians, its court peers and its country peers, its proto-Tories and its proto-Whigs. Unity now meant the agreement of the like-minded rather than the conversion of the scrupulous. If majorities were not preferable they were practical, and practicality – not for the first time – overcame ideals. The transformation of the selection of members to Parliament mirrored the political transformation among those who selected them.

Yet for all that was different, much survived between old and new. The efflorescent aristocratic classes continued to dominate the process, maintaining their stranglehold on candidacy and, with the increasing importance of patronage, actually expanding their influence. The later seventeenth century witnessed a consolidation of gentry and aristocracy after years of flux. The descendants of the Jacobean parvenus at whom Elizabethan gentlemen had sneered were now part of the ancient lineage of county communities. In many cases they had made their way into the expanded ranks of the titular nobility and now pushed their sons into county seats. The rapid geographical mobility into and out of urban areas that characterized the town elites of the Tudors appears to have slowed in the succeeding century. Progress into the upper reaches of urban oligarchies now followed a more settled course, even when replacements were needed after political purges. This helped patrons establish durable ties with ruling magistrates and allowed local oligarchs to claim their own precedence for borough seats. While the social groups that comprised the electorate expanded, the social groups that comprised the elected contracted.

With this social continuity came a traditionalism that helped to soften the edges of change within the process of selection. The child is the father of the man. As ideals, the quest for unified choice and the observance of honor and deference maintained their appeal. Rotational arrangements and patronage continued to serve as safety valves, though they now relieved different pressures, the desire to save the expense of elections most prominent among them. Meetings of county magistrates could still settle upon nominees to avoid electoral contests, and the recitation of ancient values could still persuade reluctant colleagues into acquiescence. In the political crises of 1679 and in the political reaction of 1685 unified choice sent a powerful ideological message.

While it is traditional to explain the increasing importance of contested elections in political terms, they are the terms of issue-oriented politics. In the eyes of the Whigs, who date the rise of contests to the late sixteenth and early seventeenth centuries, contested elections resulted from challenges to authority. Discontented gentry, either aspiring officeholders or Puritan malcontents, challenged the Crown and its boroughmongers. Disenfranchised denizens challenged repressive oligarchs for their natural right of political participation. Local communities challenged the stranglehold of invading patrons and their carpetbagging nominees. In each case contested elections were the opportunity for ideological struggle, and in each case their appearance furthered the advance of democracy.

Contests did result from an increasing politicization of English society, but they rarely resulted from straightforward ideological division. As the process of selection was firmly rooted in the social hierarchy of early modern English society, contests grew from conflict within the elite. As political and religious divisions sharpened after the Restoration, they became but another element in the struggle for social differentiation. Potent ideological issues, like the summoning of the Long Parliament or the Exclusion Crisis, increased competition for seats in Parliament, but these were extraordinary events whose impact was general rather than specific. It was not political issues per se, but the politicization of English society that had a decisive impact upon the process of parliamentary selection. It was this that broke apart the identity of interest within the ruling classes and gave rise to the competition so evident in electoral contests.

This was a process still in its infancy by the late seventeenth century. Far more of the social elements of selection would have to be stripped away, far more of the political elements of elections would have to grow in their place before the transformation was complete. But it was with the English Revolution that that process began, and it is to the mid-seventeenth century that we must look to understand the origins of participatory democracy. It is a surprising sight.

Selected Bibliography

Archives

British Library
Additional manuscripts
       6705 Derbyshire Collections
  11,044–51 Scudamore Papers
  22,248 Letters and Papers Relating to Election Matters at Aldeburgh, Suffolk 1584–1737
  28,175 Collections for a History of Tamworth
  29,550–51 Hatton-Finch Papers
  29,910 Correspondence of the Swynfyn Family
  32,324 Papers of the Family of Seymour of Trowbridge
  32,464 Papers Relating to the Parliament of 1614
  33,512 Sandwich Corporation Letters and Papers
  33,572–73 Hale Papers
  33,923 Transcript of the Diary of Sir John Knatchbull
  34,306 Correspondence of the Earl of Devonshire 1660–66
  37,818 Nicholas Papers: Register of Lord Zouch, Warden of the Cinque Ports, 1618–24
  37,819 Nicholas Papers: Duke of Buckingham's Register
  40,629–30 Cassonbury Papers
  44,846 Letterbook of Sir Thomas Peyton
Egerton manuscripts
      784 William Whiteway's Diary
  2644–46 Barrington Papers
  3330–31 Correspondence of Thomas Osborne, Duke of Leeds
Harleian manuscripts
       97 Papers of Sir Symonds D'Ewes
     384 Letters to Sir Symonds D'Ewes
     387 Miscellaneous D'Ewes Papers
   1929 Notebook of Randall Holme
   2105 Randall Holme's Chester Collections
   2125 Randall Holme's Chester Collections
   2313 Notes on Commons' Proceedings

Stowe manuscripts
    184 Dering Papers
    185 Miscellaneous Historical Papers
    743 Dering Correspondence
Loans
    28 Harley Papers
Microfilms
    485 Hatfield Manuscripts
    636 Verney Papers

Public Record Office
Admiralty
    2/1745–46 Papers of James, Duke of York, Lord Admiral
Chancery
    C/219 Election Indentures
Star Chamber
    STAC/5 Elizabeth I
    STAC/8 James I
State Papers
    SP/14 James I
    SP/21 Charles I
    SP/29 Charles II
    SP/44 Charles II
    SP/46 James II

Institute of Historical Research
Kingsmill Family Letters

Bristol Record Office
    AC Smythe of Ashton Court

Cumberland Record Office
    CA Carlisle City Records
    D/LONS Lowther Manuscripts

Essex Record Office
    Morant Papers
    D/DBA Barrington Papers
    D/B Maldon Papers

Hampshire Record Office
    M69 Jerviose Manuscripts

Huntington Library
    HA Hastings Manuscripts
    STT Temple-Stowe Manuscripts

Kent Archive Office

U1015 Papillon Papers
U350 Dering Papers
U47 Twysden Papers
Qb Queenborough Records
NR New Romney Records
Sa Sandwich Records

Lambeth Palace Library
Shrewsbury Manuscripts

Leeds Central Library
MX Mexborough Manuscripts

Norfolk and Norwich Record Office
NAS Gaudy Manuscripts
Walsingham Papers of Sir Edward de Grey
Aylsham Papers of Sir Arthur Heveningham
M 430–31 Townshend Manuscripts

Northamptonshire Record Office
IC Isham Correspondence
FH Finch-Hatton Papers
Montague Papers of Lord Montague of Boughton
F (M) C Peterborough Records
Northampton Town Records

Althrope House
Spencer Manuscripts

Nottinghamshire University Library
Cl Clifton Manuscripts
NeC Letterbooks of the Earl of Clere
Cl LP East Retford Papers

Somerset Record Office
DD/PH Phelips Manuscripts
DD/SF Sandford Manuscripts

Staffordshire Record Office
D1721 Bagot Papers

Wiltshire Record Office
John Hawarde's Diary

Longleat House
Whitelocke Papers

Westmoreland Record Office
D/RY Rydall Hall Manuscripts

Printed Sources

Place of publication is London unless otherwise noted.

Acts of the Privy Council of England. New series, 32 vols. 1890–1907.

de Beer, E.S., ed. *The Diary of John Evelyn.* 6 vols. Oxford and London, 1955.

Birch, Thomas, ed. *A Collection of the State Papers of John Thurloe.* 7 vols. 1742.

Blundell, Margaret, ed. *Cavalier: Letters of William Blundell to His Friends 1620–1698.* 1933.

Bond, Maurice F. *The Diaries and Papers of Sir Edward Dering.* 1976.

Braybrooke, P., ed. *The Autobiography of Sir John Bramston, K. B.* Camden Society, vol. 32. 1845.

Browning, A., ed. *Memoirs of Sir John Reresby.* Glasgow, 1936.

Bruce, J., ed. *Notes of Proceedings in the Long Parliament. . . by Sir Ralph Verney.* Camden Society, vol. 31. 1844.

Bruce, J., W. D. Hamilton, and S. C. Lomes, eds. *Calendar of State Papers, Domestic Series, of the Reign of Charles I.* 12 vols. 1858–97.

Buckley, W. E. *Memoires of the Earl of Ailesbury.* 2 vols. Roxburghe Club. 1890.

Challenor, Bromley. *Selections from the Municipal Chronicles of the Borough of Abingdon.* Abingdon, 1898.

Chanter, J. R., and T. Wainwright, eds. *Barnstaple Records.* 2 vols. Barnstaple, 1900.

Cooper, W. D. *Saville Correspondence.* Camden Society, vol. 71. 1858.

Cope, Esther, ed. *Proceedings of the Short Parliament of 1640.* Camden Society, fourth series, vol. 19. 1977.

Courtenay, Thomas P. *Memoirs of the Life, Works, and Correspondence of Sir William Temple, Bart.* 2 vols. 1936.

Day, William Ansell. *The Pythouse Papers.* 1879.

Domestick Intelligencer. Edited by Benjamin Harris.

The Domestick Intelligencer. Edited by Nathaniel Thompson.

Duckett, George. *Penal Laws: Test Act.* 2 vols. 1882–83.

East, R., ed. *Extracts from Records in the Possession of the Municipal Corporation of the Borough of Portsmouth.* Portsmouth, 1891.

Firth, C. H., ed. *The Clarke Papers.* Camden Society Publications. 4 vols. 1891–1901.

Firth, C. H., and R. S. Rait, eds. *Acts and Ordinances of the Interregnum.* 3 vols. 1911.

Gardiner, Dorothy, ed. *The Oxinden and Peyton Letters 1642–1670.* 1937.

Gilmore, G. D. "The Papers of Richard Taylor of Clapham." *Bedfordshire Record Society Publications,* 25 (1947): 104-9.

Glanville, John. *Reports of Certain Cases Returned and Adjudged by the Commons in Parliament.* 1775.

Goldney, F. H., ed. *Records of Chippenham.* 1889.

Greaves, R. W., ed. *The First Ledger Book of High Wycombe.* Archaeological and Architectural Society of Buckinghamshire Records Branch Publications, vol. 11. Buckingham, 1956.

Green, M. A. E., F. H. B. Daniell, and F. Berkley, eds. *Calendar of State Papers, Domestic Series, of the Reign of Charles II.* 28 vols. 1860–1939.

Gribble, Joseph. *Memorials of Barnstaple.* Barnstaple, 1830.

Gurney, Hudson. "Extracts from the Proceedings of the Corporation of Lynn Regis." *Archaeologia*, 24 (1832): 317–28.

Historical Manuscripts Commission Reports. *5th Report* (manuscripts of the Duke of Sutherland; Sir Alexander Malet; Sir Nicholas Lechmere; Reverend E. Field; Cholmondeley manuscripts). 1876.

6th Report (manuscripts of Sir Robert Paston). 1877–8.

7th Report (manuscripts of Sir Harry Verney; G. E. Frere; G. A. Lowndes; W. More-Molyneux). 1879.

9th Report (manuscripts of the corporation of Ipswich). 1883–84.

10th Report, Appendix IV (More manuscripts). 1885.

11th Report, Appendix III (manuscripts of the corporation of King's Lynn). 1887.

11th Report, Appendix V (manuscripts of the Earl of Dartmouth). 1887.

11th Report, Appendix VII (manuscripts of the Duke of Leeds; Reading Corporation). 1888.

12th Report, Appendix I (manuscripts of the Earl Cowper, Sir John Coke). 1888.

12th Report, Appendices IV & V (manuscripts of the Duke of Rutland). 1888–1905.

12th Report, Appendix VII (manuscripts of S. H. LeFleming). 1890.

12th Report, Appendix IX (manuscripts of the Duke of Beaufort). 1891.

13th Report, Appendices I & II (manuscripts of the Duke of Portland). 1891–93.

13th Report, Appendix IV (records of the corporation of Rye; Dovaston mss.; manuscripts of Captain Loder-Symonds). 1892.

13th Report, Appendix VI (manuscripts of Sir William Fitzherbert). 1893.

14th Report, Appendix IV (manuscripts of the Lord Kenyon). 1894.

14th Report, Appendix IX (manuscripts of the Earl of Lindsey). 1895.

15th Report, Appendix VII (manuscripts of the Duke of Somerset; the Marquis of Ailesbury). 1898.

Report on the Manuscripts of the Marquis of Salisbury. 24 vols. 1883–1981.

Report on the Manuscripts of the Duke of Buccleuch and Queensberry. 3 vols. 1899–1926.

Report on the Manuscripts of F. W. Leybourne-Popham. 1899.

Report on the Manuscripts of Lord Montague of Beaulieu. 1900.

Report on the Frankland–Russell–Astley Manuscripts. 1900.

Report on the Manuscripts in Various Collections. 8 vols. 1901–14. Volume II, *Report on the Manuscripts of Sir George Wombwell; Miss Buxton; Mrs. Wentworth;* Volume IV, *Report on the Manuscripts of the Corporation of Aldeburgh; Orford; and Salisbury;* Volume VII, *Report on the Manuscripts of the Dissolved Corporation of Dunwich.*

Calendar of the Manuscripts of the Marquis of Ormond. 8 vols. 1902–20.

Report on the Manuscripts of the Earl of Verulam. 1906.

Report on the Manuscripts of Allan George Finch. 2 vols. 1913–22.

Report on the Manuscripts of R. R. Hastings. 4 vols. 1928–47.

Hobson, M. G., and H. E. Salter, eds. *Oxford Council Acts 1626–1665.* Oxford Historical Society Publications, vol. 95. Oxford, 1933.

Hull, Felix, ed. *The White and Black Books of the Cinque Ports.* 1966.

Johnson, R. C., M. F. Keeler, M. J. Cole, and W. B. Bidwell, eds. *Proceedings in Parliament 1628.* 6 vols. New Haven, 1977–83.

Kempe, A. J. *The Loseley Manuscripts.* 1836.

Knowler, William, ed. *The Earl of Strafford's Letters and Dispatches.* 2 vols. 1739.

Larking, L. B. *Proceedings in the County of Kent in Connection with the Parliaments Called in 1640.* Camden Society, vol. 80. 1862.

Latimer, John. *The Annals of Bristol in the 17th Century.* Bristol, 1900.

Leach, Arthur F., ed. *Beverley Town Documents.* Selden Society. 1900.

Lemon, R., and M. A. E. Green, eds. *Calendar of State Papers, Domestic Series, of the Reigns of Edward VI, Mary, Elizabeth and James I.* 12 vols. 1856–72.

Lewis, T. T., ed. *Letters of Lady Brilliana Harley.* Camden Society, vol. 58. 1854.

McClure, N. E., ed. *The Letters of John Chamberlain.* 2 vols. Philadelphia, 1939.

Markham, C. A., and J. C. Cox, eds. *The Records of the Borough of Northampton.* 2 vols. Northampton, 1897.

Marsham, Robert. "Poll for Norfolk Members, 1656." *Norfolk Archaeology* 1 (1847): 67.

Mayo, C. H. *The Municipal Records of the Borough of Shaftesbury.* Sherbourne, 1889.

Municipal Records of Dorchester, Dorset. Exeter, 1908.

Notestein, W., and W. H. Coates, eds. *The Journal of Sir Symonds D'Ewes.* 2 vols. New Haven, 1923–42.

Notestein, W., F. H. Relf, and H. Simpson, eds. *Commons Debates, 1621.* 7 vols. New Haven, 1935.

Ogle, O., W. H. Bliss, and C. H. Firth, eds. *Calendar of the Clarendon State Papers.* 4 vols. Oxford, 1872–1938.

Palmer, C. R., ed. *The History of Great Yarmouth by Henry Manship.* 2 vols. Great Yarmouth, 1854–56.

Return of Every Member of the Lower House of the Parliament of England. . . 1213–1874. 2 vols. 1878.

Robbins, Caroline. "Election Correspondence of Sir John Holland of Quidenham, 1661." *Norfolk Archaeology* 30 (1952): 130–39.

Rutledge, F. J., ed. *Calendar of the Clarendon State Papers.* vols. IV and V. Oxford, 1932, 1970.

Rutt, John T. *Diary of Thomas Burton.* 4 vols. 1828.

Sainty, J. C. *Lieutenants of Counties, 1585–1642.* Bulletin of the Institute of Historical Research, special supplement no. 8. 1970.

Salter, H. E. *Oxford Council Acts 1583–1626.* Oxford Historical Society Publications, vol. 87. Oxford, 1928.

Saxton, E. B. "Fresh Light on the Liverpool Election of 1670." *Historical Society of Lancashire and Cheshire* 93 (1941): 54–68.

Scrope, R., and T. Monkhouse, eds. *State Papers Collected by Edward, Earl of Clarendon, Commencing 1621.* 3 vols. Oxford, 1767–86.

Smith, John. *The Life, Journals, and Correspondence of Samuel Pepys.* 2 vols. London, 1841.

Stevenson, W. H., et al., eds. *Records of the Borough of Nottingham.* 9 vols. London and Nottingham, 1882–1956.

Tanner, J. R., ed. *Further Correspondence of Samuel Pepys 1662–1679.* 1929.

Thompson, E. M., ed. *Correspondence of the Family of Hatton.* 2 vols. Camden Society, new series, vols. 22–23. 1878–9.

Tighe, R. R., and J. E. Davis. *Annals of Windsor.* 2 vols. 1858.

Timings, E. K., ed. *Calendar of State Papers, Domestic Series, of the Reign of James II.* 3 vols. 1960–72.

Trollope, Andrew. "Hatcher Correspondence Relating to Parliamentary Elections."

Associated Architectural and Archaeological Societies' Reports 23 (1895–96): 134–42.

Turner, W. H. *Selections from the Records of the City of Oxford.* Oxford, 1880.

The Victoria County History of England. *The City of York.* 1961.

  The County of Buckinghamshire. 4 vols. 1905–27.

  The County of Cheshire. 3 vols. 1979–80.

  The County of Oxford. 12 vols. 1955–83.

  The County of Somerset. 21 vols. 1906–78.

  The County of Wiltshire. 12 vols. 1955–83.

  The County of York: The East Riding. 5 vols. 1969–1984.

Warner, G. F. *The Nicholas Papers.* 4 vols. Camden Society Publications. 1886–1920.

Whithed, Henry, Sir. *Sir Henry Whithed's Letter Book 1601–1614.* Hampshire Record Series 1. Portsmouth, 1976.

Williams, P. R., ed. *The Court and Times of Charles I.* 2 vols. 1848.

Secondary Works

Abbott, W. C. "The Long Parliament of Charles II." *English Historical Review* 21 (1906): 21–56, 254–285.

Adams, S. L. "Office-Holders of the Borough of Denbigh." *The Denbighshire Historical Society Transactions* 25 (1974): 92–113.

Albery, W. A. *Parliamentary History of Horsham.* 1927.

Ashford, L. J. *The History of the Borough of High Wycombe from its Origins to 1880.* 1960.

Ashmole, Elias. *The Antiquities of Berkshire.* Reading, 1736.

Atkinson, W. A. "A Parliamentary Election in Knaresborough in 1628." *Yorkshire Archaeological Journal* 34 (1939): 213–21.

Aubrey, E. R., ed. *The History and Antiquity of Southampton.* Publications of the Southampton Record Society, no. 8. Southampton, 1909.

Aylmer, G. E. *The King's Servants.* 1961.

  The State's Servants: The Civil Service of the English Republic 1649–60. 1973.

Bagot, William Baron. *Memorials of the Bagot Family.* Blithfield, 1824.

Bailey, Thomas. *Annals of Nottinghamshire.* 4 vols. London and Nottingham, 1852–55.

Baker, Joseph B. *The History of Scarborough from the Earliest Date.* 1882.

Ballard, Adolphus. *Chronicles of the Royal Borough of Woodstock.* Oxford, 1896.

Banks, G. *The Story of Corfe Castle.* 1853.

Barnes, Thomas. *Somerset 1625–1640.* 1961.

Barnes, W. Miles. "Election of the Knights of the Shire for Dorset in 1625/6." *Somerset and Dorset Notes and Queries* 4 (1895): 23–24.

Bean, W. W. *The Parliamentary Representation of the Six Northern Counties of England.* Hull, 1890.

Beesley, Alfred. *The History of Banbury.* 1841.

Benham, W. Gurney. "The Essex Petition of 1679–80." *Essex Review* 43 (1934): 193–203.

Bennett, J. *History of Tewkesbury.* Tewkesbury, 1830.

Benson, R., and H. Hatcher. *Old and New Sarum, or Salisbury.* 2 vols. 1843.

Bettey, J. H., ed. *Calendar of the Correspondence of the Smyth Family of Ashton Court.* Bristol Record Society's Publications, vol. 35. Bristol, 1982.

Black, Sir F. *The Parliamentary History of the Isle of Wight.* Newport, 1939.

Bohannon, M. E. "The Essex Election of 1604." *English Historical Review* 48 (1933): 395–413.

Boyle, J. R. *The Early History of the Town and Port of Hedon.* Hull and York, 1895.

Bradley, A. C. *Coriolanus.* British Academy Annual Shakespeare Lecture, no. 2. 1912.

Bridges, W. B. *Some Account of the Barony and Town of Okehampton.* Tiverton, 1889.

Brown, Louise F. "The Religious Factors in the Convention Parliament." *English Historical Review* 22 (1907): 51–63.

"Ideas of Representation from Elizabeth to Charles II." *Journal of Modern History* 11 (1939): 23–40.

Browning, Andrew. *Thomas Osborne, Earl of Danby and Duke of Leeds, 1632–1712.* 3 vols. Glasgow, 1951.

Brunton, D., and D. H. Pennington. *Members of the Long Parliament.* Cambridge, 1954.

Bushman, R. L. "English Franchise Reform in the Seventeenth Century." *Journal of British Studies* 3 (1963): 36–56.

Cannon, John. *Parliamentary Reform 1640–1832.* Cambridge, 1973.

Carew, Thomas. *An Historical Account of the Rights of Elections of the Several Counties, Cities and Boroughs of Great Britain:. . .* 2 parts. 1755.

Carroll, Roy. "Yorkshire Parliamentary Boroughs in the Seventeenth Century." *Northern History* 3 (1968): 70–104.

Cartwright, J. J. *Chapters in the History of Yorkshire.* Wakefield, 1872.

Chanter, J. R. *Sketches of the Literary History of Barnstaple.* Barnstaple, 1866.

Chichester, Sir Alexander. *History of the Family of Chichester.* 1871.

Christie, William D., ed. *Memoirs, Letters and Speeches of Anthony Ashley Cooper, First Earl of Shaftesbury.* 1859.

Christie, William D. *A Life of Anthony Ashley Cooper, First Earl of Shaftesbury 1621–1683.* 2 vols. 1871.

Clark, Peter. "Thomas Scott and the Growth of Urban Opposition to the Early Stuart Regime." *Historical Journal* 21 (1978): 1–26.

Clarke, G. R. *History and Description of the Town and Borough of Ipswich.* Ipswich, 1830.

Clarkson, Christopher. *The History of Richmond in the County of York.* Richmond, 1814.

Cliffe, J. T. *The Yorkshire Gentry from the Reformation to the Civil War.* 1969.

Coate, Mary. "William Morice and the Restoration of Charles II." *English Historical Review* 33 (1918): 367–77.

Cooper, C. H. *Annals of Cambridge.* 5 vols. Cambridge, 1842–53.

Cooper, William D. *The History of Winchelsea.* 1850.

Courtney, William P. *The Parliamentary Representation of Cornwall to 1832.* 1889.

Coward, B. "The Lieutenancy of Lancashire and Cheshire in the Sixteenth and Early Seventeenth Century." *Transactions of the Historic Society of Lancashire and Cheshire* 119 (1969): 39–64.

"The Social and Political Position of the Earls of Derby in Later Seventeenth

Century Lancashire." *Transactions of the Historic Society of Lancashire and Cheshire* 132 (1982): 127–54.

The Stanleys, Lords Stanley and Earls of Derby 1385–1672. Chetham Society, third series, no. 30. Manchester, 1983.

Crissey, Merrill, and Davies, Godfrey. "Corruption in Parliament 1660–1677." *Huntington Library Quarterly* 6 (1942–43): 106–114.

Cunnington, E. B. Howard. *Some Annals of the Borough of Devizes.* Devizes, 1925.

Cust, R. P., and P. G. Lake. "Sir Richard Grosvenor and the Rhetoric of Magistracy." *Bulletin of the Institute of Historical Research* 54 (1981): 40–53.

Davies, Godfrey. "The Political Career of Sir Richard Temple (1634–1697) and Buckingham Politics." *Huntington Library Quarterly* 4 (1940): 47–83.

"The By-Election at Grantham, 1678."*Huntington Library Quarterly* 7 (1943–4): 179–182.

"The Elections to Richard Cromwell's Parliament, 1658–9." *English Historical Review* 63 (1948): 488–501.

"The General Election of 1660." *Huntington Library Quarterly* 15 (1952): 211–35.

Davies, Godfrey, ed. "Memoirs of the Family of Guise." *Camden Society,* third series, vol. 28 (1917): 85–177.

DeBeer, E. S. "Members of the Court Party in the House of Commons 1670–1678." *Bulletin of the Institute of Historical Research* 11 (1933–1934): 1–23.

Dennett, J., ed. *Beverley Borough Records 1575–1821.* Yorkshire Archaeological Society, vol. 84. York, 1933.

Dodd, A. H. "Wales's Parliamentary Apprenticeship (1536–1625)." *Transactions of the Honorable Society of Cymmrodorion* (1942): 8–72.

"Wales in the Parliaments of Charles I." *Transactions of the Honorable Society of Cymmrodorion* (1945): 16–49; (1946–7): 59–96.

Donagan, Barbara. "The Clerical Patronage of Robert Rich, Second Earl of Warwick, 1619–1642." *Proceedings of the American Philosophical Society* 120, no. 5 (1976): 388–419.

Drakard, John. *The History of Stamford in the County of Lincoln.* Stamford, 1822.

Evans, John T. *Seventeenth-Century Norwich.* Oxford, 1979.

Everett, Alan. *The Community of Kent and the Great Rebellion.* Leicester, 1966.

Farnham, Edith. "The Somerset Election of 1614." *English Historical Review* 46 (1931): 579–99.

Firth, C. H. *The Last Years of the Protectorate 1656–58.* 2 vols. 1909.

Fletcher, Anthony. "Sir Thomas Wentworth and the Restoration of Pontefract as a Parliamentary Borough." *Northern History* 6 (1971): 88–97.

Forster, G. C. F. "The North Riding Justices and Their Sessions 1603–25." *Northern History* 10 (1975): 102–125.

Forster, John. *Sir John Eliot: A Biography.* 2 vols. 1864.

Galpin, F. W. "The Household Expenses of Sir Thomas Barrington." *Transactions of the Essex Archaeological Society,* new series, 13 (1915): 203–24.

Gardiner, S. R. "The Use of Member of Parliament." *English Historical Review* 8 (1893): 525.

History of the Commonwealth and Protectorate (1649–1656). 3 vols. 1894–1901.

Gay, Edwin F. "The Rise of an English Country Family: Peter and John Temple to 1603." *Huntington Library Quarterly* 1 (1937–38): 367–90.

"Sir Richard Temple: The Debt Settlement and Estate Litigation, 1653–1675." *Huntington Library Quarterly* 6 (1942–43): 255–91.

George, M. D. "Elections and Electioneering 1679–81." *English Historical Review* 45 (1930): 552–78.

Gillett, E., and K. A. MacMahon. *The History of Hull.* 1980.

Gooder, Arthur, ed. "Parliamentary Representation of the County of York, 1258–1832." *Yorkshire Archaeological Society Record Series,* vol. 2, no. 96 (1938).

Greaves, R. W. "The Earl of Huntingdon and the Leicester Charter of 1684." *Huntington Library Quarterly* 15 (1952): 371–91.

Groome, A. N. "Higham Ferrers Elections in 1640." *Northamptonshire Past and Present* 2 (1958): 243–51.

Grosvenor, Ian D. "Catholics and Politics: The Worcestershire Election of 1604." *Recusant History* 3 (1978): 149–62.

Gruenfelder, John K. "The Elections for Knights of the Shire for Essex in the Spring 1640." *Transactions of the Essex Archaeological Association,* third series, 2 (1968): 143–46.

"Rye and the Parliament of 1621." *Sussex Archaeological Collections* 107 (1969): 25–35.

"The Election to the Short Parliament, 1640." *Early Stuart Studies,* ed. H. S. Reinmuth, Jr., pp. 180–230. Minneapolis, 1970.

"The Parliamentary Election for Shrewsbury 1604." *Transactions of the Shropshire Archaeological Society* 59 (1973–74): 272–77.

"The Lord Wardens and Elections, 1604–28." *Journal of British Studies* 16, no. 1 (1976): 1–23.

"Two Midland Parliamentary Elections of 1604." *Midland History* 3 (1976): 241–55.

"Dorsetshire Elections, 1604–1640." *Albion* 10 (1978): 1–13.

"Gloucester's Parliamentary Elections, 1604–40." *Bristol and Gloucestershire Archaeological Society Transactions* 96 (1978): 53–59.

Gruenfelder, J. K. *Influence in Early Stuart Elections, 1604–1640.* Columbus, Ohio, 1981.

Guilding, J. M., ed. *Records of the Borough of Reading.* 4 vols. Reading, 1892–96.

Gurney, Hudson. "Norfolk." *Norfolk Archaeology* 1 (1847): 47.

Haley, K. D. H. *The First Earl of Shaftesbury.* Oxford, 1968.

Hanham, H. J. "Ashburton as a Parliamentary Borough, 1640–1868." *Transactions of the Devonshire Association* 98 (1966): 206–56.

Hardacre, Paul H. "William Boteler: A Cromwellian Oligarch." *Huntington Library Quarterly* 11 (1947): 1–11.

Hasler, P. W., ed. *The House of Commons 1558–1603.* 3 vols. 1982.

Hedges, John K. *The History of Wallingford.* 2 vols. 1881.

Hele, Nicholas F. *Notes or Jottings about Aldeburgh, Suffolk.* 1870.

Henning, Basil, ed. *The House of Commons 1660–1690.* 3 vols. 1983.

Hill, J. E. C. "Parliament and the People in Seventeenth Century England." *Past and Present* 93 (1981): 100–25.

Hillaby, J. "The Parliamentary Borough of Weobley 1628–1708." *Transactions of the Woolhope Naturalist Club* 39 (1967): 104–52.

Hills, W. H. *The History of East Grinstead.* East Grinstead, 1906.

Hirst, Derek. "Elections and the Privileges of the House of Commons in the Early

Seventeenth Century: Confrontation or Compromise?" *Historical Journal* 18 (1975): 851–62.

The Representative of the People? Cambridge, 1975.

Holmes, Clive. *Seventeenth Century Lincolnshire.* Lincoln, 1981.

Horsefield, T. W. *The History, Antiquities, and Topography of the County of Sussex.* Lewes and London, 1835.

Horwitz, Henry. "The General Election of 1690." *Journal of British Studies* 11 (1971): 77–91.

Houghton, K. N. "Theory and Practice in Borough Elections to Parliament During the Later Fifteenth Century." *Bulletin of the Institute of Historical Research* 39 (1966): 130–40.

Hulme, Harold. "The Sheriff as a Member of the House of Commons from Elizabeth to Cromwell." *Journal of Modern History* 1 (1929): 361–77.

The Life of Sir John Eliot 1592–1632. New York, 1957.

Hume, A. "Some Account of the Liverpool Election of 1670." *Transactions of the Historic Society of Lancashire and Cheshire* 6 (1853–4): 4–17, Appendix.

Hutchins, John. *The History and Antiquities of the County of Dorset.* 4 vols. Westminster, 1861–70.

Jessup, Frank W. "The Kentish Election of March, 1640." *Archaeologia Cantiana* 86 (1971): 1–10.

Johnson, Richard. *The Ancient Customs of the City of Hereford.* 1882.

Jones, G. F. T. "The Composition and Leadership of the Presbyterian Party in the Convention." *English Historical Review* 79 (1964): 307–54.

Jones, J. Bavington. *Annals of Dover.* Dover, 1916.

Jones, J. R. "Restoration Election Petitions." *Durham University Journal* 53 (1961): 49–57.

Jones, Madeline V. "Election Issues and the Borough Electorates in Mid-Seventeenth Century Kent." *Archaeologia Cantiana* 85 (1970): 19–27.

Keeler, M. F. "The Election at Great Marlow in 1640." *Journal of Modern History* 14 (1942): 433–48.

The Long Parliament 1640–41. Philadelphia, 1954.

Kenny, Robert W. "Parliamentary Influence of Charles Howard Earl of Nottingham, 1536–1624." *Journal of Modern History* 39 (1967): 215–232.

Kershaw, R. N. "The Elections for the Long Parliament, 1640." *English Historical Review* 38 (1923): 496–508.

Ketton-Cremer, R. W. *Norfolk in the Civil War.* Hamden, Conn., 1969.

Lambert, A. U. M. *Blechingley: A Parish History.* 2 vols. 1921.

Lawson, Philip. "Family Memoranda of the Stanleys of Alderly." *Journal of the Chester and North Wales Archaeological and Historic Society* 24 (1921-22): 81–101.

Lawson-Tancred, Thomas. "Parliamentary History of Aldborough and Boroughbridge." *Yorkshire Archaeological Journal* 27 (1924): 325–62.

Lipscomb, George. *The History and Antiquities of the County of Buckingham.* 4 vols. 1847.

Lipson, E. "The Elections to the Exclusion Parliaments, 1679–1681. *English Historical Review* 28 (1913): 59–85.

Lomas, S. C., ed. *The Memoirs of Sir George Courthop.* Camden Society, third series, vol. 13, 1907.

Lowndes, G. A. "The History of the Barrington Family." *Transactions of the Essex Archaeological Society,* new series, 2 (1884): 3–54.

Lytle, G. F., and Orgel, S., eds. *Patronage in the Renaissance*, Princeton, 1982.

MacCaffrey, W. *Exeter, 1540–1640*. Cambridge, Mass., 1958.

MacCulloch, Diarmaid. "Catholic and Puritan in Elizabethan Suffolk." *Archiv für Reformationsgeschichte* 62 (1981): 232–87.

Manning, C. R. "News-Letters from Sir Edmund Moundeford Knt., M.P., to Framlingham Gawdy esq., 1627–1633." *Norfolk Archaeology* 5 (1859): 53–73.

Marsh, A. E. W. *A History of the Borough and Town of Calne*. 1903.

Martin, Thomas. *The History of Thetford*. 1779.

Miller, John. "The Crown and the Borough Charters in the Reign of Charles II." *English Historical Review* 100 (1985): 53–84.

Moir, Thomas L. *The Addled Parliament of 1614*. Oxford: 1958.

Morrill, J. S. *Cheshire, 1630–60*. Oxford, 1974.

Muir, Ramsey. *History of Liverpool*. 1907.

Muir, Ramsey, and E. M. Platt. *A History of Municipal Government in Liverpool*. Liverpool, 1906.

Mukerjee, H. N. "Elections for the Convention and Cavalier Parliaments." *Notes and Queries* 166 (1934): 398–403, 417–21.

Mullett, M. "The Politics of Liverpool, 1660-88." *Transactions of the Historic Society of Lancashire and Cheshire* 124 (1973): 31–56.

" 'Deprived of Our Former Place': The Internal Politics of Bedford 1660 to 1688." *Publications of the Bedfordshire Historical Record Society* 59 (1980): 1–42.

Munby, Lionel M. "The Early History of Parliamentary Politics in Hertfordshire." *Transactions of the East Hertfordshire Archaeological Society for 1955–61* (1964): 72–73.

Neale, J. E. "Three Elizabethan Elections." *English Historical Review* 46 (1931): 209–38.

"More Elizabethan Elections." *English Historical Review* 61 (1946): 18–44.

The Elizabethan House of Commons. 1949.

Notestein, Wallace, ed. *The Journal of Sir Symonds D'Ewes*. New Haven, 1923.

Onslow, Earl of. "Sir Richard Onslow 1603-1664." *Surrey Archaeological Collections* 36 (1925): 58–79.

Palliser, David. *Tudor York*. 1979.

Pape, Thomas. *Newcastle-under-Lyme in Tudor and Early Stuart Times*. Manchester, 1938.

Papillon, Alexander F. W. *Memoirs of Thomas Papillon, London Merchant 1623–1702*. Reading, 1887.

Park, Godfrey R. *Parliamentary Representation of Yorkshire*. Hull, 1886.

The History of the Ancient Borough of Hedon. Hull, 1895.

Parry, Charles Henry. *The Parliaments and Councils of England*. 1839.

Parsloe, C. G. "The Corporation of Bedford, 1647–64." *Transactions of the Royal Historical Society*, fourth series, vol. 29 (1947): 151–65.

Peck, Linda. "*Goodwin v. Fortescue*: The Local context of Parliamentary Dispute." *Parliamentary History* 3 (1985): 33–56.

Picton, J. A. *Selections From the Municipal Archives and Records of Liverpool*. Liverpool, 1883.

Pinckney, Paul J. "The Cheshire Election of 1656." *Bulletin of the John Rylands Library* 49 (1967): 387–436.

Pink, W. D., and Bevan, Alfred. *The Parliamentary Representation of Lancashire*. 1889.

Plumb, J. H. "The Growth of the Electorate in England from 1600 to 1715." *Past and Present* 45 (1969): 90–116.

Porritt, Edward and Anne. *The Unreformed House of Commons.* 2 vols. 1903.

Poulson, George. *Beverlac; or the Antiquities and History of the Town of Beverley.* Beverley, 1829.

Prest, Wilfred. "An Australian Holding of Norfolk Manuscripts." *Norfolk Archaeology* 37 (1978): 121–23.

Raven, John J. *The History of Suffolk.* 1895.

Reinmuth, Howard S. "A Mysterious Dispute Demystified: Sir George Fletcher. vs. the Howards." *Historical Journal* 27 (1984): 289–308.

Rex, M. B. *University Representation in England.* 1954.

Roberts, George. *The Social History of the People of the Southern Counties of England in Past Centuries.* 1856.

Rogers, James E. T. *Oxford City Documents.* Oxford Historical Society Publications, vol. 18. Oxford, 1891.

Round, J. H. "Colchester under the Commonwealth." *English Historical Review* 15 (1900): 641–64.

Rowe, V. A. "The Influence of the Earls of Pembroke on Parliamentary Elections, 1625–41." *English Historical Review* 50 (1935): 242–56.

Ruigh, Robert. *The Parliament of 1624.* Cambridge, Mass., 1971.

Sacret, J. H. "The Restoration Government and the Municipal Corporations." *English Historical Review* 45 (1930): 232–59.

Salt, S. P. "Sir Thomas Wentworth and the Parliamentary Representation of Yorkshire, 1614–1628." *Northern History* 16 (1980): 130–68.

Seddon, P. R. "A Parliamentary Election at East Retford, 1624." *Transactions of the Thoroton Society of Nottinghamshire* 76 (1972): 26–34.

"The Nottinghamshire Elections for the Short Parliament of 1640." *Transactions of the Thoroton Society of Nottinghamshire* 80 (1976): 63–68.

Shakespeare, William. *Coriolanus.* Arden Shakespeare Library, 1922.

Simpson, Robert. *The History and Antiquities of the Town of Lancaster.* Lancaster, 1852.

Sinclair, D. *History of Wigan.* Wigan, 1882.

Slack, P. "An election to the Short Parliament." *Bulletin of the Institute of Historical Research* 46 (1973): 108–114.

Smart, T. W. W. "Extracts From the Mss. of Samuel Jeake." *Sussex Archaeological Collections* 9 (1857): 45–60.

Smith, A. Hassell. *County and Court.* Oxford, 1974.

Snow, Vernon. "Parliamentary Reapportionment Proposals in the Puritan Revolution." *English Historical Review* 74 (1959): 409–42.

Statham, Samuel P. H. *The History of the Castle, Town, and Port of Dover.* 1899.

Stone, Lawrence. "The Electoral Influence of the Second Earl of Salisbury, 1614–68." *English Historical Review* 71 (1956): 384–400.

Tawney, R. H. *Religion and the Rise of Capitalism.* 1922.

Thompson, Christopher. "The 3rd Lord Rich and the Essex Election of 1604." *Essex Journal* 14 (1979): 2–6.

Thompson, James. *History of Leicester.* 1849.

Toy, Henry Spencer. *The History of Helston.* 1936.

Trollope, Andrew. "Hatcher Correspondence Relating to Parliamentary Elections." *Associated Architectural and Archaeological Societies' Reports* 23 (1895–6): 134–42.

Underdown, D. E. "The Ilchester Elections, February 1646." *Proceedings of the Somerset Archaeological and Natural History Society* 110 (1966): 40–51.
　"Party Management and the Recruiter Elections, 1645–1648." *English Historical Review* 83 (1968): 235–64.
De Villiers, Evangeline. "Parliamentary Boroughs Restored by the House of Commons 1621–41." *English Historical Review* 68 (1952): 175–202.
Wedgwood, J. C. "Parliamentary History of Staffordshire." *Historical Collections of Staffordshire.* 2 vols. William Salt Archaeological Society, 1919–22.
Weeks, W. S. *Clitheroe in the Seventeenth Century.* Clitheroe, 1927.
Weinbaum, Martin, ed. *British Borough Charters 1307–1660.* Cambridge, 1943.
Weinstock, Maureen, ed. *Weymouth & Melcombe Regis Minute Book, 1625–1660.* Dorchester, Dorset Record Society, 1964.
Weyman, Henry T. "Shropshire Members of Parliament." *Transactions of the Shropshire Archaeological Society,* fourth series, no. 11: 1–48, 153–84.
Wheeler, W. A. *Members of Parliament for Salisbury.* Salisbury, 1883.
Whitaker, T. D. *A History of the Original Parish of Whalley and Honor of Clitheroe.* 4th ed., revised and enlarged by J. G. Nichols and P. A. Lyons. 2 vols. 1872–76.
Wilkes, George. *The Barons of the Cinque Ports and the Parliamentary Representation of Hythe.* Folkestone, 1892.
Williams, John. *Ancient and Modern Denbigh.* Denbigh, 1856.
Williams, Penry. "Government and Politics in Ludlow 1590–1642." *Transactions of the Shropshire Archaeological Society* 56 (1957–60): 282–94.
Williams, W. R. *Parliamentary History of the Principality of Wales.* Brecknock, 1895.
Woodruff, C. E. "Notes on the Municipal Records of Queenborough." *Archaeologia Cantiana* 22 (1897): 169–85.

Theses and Unpublished Works

Abernathy, George. "The Borough of Buckingham, 1660–1697: A Struggle for Control." Unpublished paper.
Ball, J. N. "The Parliamentary Career of Sir John Eliot 1624–9." Ph.D. dissertation, Cambridge University, 1953.
Barre, Dianne. "Worcestershire Politics and Elections 1679–1715." Master's thesis, Birmingham University, 1971.
Barrows, Floyd D. "The House of Commons of 1685." Ph.D. dissertation, University of California, Los Angeles, 1967.
Calnan, Julie B. "County Society and Local Government in the County of Hertfordshire 1580–1630." Ph.D. dissertation, Cambridge University, 1979.
Carroll, Roy. "The Parliamentary Representation of Yorkshire 1625–1660." Ph.D dissertation, Vanderbilt University, 1964.
Chivers, G. V. "The Members from the Northern Counties in Richard Cromwell's Parliament." Master's thesis, Manchester University, 1954.
Cust, Richard P. "The Forced Loan and English Politics, 1626–28." Ph.D. dissertation, University of London, 1983.
Durston, C. G. "Berkshire and its County Gentry 1625–49." Ph.D. dissertation, Reading University, 1977.

Evans, T. W. "Hyde and the Convention Parliament of 1660." Master's thesis, University of London, 1964.

Fuidge, Norah M. "Personnel of the House of Commons 1563–7." Master's thesis, University of London, 1950.

Gabriel, R. C. "Members of the House of Commons 1586–7." Master's thesis, University of London, 1954.

Helms, Mary W. "The Convention Parliament of 1660." Ph.D. dissertation, Bryn Mawr College, 1963.

Hodges, Vivienne J. "The Electoral Influence of the Aristocracy 1604–1640." Ph.D. dissertation, Columbia University, 1977.

Jones, Madeline V. "The Political History of the Parliamentary Boroughs of Kent, 1642–62." Ph.D. dissertation, University of London, 1967.

Lansberry, H. C. F. "Politics and Government in St. Albans 1685–1835." Ph.D. dissertation, University of London, 1964.

Levy, Jacqueline, "Perceptions and Beliefs: The Harleys of Brampton Bryan and the Origins and Outbreak of the First Civil War." Ph.D. dissertation, University of London, 1983.

Matthews, Hazel. "Personnel of the Parliament of 1584–5." Master's thesis, University of London, 1948.

Mort, Margaret K. "The Personnel of the House of Commons in 1601." Master's thesis, University of London, 1952.

Mullett, M. "The Crown and the Corporations." Master's thesis, Cambridge University, 1972.

Pickavance, R. G. "The English Boroughs and the King's Government: A Study of the Tory Reaction of 1681–5." Ph.D. dissertation, Oxford University, 1976.

Pinckney, P. J. "A Cromwellian Parliament: The Electoral Personnel of 1656." Ph.D. dissertation, Vanderbilt University, 1962.

Plumb, J. H. "Elections to the House of Commons in the Reign of William III." Ph.D. dissertation, Cambridge University, 1935–36.

Quintrell, B. W. "The Government of the County of Essex 1603–42." Ph.D. dissertation, London University, 1965.

Roberts, J. C. "The Parliamentary Representation of Devon and Dorset 1559–1601." Master's thesis, University of London, 1958.

Robinson, Rudite P. "The Parliamentary Representation of Gloucestershire 1660–1690." Ph.D. dissertation, Yale University, 1975.

Silcock, R. H. "County Government in Worcestershire." Ph.D. dissertation, University of London, 1974.

Sommers, Kathleen. "Court, County, and Parliament: Electoral Influences in Five English Counties, 1586–1640." Ph.D. dissertation, Yale University, 1978.

Spence, R. T. "The Cliffords, Earls of Cumberland, 1579–1646." Ph.D. dissertation, University of London, 1959.

Stuart, D. G. "Parliamentary History of the Borough of Tamworth, Staffordshire 1661–1837." Master's thesis, University of London, 1958.

Taffs, Winifred. "The Borough Franchise in the First Half of the 17th Century." Master's thesis, University of London, 1926.

Thomas, J. D. "A Survey of the Parliamentary Elections of 1625, 1626, and 1628." Master's thesis, University of London, 1952.

Trafford, Evelyn E. "Personnel of the Parliament of 1593." Master's thesis, University of London, 1948.

Ward, Cedric. "Disputed Elections in the House of Commons 1604–1641." Ph.D. dissertation, University of Nebraska, 1974.

Ward, Pamela W. U. "Members of Parliament and Elections in Derbyshire, Leicestershire and Staffordshire between 1660 and 1714." Master's thesis, Manchester University, 1959.

Index